POINT MAN

POINT MAN

Inside the Toughest and Most Deadly Unit in Vietnam by a Founding Member of the Elite Navy SEALs

Chief James Watson and Kevin Dockery

WILLIAM MORROW AND COMPANY, INC.
New York

It is the policy of William Morrow and Company, Inc., and its imprints and affiliates, recognizing the importance of preserving what has been written, to print the books we publish on acid-free paper, and we exert our best efforts to that end.

Library of Congress Cataloging-in-Publication Data

Watson, James, Chief.
 Point man / by James Watson and Kevin Dockery.
  p. cm.
 Includes index.
 ISBN 0-688-12212-4
 1. Vietnamese Conflict, 1961–1975—Commando operations.
2. Vietnamese Conflict, 1961–1975—Regimental histories—United States. 3. United States. Navy. Sea, Air, Land Teams—History.
4. Vietnamese Conflict, 1961–1975—Personal narratives, American.
5. Watson, James, Chief. I. Dockery, Kevin. II. Title.
DS558.92.W39 1993
959.704'3373—dc20   93-20226
                          CIP

Printed in the United States of America

2 3 4 5 6 7 8 9 10

BOOK DESIGN BY PAUL CHEVANNES

This book is dedicated to my late wife, Betty, who first
encouraged me to get my story down on paper.
And also to my four children, the ones who really paid
the price for their father being a professional military man:

James D. Watson IV ("Little Jim")
Helene R. Watson ("Angel")
Patricia Watson ("Pat Pat")
Jean Watson ("Jeannie")

And to all of my fallen teammates who gave their lives
or were disabled for our belief in freedom.

Though no SEALs or UDT operators were ever left behind, living
or dead, a great many Americans, as POWs and MIAs, have been
lost and unaccounted for.

This book is also dedicated to those POWs and MIAs of Vietnam
and other of our country's conflicts, and to the man who has done
the most to bring those missing men home or account for them:
Mr. Ross Perot.

This book is dedicated to my late wife, Betty, who first
encouraged me to get my story down on paper.
And also to my four children, the ones who really paid
the price for their father being a professional military man:

James D. Watson IV ("Little Jim")
Helene R. Watson ("Angel")
Patricia Watson ("Pat Pat")
Jean Watson ("Jeannie")

And to all of my fallen teammates who gave their lives
or were disabled for our belief in freedom.

Though no SEALs or UDT operators were ever left behind, living
or dead, a great many Americans, as POWs and MIAs, have been
lost and unaccounted for.

This book is also dedicated to those POWs and MIAs of Vietnam
and other of our country's conflicts, and to the man who has done
the most to bring those missing men home or account for them:
Mr. Ross Perot.

ACKNOWLEDGMENTS

I would like to acknowledge the men who played a big part in my becoming a Navy SEAL and surviving the experience:

Lieutenant Commander Roy Boehm, United States Navy (Retired), who gave me the chance to become one of the first SEALs.

Master Chief Boatswain's Mate Rudy Boesch, United States Navy (Retired), who guided me through the rough years first as a junior, and later as a senior petty officer.

Chief Warrant Officer Robert Gallagher, United States Navy (Retired), who taught me how to be a leader as well as how and what it meant to earn your men's respect.

Commander Richard Marcinko, United States Navy (Retired), who taught me the way to get things done the first time as well as the value of teamwork combined with training. He always backed his men, regardless of the consequences to himself. The bottom line was always the success of the mission.

And to all of the officers and men of SEAL Team Two, who have made the Team, and are making the Teams what they are today . . . the best in the world.

CONTENTS

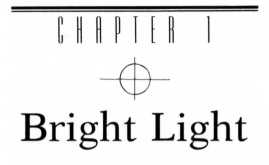

Bright Light

Here it was, a POW rescue operation. These ops were so important that the high command had given them their own code name, Bright Light. And my SEAL platoon was going in on the first Bright Light operation of the Vietnam War. As the lead helicopter of our assault group came close to the ground, John Porter and I were just getting ready to jump out when the door gunner and crew chief grabbed us. "No!" they shouted.

I looked to the pilot in the right-hand seat just in time to see him pull all the way up on the collective while turning the throttle to full open. He was trying to get the bird up and out of there, and the chopper wasn't moving.

All I heard at the time was the fading scream of the turbine slowing to a stop. We had lost the engine. We were taking fire from the ground.

I saw the pilot slap the stick over to the side. He was trying to put the bird in on her side so that the blades wouldn't slice us into chopped meat when we bailed out. If we went in straight, it would be a toss-up whether the engine and transmission coming through the roof would crush us before the blades had a chance at us. Below us was double-canopy jungle—we had overshot the insertion point.

Holy shit, we're gonna crash! I thought to myself. We're gonna plow into the ground, burn, and die! What the hell did I get myself into this time?

Though I didn't know it until later, when the pilot turned the chopper on her side, Füks, our native interpreter, fell out of the bird! Because we were so close to the ground, Füks wasn't hurt when he landed. He had a small Instamatic camera in his shirt pocket and actually snapped some pictures of the crash.

There wasn't time for more than a moment's thought when *wham*, we were into the ground. The chopper went in on her right side, plowing through the trees and into the jungle floor. Blades snapped as they sliced into the rotting vegetation that covered the ground.

Metal groaned as it bent and screamed as it tore. We were all tossed around like gravel in a cement mixer. Finally the stricken bird came to a stop. The sharp odor of fuel leaking from ruptured lines overwhelmed the normal stench of the jungle.

Miraculously, nobody was hurt in the crash. We were all shook up, but even the right-hand door gunner got out without much more than a banging-up. We had to sort out the tangled mass of men in the dead chopper and scramble out and away from the downed bird before she caught fire. Quickly organizing the team away from the helicopter, I took stock of our situation.

I was running very light in terms of weapons. I only had a .45 automatic pistol and the radio on my back. Originally, I had figured I would be too busy on the radio to worry about a shotgun. A radio is the biggest "gun" a man can carry, because with it you can call in all the available fire support, and I almost always carried my own radio. John was right there at my side with his Stoner light machine gun at the ready when we all scrambled out of the crippled bird.

After we were safely on the ground I understood the situation a little more clearly. I had a pilot, copilot, two door gunners, Füks, the prisoner, John, and several VNs on my hands, most of them even more scared than I was, if that was possible. I had never been in a crash before.

We needed to get away from the downed bird as quickly as we could. I had no idea if there would be a fire or not. After putting some distance between ourselves and the crash, I could see that the next thing I had to do was calm everyone down a little bit. We were deep into Jap country, and the natives had already proved themselves restless. (A legacy from the UDT of World War II, enemies in Asia were "Japs.")

The copilot, who was Vietnamese, had left his weapon back in the bird and was really shook about not being armed. "John, stay in my pocket," I said to Porter as I handed the VN my pistol. That made the VN smile a bit, and then I turned my attention to the pilot.

"Sir," I said, "if you had to get shot down, you just got shot down with the best in the world. We're going to get you all out of here. I don't give a damn if we have to walk for a week, I'm getting you out of this. You have no problem—we just don't need you getting excited. Just do as I tell you, move when I tell you, and we're going to be all right. We've survived this, and we can get out."

The two door gunners were all ears and listened to my every word. The only weapon they could have reached was a .50 caliber machine gun mounted in the left door, and there was no way we were going to take that. The M60 that had been in the right door was buried under the bird. The VNs could all speak a little English, and I had succeeded in getting everyone calmed down. Now if only someone would give me a pep talk!

The clearing where we were supposed to land was, I thought, to our north. I took a fast compass sighting and pointed. "John, that way, go." I had no idea whether the bird would explode if we threw a grenade or Mark 13 signal flare into it. Anyway, I wanted to get away and call in my air support.

I had all the air cover in the world at my disposal. My plan was to get away from the bird and call the guns in to bust it. That thought kept me from worrying about leaving weapons behind for Charlie to recover. What I was thinking about was moving as fast as we could to get away from the area and to a clearing where they could pick us up. If we couldn't get out, maybe if we could get to the original landing zone (LZ) we had been going to use, I could bring in the rest of the team and still complete the mission.

The radio was my big gun, and that was most important to me right now, only the radio wasn't working! Jesus Christ, I thought, of all times for the radio to quit working. It had probably been damaged when we crashed. The only casualty of the bunch, and it had to be the radio!

I grabbed John, who was just in front of me. "John, check this out," I said quietly, and I bent over in front of him so he could see the top of the radio.

"The damned thing's off, Chief," John said, turning the control switch to the on position. I was too relieved to feel foolish just then. It must have gotten switched off during the crash, I thought as I put the headset to my mouth.

"Bird down! Bird down!" I heard over the headset. "No smoke, I see no smoke. Abort! Abort the operation! Abort!" All sorts of stuff was flying through the air as I came into the net.

"Break! Break! This is Whiskey Sour, this is Whiskey Sour, we're down and we're out, everyone's okay." I wasn't going to tell them what direction I was heading in. Charlie has radios too.

"When I get farther away, I will identify with the night end of a Mark 13." I did not want to pop smoke—it would linger in the area and Charlie would know where we were.

"Bust the bird! We're out of it. I repeat, bust the bird, we couldn't take the gear with us." I didn't want to come right out and say "weapons," but Charlie wasn't that stupid. He could figure out what I was talking about if he was listening.

There was sporadic gunfire coming from the direction of the camp, to our rear, but we weren't paying any attention to it. I expect we really shook things up at that POW camp. Everybody there seemed to be firing in all directions, but we couldn't hear anything whistling by our heads. The VC were "reconning by fire," shooting in the hopes of our shooting back. But none of my men got trigger-happy, not even the VNs; fire discipline was important, and our training stuck with us. With none of the fire coming near us, we were able to keep going.

After we had moved some distance I popped the night (flare) end of a Mark 13 and called up to the circling aircraft. "Do you identify me?" I called into the radio. They answered back that they did. Now those aircraft could see the situation one hell of a lot better than I could. I called up to them to vector me in to the break in the canopy.

"Okay, you see us," I transmitted. "What direction do I go for the nearest clearing?" They told me, and we moved out. "John, that way," I said, pointing.

We reached the clearing. John covered us with his Stoner while Füks and I cut down some small trees and bushes with our knives enlarging the cleared area enough for a helicopter to land fully. The other people from the chopper stayed under the cover of the trees.

While we were working on the clearing, John moved through the bush, securing the area. He was facing VC just by himself, with only his Stoner for support. If we were discovered or started taking direct fire, John was ready to lead the enemy off after him. He would sacrifice himself to protect the team. Later, I put John in for the Silver Star for those actions; he got it.

As soon as we had cleared the area, I got back on the radio. Now I had a C&C (Command and Control) bird on the net.

"All right," I called, "we're ready for extraction—we have the LZ secured. Come in and take out your pilot and crew. We will remain behind and cover the extraction in and out. Then come back for us. Send me one of your best pilots—it's a very tight LZ."

Well, that really rattled somebody's cage up there. "How do you know what's needed?" came over the radio, along with a bunch of other garbage. Apparently there was a full bird colonel in the C&C chopper and he was not going to take advice from a lowly Navy chief.

I do *not* need this right now, I thought as I answered him. Thinking fast, I came up with something I figured would impress an Army officer. The Army believes in its Rangers, and its Rangers are good. I had been one of the first SEALs to attend Ranger School back in 1965 and had graduated as the top NCO of Class 7.

"For everyone's information," I transmitted, "I am Army Ranger–qualified. I went to your Ranger School. Watch me when you come in. I will watch the tail rotor and ground-guide the craft. Tell the pilot to watch me and I will keep his tail rotor out of trouble." In a tight LZ, if the pilot lets his tail rotor get snarled, he goes down fast. I did not want any more company with me on the ground. Ranger School had taught me how to guide a chopper in and which signals to use.

Apparently, that satisfied the Army. In came the chopper, and it extracted the first bird's crew without incident. Well, almost without incident.

The Viet Cong prisoner who had been acting as our guide on the operation hadn't been giving us any trouble. If Charlie was to catch him in our company, he would be executed immediately for talking. As our pilot and crew moved out to the extraction bird, off went the prisoner, straight to the chopper. Füks and John wanted to drill the guy right there, but I told them not to. I was so relieved the situation hadn't gotten any worse that I was able to be a little generous.

"No, let him go," I said. "It wasn't his fault. He did his job."

The chopper took off with the first extraction. Now there were only John, Füks, me, and about six of Father Wa's Vietnamese mercenaries left in the clearing. John came up to me and spoke softly so none of the others could hear. "Jim," he said, "if you EVER let me talk you into changing your mind again, I'll kill you." According to my original plan, John was supposed to have been in the second bird, not in the first with me. But he had argued his way aboard the first bird before the operation started.

Everyone was staying cool. We had arrived at an extraction site, and all we had to do was wait for another chopper to come in and pick us up. Father Wa's people were just standing by. We had earned the trust of these men many times in the past, and they knew we wouldn't leave them now.

Now we started noticing rounds zipping by. The pop-zip of small-arms fire was starting to get close. I got back on the radio and began directing gunships to fire on the targets around our position. We did not want to do any shooting—we let the gunships take care of that for us.

"Saturate north of me. Saturate northeast of me. There is gunfire on my position coming from there," I radioed to the circling gunships. Overhead were Cobras, Army gunships, Black Ponies, Seawolves, every kind of air support imaginable waiting to assist us; a man couldn't have asked for more. They were not actually circling our position. Charlie still didn't know where we were, but if he saw a bunch of gunships circling a patch of jungle, he would quickly figure there was something in the center of the circle the gunships were protecting. But all that flying hardware stayed real close by to where we were.

Then that officer in the C&C ship came back on the net. "Whiskey Sour, Whiskey Sour. Calm down, you aren't getting shot at."

That really popped my cork. Who was this jerk? "How the fuck would you know?" I snarled into the radio. "You're up there at about four thousand feet by now, for Christ's sake."

"Well, you just hang loose there, Whiskey Sour. We have some decisions to make up here. We'll get you out."

Oh, great, I thought. They had some decisions to make. I hoped Charlie would give them all the time they'd need to straighten out their pointy little heads.

Meanwhile, I had some men to take care of. I reassured everyone that things were going fine. John noticed something was going on as I quietly flexed my hands, imagining them around a certain officer's throat. I had never thrown a prisoner from a chopper, but I would have liked to see that colonel's wings work.

They made us wait in that stinking jungle for several hours while they made their "decisions." The C&C bird came back on the radio. He wanted me to go back to the downed aircraft!

"You have got to be shitting me!" I answered. "You didn't bust it?" By this time Charlie would have built a jungle workshop on the site. "Didn't you hear me? There was gear on that bird!"

"No, no, that's not important. We want you to go back and secure the bird so we can hook it out."

They wanted us to go back through a jungle where Charlie was already looking for us and secure the area? This dimwit colonel wanted to bring in a big, slow cargo chopper and lift the wreck out with a hook. Who was this man and where did he think we were— Fort Hood, Texas?

"Fuck you! I don't know the way you were trained in your Army, but we know different. All my training says that if you're shot down in a hostile area, get as far away from the bird as you can as quickly as possible. And if you think I'm going back to that bird, you're crazy. There are probably VC all over it by now, getting whatever was in it out of it."

That really made the colonel hot. "I'm giving you a direct order," he said. "Go back and secure the bird."

"I don't give a shit what you say. I am not taking my men back through that jungle just so you can save a dead bird. We will walk out if we have to. And if we do walk out of here, I *will* find out who you are and *where* you are!"

After a while, one of the circling Cobra gunships came onto the net. "Whiskey Sour. On behalf of the United States Army and especially us pilots, number one, I want to thank you for getting our people out. Number two, I want to apologize for the assholes who are leaving you down there."

Immediately the C&C ship came up on the net. "Who is that? Who is that? What's your call sign? Identify yourself!"

"To repeat Whiskey Sour's earlier remark, fuck you! Whiskey Sour, regardless of what happens, I will not leave you! And neither will most of the other gunships—you got our people out." And the airways were clear.

Well, then things started happening. They came in and got us without any more garbage about hooking out the bird. And after all that, I never did find out if they busted it. I didn't see or hear it go while we were on the ground. But the way things were happening, I couldn't have cared less. Getting my people out of there was my primary concern.

I did find out what the colonel had wanted to do. He was trying to prove pilot error caused the crash! When something goes wrong, the higher echelon wants to hang somebody. That colonel did not believe that we had been shot down. That officious bastard figured that the pilot had done something wrong and had a flameout. If they had pulled the bird out and it hadn't had any bullet holes in it, they could have nailed the pilot.

It wasn't until much later, when the platoon was back at Little Creek, that I learned we had the evidence all along, because Füks had taken pictures of the crash. All over the underside of the aircraft were plainly visible bullet holes. So much for the colonel's flameout.

As it turned out, some good did result from the operation. When we hit the area, the guards at the camp went absolutely shithouse. In the confusion, about twenty VN POWs were able to get away. But we never did find out about any Americans who might have been in that camp.

Duke Leonard came over and threw his arms around me.

"Chief," he said, "Chuck almost shot that other pilot because of what happened."

"What are you talking about, Duke?" I asked. "And where is Chuck, anyway?"

"He's over in the ammo locker counting bullets," Duke said. "He expects the shore patrol to come along any minute and drag him away to a court-martial."

Remembering my own lack of military courtesy to a certain colonel in a C&C bird, I started wondering. "What court-martial? Just what the hell are you talking about, Duke?" I asked. It was then that I learned what had happened in the second bird.

Eight of the ten helicopters in my assault group had one SEAL from my platoon on board. The SEAL would be leading a group of Father Wa's people who were on the chopper with him. The first two birds each had two SEALs on board to provide immediate extra leadership on the ground. Duke and Chuck had been the two SEALs on the second bird.

"The door gunner had spotted some people moving around on the ground just before you went in," Duke said. "He wanted to take them under fire, and there wasn't anything I could do to talk him out of it. So I did the next-best thing. My Stoner was pointed in his direction, and I told him that if he opened fire so would I. Chuck was up in the cockpit and he saw you go down. Since I was in back, I couldn't see what the hell was going on. Besides, I had my hands full with the door gunner.

"The pilot told Chuck, 'We've aborted—the lead bird went in.' And that sonofabitch was going to leave you, Jim," Duke said. "Only he didn't recon with Fellers. Chuck told him, 'That's my chief down there. We aren't going to leave him there alone.' Then, so help me, Jim, Chuck took his Stoner and laid the barrel up against the pilot's head! Then the copilot took his .45 and put it up to Chuck's head! We had a Mexican standoff right there in the cockpit of a Huey.

"Since I was busy with the door gunner, I couldn't back Chuck," Duke continued. "The pilot was trying to tell Chuck that the rest of the flight and support teams were backing you up, but we couldn't see what was going on with the other birds. Chuck finally let the pilot go back to the field. But I don't think that VN copilot took his eyes off of Chuck for one second during the return flight. All Chuck had wanted to do was get in close enough so we could jump out and back you up. Right now, he's figuring that pilot's going to have him charged with assaulting a superior officer or something." As it turned out, the pilot never tried to have Chuck charged.

All the SEALs are good men. Some just excel a little bit more than the others. When you have gone through as much as we had just getting through training, you become very close with your teammates. The guys in the other birds just knew that the mission had been aborted. They didn't know that I had been shot down until they were back at the LZ. Only Chuck actually saw me go down; otherwise the stories in the other birds might have been a lot different.

CHAPTER 2

Home and Hearth

I have been a professional military man for most of my adult life. Even my earliest memories revolved around war. I was born in 1937 and so was too young to remember the beginning of World War II, but my whole life centered around my family's reactions to it.

My father had been a mechanic for a bus company in New Jersey during 1941 and '42. As the country geared up for defense production, Dad moved the family to Pennsylvania. We stayed with my grandparents in Sharon Hill, on the outskirts of Philadelphia, along with most of the rest of the family. My grandparents had a large three-story house with pillars on the front porch. The porch wrapped most of the way around the building. We played on that huge porch during the summer.

It seemed like the whole family had moved in with Grandma and Grandpa. Uncle Buck and Aunt Mary were there along with their two sons, Jimmy and Skip, and my Aunt Pearl and Aunt Chick (just kids at the time), and Mom and Dad, my little brother Bob, and myself.

Dad had become the head test driver at the Baldwin Locomotive Company. Baldwin had switched production from rolling stock to tanks for the duration, and both Dad and Uncle Buck had become test drivers. The whole family worked at Baldwin—my aunts, uncles, and grandfather all worked as welders and general workers constructing Sherman tanks for the war effort.

Since Baldwin was an important production plant in a critical defense industry, most of the workers were exempt from the draft. In fact, some of the jobs were considered so important that the workers holding them weren't eligible for military service. Dad and Uncle Buck were in this exempt category. Therefore it was a complete surprise when Uncle Buck came home from work one evening and told us that he would not be going back to the plant in the morning—he had enlisted in the Army! In spite of his job classification, Uncle Buck had found a way around the rule and was reporting for induction the next day.

The situation at home was now a little different. The whole family was working not just for the war effort but also to support Uncle Buck at the front. Since things were getting crowded at Grandma's, Dad moved the family to nearby Glenolden in some new housing that had been constructed for the defense workers at Baldwin.

I started school during the war just down the street from where we lived. The whole class participated in air-raid drills, scrap drives, and other activities. It was a difficult time for the country. The enemy could be clearly seen and his intentions were obvious. Everyone seemed to work together for the common good. Though I didn't really understand what it meant at the time, Uncle Buck had joined the U.S. Army Rangers and took part in fierce fighting in Italy.

Toward the end of the war, Dad moved the family back to New Jersey. We were living in Jersey City next door to where my Uncle Walter and Aunt Muriel and their two daughters lived. Just across the river from our house, you could see the Empire State Building reaching into the sky.

There had been a lot of false alarms about the war being over in Europe. Every now and then someone would get a little trigger-happy and the bells in the town would start ringing. When VE Day (Victory in Europe) finally did take place, the whole town went crazy. People were crowding into the streets, laughing and yelling.

It was the biggest party I had ever seen. But just a few months later, on VJ Day (Victory in Japan), the war was completely over, and that party was even bigger.

When Uncle Buck returned home, our family went back to Pennsylvania to greet him. Back then, when a man came home from the service, the whole block would turn out to greet him and have a large block party. When you drove into town and got near Uncle Buck's block you could see banners and signs all over reading "Welcome Home Buck." I've never forgotten those signs.

But things weren't all well with Uncle Buck. While in Italy, he had been seriously wounded in the stomach. Though I didn't know it at the time, the Rangers had seen a long period of action against the Germans. In part because of this long stretch of fighting, Buck had some problems in adjusting to civilian life.

There was a firehouse in town that sounded its siren every day at noon. We were all used to it, but we quickly learned we had to warn Buck that the siren was going to sound or he'd take cover or have a case of the shakes. It would be a long time before I would come to understand what had happened to Uncle Buck.

But all of this had little lasting effect on a young growing boy in postwar America. Being a rowdy lad, I quickly became interested in sports, playing sandlot football with a neighborhood team. Despite my small stature, I was a feisty kid who could snap the ball as center and run like a sonofabitch.

I liked to play center. Even into high school when I started to fill out, I liked to be in the middle, where the action was. My brother Bob was even slighter than I was and didn't lean toward sports at all. But I wasn't just a musclehead young jock-to-be; I liked some of the academic aspects of school too.

While I was learning how to play football with the team, I also picked up on playing a musical instrument, the baritone horn. The Drum Corps of the Jersey City Recreation Department soon had another enthusiastic, but none too skilled, young marcher staggering along under a horn half as big as he was.

I strove to be the best, or at least with the best, at everything I did. Hard work paid off with my horn playing. When I was sixteen, I qualified to join the St. Vincent's Drum and Bugle Corps of Bayonne, New Jersey. Competition with the corps led to my winning the Tri-State Baritone Bugle Individual contest in Reading, Pennsylvania, in 1953. As it turned out, playing a horn was to also affect my later Navy career.

But horn playing was not the reason I was going to school. I had decided to become a doctor. My first step toward this goal was to enter the college preparatory curriculum at Dickinson High School. My second step was to plan ahead for paying for college. My dad worked very hard for our family, but paying a son's college bill was a little more than he could handle at the time. Since I was already involved in sports, I decided to try for a football and track and field scholarship. In track and field I had been able to hold my own as a half-mile runner and cross-country runner as well as competing in the high jump and pole vault.

But an injury prevented me from being able to continue in football and track and ended my chances for a scholarship. At the end of the season I decided to quit school and take a paying job to help my family. Dad helped me get a job working as a truck driver's assistant in February of 1955. I loaded and unloaded trucks, mostly on the piers of New York. Though it was honest work, by that fall, I had decided that it was time for something else.

A few summers earlier, a group of friends and I had caught a Saturday-afternoon matinee that I would never forget. It was at the Five Corners Orpheum Theater in Jersey City. It was *The Frogmen*, starring Richard Widmark.

No other film I have ever seen impressed me as much as this one did. Here were Navy sailors trained as UDT (Underwater Demolition Team) swimmers taking on the Japanese during World War II. The teamwork and camaraderie among the swimmers reminded me a little of the best parts of being on a football team—a winning team.

One scene that has always stuck with me showed the men rolling off a speeding boat and later being snatched out of the water with a rubber loop. Boy, these men were the best in the Navy, and I wanted to be one!

Several friends I had grown up with were feeling just like me in the fall of 1955—it was time to fish or cut bait. Johnny O'Connor enlisted in the Air Force, and ended up making it a lifetime career. Tom Garrahy joined the Marines, and stayed with the Corps for ten years. Tippy Larkin, one of the smart ones, decided to stay home and take care of the women we were leaving behind. As for myself, it was the Navy, and I was going to be a frogman.

Johnny, Tom, and I all entered the service within about thirty days of each other. My dad decided to give us all a party before we left. We were still too young to drink legally, but my dad figured since we were willing to serve our country, he could serve us. We thought it was real smart to drink vodka, since nobody could smell it, or so we'd heard. At the end of the party, my friends and I were pretty drunk, although there was still most of a bottle of vodka left. Dad took the bottle and stashed it away. The idea was that when the three of us were all back and out of the service we would unseal the bottle and finish it. I think Dad still has that bottle.

There was a young lady that I was very serious about. Lynn Burdell had been a snare drummer in an all-girl drum corps, the Bon Bons of Audubon, New Jersey. The game plan was that I would join the Navy and when I was assigned to a ship, Lynn and I would get married. We had been going together for quite a few years, and I was very much in love with Lynn. We announced our engagement, and Lynn's stepfather threw me a going-away party before I left for basic training. They were all good people, and I was looking forward to us all becoming a family. But first I had to get my Navy training behind me. On October 26, 1955, I reported to boot camp for recruit training.

At the time, boot camp for a seaman recruit such as myself was at the Naval Training Center in Bainbridge, Maryland. It was something of a lonely time for me. I didn't know anyone, and it appeared that my recruit company was mostly made up of country boys. As a tough sophisticated city boy who had worked on the docks of New York, I thought I was bigger and badder than these simple country lads. It didn't take long for some of them to broaden my outlook. Man, could those country boys tear ass. They tossed me around like a bale of hay with hands that had been work-hardened to the consistency of wooden mallets. This city boy, at least, couldn't always stand up to them.

The instructors taught us much of what we had to know to become good sailors. All sorts of really salty information crept into our eager young ears. The pointy end of the boat is the bow; port is left (four letters, just like left!); when you're facing the bow, starboard is the side that isn't port; you pee in the head; if it floats and you can carry it on board it's probably a boat; if it's too big, call it a ship; and the captain of a ship is "The Almighty One," but he does listen to advice from his senior chiefs.

The close-order drill and marching gave me no trouble, thanks to my years with the drum corps and competitions. But why was I doing it? How much marching can you do aboard ship? Besides, I was still going to be a frogman! Just where was UDT training, anyway?

Surprise—UDT is a qualification and not a specialty, and you cannot volunteer and be accepted to Underwater Demolition Team Replacement training, the school for new men entering the UDT, without having a specialty. What is a specialty? It's a job such as boatswain's (bosun's) mate, quartermaster, or even cook. To acquire a specialty you had to attend either a service school or a training course after passing boot camp. The rating, or rank, you would earn in your future naval career would be based in part on your being tested in your specialty. Here was a situation I could deal with, and I had a pretty good idea what job I could handle.

Boot camp had a recruit training drum and bugle corps. I would hear it practicing almost every morning. This was something familiar to me, and I knew I was good at it. Earlier that year I had come in second place in the VFW national competition, so I knew I could prove myself with an instrument. Not only was I certain that I could do well in the corps, but musician was a specialty! If I made the grade I could be more quickly assigned and Lynn and I could be married that much sooner.

I kept bugging my company commander to let me try out for the unit, and finally he took me over there. But I was still a boot and scared shitless about what might happen. I had my own custom-made mouthpiece in my pocket, and I hung on to it as a good luck charm. When I had enlisted, the recruiters had told me about the boot camp band. My mouthpiece had been in my gear all this time, and now was my chance to put it to use. I was introduced to the man in charge of the corps, a bosun's mate first class named Quackenbush. Quackenbush was the biggest, ugliest man I ever met in my life. His hands were so large that he had to have gloves specially made for him—the government didn't stock them that size.

Quackenbush asked me what I played. "Baritone horn, sir," I answered. He handed me a horn and told me to go into a back room and warm up, then continued with his conversation with my commander.

I was in a corner playing "The Carnival of Venice" in triple-time. Suddenly Quackenbush came flying into the room shouting, "Who's playing that?"

I answered, "I am."

"What's your name?" asked Quackenbush. "Where did you learn to play like that?"

I told him who I was and some of the playing I had done, and he turned and went out of the room. I was puzzled. What was going on? Then he came back into the room and hauled me into his office. He had a copy of *Drum Corps World* spread out on his desk. "Are you that James Watson?" asked Quackenbush, pointing at the paper.

The paper was turned to a report on the VFW national individuals competition standings. "Yes sir," I said. That was the beginning of a beautiful friendship.

On January 19, 1956, I graduated boot camp and my rating was changed from seaman, recruit (SR) to seaman, apprentice (SA). I was now a sailor, or at least closer to being one than I had been working on the piers. Quackenbush immediately saw to it that as soon as I had graduated I was assigned to the corps as an instructor.

So here I was, still without the qualifications that could get me into UDT training, but I was instructing and leading other seamen. Still being quite a bullheaded young man, I insisted on doing things my way. I began teaching the other players some of the current music that I had played in civilian competitions. Besides "Anchors Aweigh" and other traditional naval tunes, the sounds of "Memories Are Made of This" and "Cherry Pink and Apple Blossom White" could be heard coming from the practice area.

This didn't go over very well with the higher-ups at the base. The word came down from regiment that the drum corps would play military marches only. Well, graduation was coming up, and about eight or ten guys from the drum corps would be leaving to go to other duty stations. A few of these guys I had known from civilian drum corps before we were in the Navy. We performed at graduation and were quite well received. As we were marching off the drill field some of the guys started calling out, "Mr. Watson,

Mr. Watson, 'Cherry Pink,' 'Cherry Pink.' " I figured we were clear of the drill field and since it was their graduation, what the hell.

One of the players stuck a horn into my hands and said, "Here, you take it." We called for a roll-off from the drums, and I started out into the slur where the most popular part of the music begins. As it turned out we were still well within earshot of the drill field, and "Cherry Pink" might be considered something of a mistake. After I had received my first official Navy ass-chewing over the incident, I tended to follow official directives a bit more closely.

I stayed at Bainbridge with the corps for about six months. All the time I was there I was an instructor, and I'm pretty certain I was the lowest-ranked instructor in the Navy. I might have remained at Bainbridge with the drum and bugle corps for considerably longer than I did, but not everything in this life goes according to plan.

Because I had become an instructor, I figured it was time to get married. Plans were finalized with Lynn, reservations were made at a lodge in the Poconos for the honeymoon, and a full spread was laid on. As I was the first in my generation of our family to get married, my dad put a lot of money out to see his son off right.

I had been going home almost every weekend to see Lynn and my family. Lynn lived in Belmawr in south Jersey, and it was easy to see her and my folks on a weekend and still get back to the base on time for Monday duty. One weekend I was home and all Lynn wanted to talk about was her acceptance to nursing school. All her thoughts were on the coming fall and her future career. It was a long weekend.

I returned to the base and my duties, a little concerned about Lynn's preoccupation but sure that everything would work out. It was on Thursday that things worked out. I went down to the mail room to pick up my mail. The clerk, along with most of the base, knew that I was soon getting married. I didn't exactly hide my feelings and ended up being the target of more than a few jokes. The clerk handed me my letter and said, jokingly, "Here's your Dear John."

I took the ribbing in good humor, but within a few minutes I was accusing the clerk of having opened and read my mail. I really popped my cork when it turned out that the letter was indeed a

Dear John from Lynn. She was calling the wedding off and hoped I would understand.

Well, I didn't understand, but Lynn had made up her mind and there was nothing that I could do to change it. I took it pretty badly. I suppose that I went off the deep end for a while; at any rate, my folks were very worried about me and wanted me to come home for a visit. So one weekend I climbed into the big Buick and headed to Jersey.

My dad had long spoken about getting back up on the horse after you're thrown, so he did what he could to find me another horse. As it turned out, Marlene MacMullen wasn't any kind of horse, and she probably would have popped me if I'd been rude enough to call her one. Marlene worked in the office of the same trucking company that Dad worked for and that I had worked for before joining the Navy.

Pushed by Dad, I called Marlene and asked her out, and things worked out well between us. We started going together on weekends when I could get home, and one thing led to another. I suppose that I was just determined at the time, and Marlene seemed very agreeable to the idea. Marlene and I finally got married, and she moved in with my mom and dad for a while, waiting for me to be assigned to a ship.

The Navy was phasing down Bainbridge, since Korea was over. While I was there, it had been turning out fifteen thousand recruits a year. Since the Navy didn't need as many training stations as it had, Bainbridge saw great reductions in its work force in 1957. So I soon found myself receiving a new set of orders. While an instructor, I had taken my examinations through the book and had been promoted to seaman. But I still didn't have a designator, a specific skill, yet.

I found myself assigned to the USS *Gwin*, a destroyer/minelayer based out of Charleston, South Carolina. I flew down to the airport in Charleston and took a cab to the docks. Being a very new sailor, and quite full of myself, I tried to sound real salty while talking to the cab driver. At the time, I didn't know a destroyer from a meat ax, but I wasn't about to let this cabbie know that.

The *Gwin* was the biggest ship I had seen up to that time, and I was really impressed. She was 376 feet long, gray, with "33" painted on her sides in big white numbers. As a naval boat she was armed with six 5-inch guns in three twin mounts and eight quadruple 40mm mounts along her sides. I was going to be one of a complement of 343 man-o'-war's men who crewed her.

I reported aboard as a seaman with no designator, so in keeping with long-standing naval tradition I was assigned to the deck force—read that chip, paint, and sweep. "Away, sweepers" was an order I became intimately familiar with.

The first time they called "Away, sweepers" and I was on my own, I just picked up my broom and started to sweep out my assigned part of the ship. Extending through my area, roughly the middle (amidships) of the right (starboard) side, were the tracks used for laying mines off the stern of the ship. The tracks were like a small railway slightly elevated above the deck and gradually sloping to the stern. Since we were at sea and a fresh breeze was blowing, a lot of the trash that I was trying to sweep up was blowing under the tracks.

I was watching this stuff blow under the tracks and asking myself, "Wow, I don't have to get a foxtail brush and a dustpan and go crawl under those tracks, do I?" Bosun's Mate First Class Bull Rhodes—he was the senior bosun's mate on the ship—was leaning against the rail nearby watching me with a cup of coffee in his hands.

Bull growled at me, "Hey, boy, how are you going to get that stuff out from under those mine tracks?" I was still a very smart-mouthed young kid and answered him, "I dunno, Boats, I haven't figured that out yet."

Bull was a very large bosun's mate of the old school and he let me know his displeasure at my answer. "Well, you better start fucking figuring, *now!*" he bellowed at me.

Not being a complete idiot, I snapped to. "Yessir!" I answered as I grabbed a foxtail brush and dustpan and dove under the tracks. I swept out under every damn plate, corner, and groove beneath those tracks with Bull leaning on the rail and watching me every minute.

That was my introduction to the deck force. It was just my first lesson in being a good shipboard sailor. I was beginning to realize that there was an awful lot of Navy learning I had missed while being an instructor at the drum corps. I got another lesson when we were returning to port from that first trip.

The first time we were coming in to anchor at the sea buoy, my division was standing on the deck preparing to secure the ship to the buoy. As I was a seaman, the second class in charge turned to me and said, "Go down to the bosun's locker and bring me up about four fathoms of marline." By this time I knew that a fathom was six feet, but what the hell was marline? I got to the bosun's locker where cordage was stowed and looked in.

There was every type of rope, line (small stuff), hawsers, and cables in the locker. I thought, Oh shit, which one is marline? So, taking the chance that I would bring up the wrong thing, I took up about three fathoms of line that I later learned was white line. I knew the second class wanted small stuff, which is what the Navy calls lines that are smaller than rope, so I figured I'd bluff my way through.

I went back topside and walked up to the second class. "I couldn't find any marline down there, Boats. Will this work?"

"Yeah, that's fine," he answered, taking the line from me.

Boy, would I have been in a world of trouble if that had been marline I was holding!

While I was at Bainbridge in the drum corps, especially as an instructor, everything was very spit-and-polish. I kept up this pride in appearance even while serving on the deck force. After I'd been on the ship only a few weeks, a chief quartermaster came up to me to talk about other duties.

"Seaman Watson," he said, "I noticed that you're always squared away and have a clean and neat appearance. How would you like to be a quartermaster?"

I of course immediately jumped at the chance to impress this chief with my knowledge of the Navy. "What the hell's a quartermaster?" I asked.

Instead of tearing my head off and kicking it out over the side, the chief gave me a straight answer. "We work up there on the bridge around all the officers. Now do you want to stay down here and swab decks and scrape paint all the time or come work with me?"

"I really don't understand," I told him.

"If I get you assigned to me for a couple of weeks to see what goes on up there and what the job is about, will you keep that smart mouth of yours shut and give quartermaster a try?"

I had a momentary flash of intelligence and simply said yes. The chief got me assigned TAD, or Temporary Additional Duty, to the quartermaster gang, and I never regretted it. Sure we had our share of swabbing, but it wasn't nearly as much as when I was on the deck gang. Besides all this, quartermaster was a specialty. I now had a rate!

Things went along pretty well for a while. I studied hard in my quartermaster rate, passed the written tests, and made third class petty officer. The Navy transferred me to an MSO (Mine Sweeper, Ocean), the USS *Detector*. While I was assigned to the *Detector*, Marlene was due to have our baby about the same time as we were scheduled to go on a cruise and minesweeping exercise. I had asked to stay behind, but the request was turned down. My mother had come down and was staying with us, so Marlene wasn't alone when my son, James Dennis Watson IV, was born.

When I heard the news I was up on the bridge like all good quartermasters. My neighbor at the apartment was a Navy signalman, and I could see him on the pier signaling to my ship in semaphore. The two waving flags used to pass messages in semaphore were a common sight in the Navy. But this was the first time I received a personal semaphore message. Learning and using semaphore was part of a quartermaster's duties. Picking up my own flags, I went out on deck in time to see my neighbor signal, "Hey, Dad."

"What's this dad stuff?" I signaled back.

"How does it feel to be a daddy?" he waved.

Again, I signaled, "I don't know what you're talking about."

"Jim," he waved, "You're the father of a seven-pound-fourteen-ounce boy. Your mother is with them and they are both doing fine."

I almost fell off the bridge! When the ship had finally docked, I arranged for a seven-day leave, grabbed a cab, and rushed home to see my new son. Jimmy was only six weeks old and became very sick the last Sunday I was home. Dad wasn't home to take the baby to the hospital and no one else could drive, but I had to catch the train to get to my ship by morning. I sent a telegram to the ship

explaining the situation and requested an emergency twenty-four-hour extension, and without waiting for a reply I headed for the doctors.

Jimmy was going to be all right, which was more than I could say for myself. When I arrived at my ship, I learned that they had never granted the extension. I was AOL (absent over leave) as of May 8, 1958. I had just made third class a short time before and I was sure that I would be busted at my captain's mast. The captain gave me a suspended bust and two weeks' restriction to the ship. The punishment wouldn't have been too bad except that the captain said restriction days didn't run while the ship was at sea.

We were just about to leave for northern Europe, and I spent most of our time in port on that cruise on board the ship. So much for seeing the world in the Navy!

While on the *Detector* I was told that if I wanted to get out of all the manual labor of sweeping and swabbing again, I would have to make second class. So I studied my ass off, passed the test, and made the rate.

When I had made second class, the Navy transferred me to an MSC (Mine Sweeper, Coastal), the *Frigate Bird*. I had worked very hard at learning my specialty well, and it paid off. I was made the flag quartermaster—that is, the main quartermaster of the flagship. Now I was the leader for all the other quartermasters in our group of ships, responsible for the way the charts would be set and updated and the records kept, and for some procedures followed for navigating all of the ships.

Because of this responsibility, I was taken to the other minesweepers in the mine division and introduced to the other quartermasters. I was the commodore's fair-haired boy, and he wanted to keep me around.

I had a little over three years in the Navy and was coming up for reenlistment. I was planning to stay in the Navy but still wanted to join UDT. Over the years I had been constantly putting in requests for UDTR training, but they were always turned down. The commodore himself, a mustang officer who had come up through the ranks, wanted me to reenlist. Quartermaster was a critical rate, and the Navy did not want to lose trained men.

I had learned during my time in service, and I was going to use the situation to my advantage. The commodore called me into his stateroom to discuss my reenlistment. He wanted me to reenlist as a quartermaster and remain with him. I told the man no, that I hadn't joined the Navy to be a quartermaster, that I wanted to be a UDT man. I went on to say that I had repeatedly requested UDT training but had never received any orders.

I realized that I was in a good bargaining position and decided to go for broke. "I tell you what, sir," I said. "If you get me UDT training, I'll reenlist."

"You've got a deal," he said. "Reenlist."

"Ah, no, sir, that's not the way I want to play the game. If you can first show me the orders to UDT training, I'll reenlist." I was sweating a bit by this time, but once you've started to push, I had learned, it's a bad idea to back down. Well, the commodore thanked me for coming and I left his office wondering just what would come next.

It was only about a week later that I was called in and shown my new orders. "Upon reenlistment," the orders read, "report to Little Creek, Virginia, Naval Amphibious Base for Underwater Demolition Team Replacement training." I had made it—I was going to be a frogman! But that wasn't the end of the orders. They went on further to say, "Upon dropping out, quitting or otherwise leaving the course, you will immediately report to the USS *Frigate Bird* for duty."

Well, the Navy didn't know it, but the last bit was the best motivation I could have received. I wasn't able to report directly to UDTR training, because the class wouldn't start until the first of the year. I reenlisted on August 7, 1959, and remained with the division until the end of December. I transferred to the USS *Limpkin* for duty until my report date for training.

UDTR training, I had been told, was one of the toughest training routines in the U.S. military. That it was hard I didn't doubt, but I knew that since other men had made it, so could I. One of the main things to do was to get your body in gear and put your brain in neutral. For myself, I figured putting my big mouth in park wouldn't be a bad idea either.

I still worked out some during my off-duty time. I would run and do push-ups, sit-ups, and other calisthenics, but I had never been a serious body builder. UDTR wasn't actually all that much about the physical end of things, even though physical activity appeared

to be what everything centered around. It was more about a certain attitude. Training you can always give a man, but if he hasn't got the heart needed for the job, you're just wasting time.

I had to work hard not to show up at UDTR with the wrong attitude, and the Navy sure didn't help. My admin section aboard the minesweeper kept me through the Christmas leave. They said that since my school was just down the road I could stay and give the other men a chance to go home for Christmas. Yeah—as if I was going to have a lot of spare time during training!

But still, it finally happened. On December 28, 1959, I left the USS *Limpkin* with orders to report to the CO of NAVPHIBSCOL Little Creek for UDTR school at 0700 hours on December 31, and I never looked back.

CHAPTER 3

Volunteers!

Attended UDT Replacement Training Course (B.11) NAVPHIBIS-
COLCREEK NAVPHIBASE, NORVA. Class # XXIII, 16 week course,
graduated 22 Apr standing 8th in 14, final mark 91.70 with 62.5 as
passing.

That is what can be read in my records about my activities
during the early months of 1960. Those few lines summarize one of
the most important and pivotal actions of my life.

I was anything but sure as I opened the doors to the quarterdeck
at UDTR school. It was December and cold outside for Virginia,
but I swear my hands were sweating when I stepped inside. I didn't
know whether to talk to the man at the desk or wait till he heard
my heart beating, it was thumping so loud in my ears.

I had first reported to the admin section over at the Amphibious
School and had my paperwork processed. From there, I went to
check in with the master-at-arms of the UDTR school. The master-
at-arms was Bernard Waddell, one of the few black men in the
Team at that time. Waddell had been in UDT for only about four
years, but he was already something of a legend.

I was six feet tall and Waddell was only a few inches taller, but

I still felt I had to look up to see him, and he was sitting down! As I handed him my paperwork I was thinking, That is one very big black man.

Many trainees were checking in and there were people everywhere, not a familiar face among them. Waddell and his people were very efficient in handling us. Even so, entering training was one of the scariest times of my life. The little bit of activity that I had allowed myself to see around the base told me that UDTR training was a lot like boot camp, only three times longer and about a thousand times harder. I tried not to think too much about what was coming up while I was at home with Marlene.

That first day we received our Quonset hut assignments, our basic issue, and an idea as to what would be coming next. We had been issued green cotton utility uniforms, heavy "boondocker" boots, and red-painted pressed-fiber helmet liners with our last names stenciled on them. We were to wear that helmet liner constantly, only taking it off when we were told to or were inside a building. To take off the helmet was to signify that you were quitting the program. I had no idea how much you could learn to hate an inanimate object. The liner even acted as an indicator that you were carrying your share of the load. The top of the helmet would be checked by the instructors to see if the paint was wearing off and you were carrying part of the weight of the boat we lugged around with us—a training feature I'll have more to say about.

The Quonset huts we were to live in were old constructions from World War II with rough wooden floors and steel walls. The shower and the head were in a separate building, making for a cold walk in the middle of winter.

When we were assigned to our huts, all the buildings were full, sixteen students to a hut. As time went by, the buildings gradually emptied as students quit. When a building got too empty, down to one or two men, they would move into another hut farther up the line. The hut I had been assigned to was at the head of the line, next to where the instructors lived. As the class got smaller, other students moved, but my group stayed in the same hut. We started with 126 students in the class. By the time of graduation, the whole class consisted of eighteen men.

In the class, officers and men were officially treated the same, except that officers were called "sir" by the instructors. Our ranking was simple—instructors were at the top, and trainees, both officer and enlisted, were at the bottom, usually in the mud. From what I could see, being an officer was actually a disadvantage during training. I was to learn later that it was true—instructors tended to rag officers a lot more than they did the enlisted students. The reason was simple. When an officer later came to the Teams—what we called the UDT and later the SEALs—he would be your leader and would direct you in combat. Your life would literally be in that officer's hands. Every man who went through training could be sure that the officer he followed had faced everything that he had, plus a little bit more. In UDT and the SEALs, our officers received that much more respect because of what went on during training.

The first day, at about five-thirty in the morning, we were fallen out in PT uniform, boondockers, green utilities, and helmets. The order from the instructors rang out, an order that would be in effect until graduation day: "FORWARD, DOUBLE-TIME!"

By the time the last man in line had run half a mile, those 126 beginning students were spread out half a mile. They had a number of temporary instructors from the Teams to assist in handling the large number of students. But the numbers problem was quickly going to go away.

The training wasn't as strenuous then as it appears to be now, at least not at the start. They built you up a little more gradually at the beginning then. We would run for only about ten minutes, a slow jog more than a hard run, and then we would be walked for about three minutes. And that's the way it went for some distance, run, walk, then run again, adding more time every day. Within the first week, as we got into shape, we weren't walking anymore, and the runs were an hour long or more. Gradually they became hard pounding runs in heavy boondocker boots, hot uniforms, and bouncing helmets. The runs didn't stay on easy terrain either. The favorite running surface for a UDTR instructor is sand, the looser the better.

The running course we eventually settled down to involved about five or six miles of sand beaches, in and out of the water's edge, with a few light obstacles to overcome. One particularly favored location was Mount Suribachi, the largest sand dune on Beach Seven, right on the shore of Chesapeake Bay, just behind the rifle range. Today at Little Creek, Beach Seven is called Normandy Beach. Running up a loose sand dune is an event not for the faint of heart, or weak of leg either. And weak legs were not something we would ever have to worry about. UDTR trainees would go everywhere at a run, *run*, RUN!

You didn't have to pass a PT (physical training) test to get into the training program then as you do now. They gave us a PT test starting our second day. There wasn't a set number you had to do of any given exercise. It was do as many push-ups as you could, do as many sit-ups as you could, do as many chin-ups as you could. And so on through a series of exercises. And the instructors really pushed us to give "every ounce you've got."

The results of all these exercises were recorded, tallied, and ranked. Out of 126 students, I ranked as number 124. By the time graduation finally arrived, I was listed as the most physically improved. I think my rise in the rankings was partly due to the departure from the program of all those students who had ranked ahead of me.

Regardless of your shape or where you finished in every evolution, one of the instructors told me again and again, even if you were last every time, as long as you didn't quit and kept going you would make it to graduation and the Teams. Any exercise, problem, or obstacle was called an evolution. As we completed them, we evolved much closer to becoming a UDT man.

That was the carrot that was held out for me and the other students. If you did come up last in every evolution, the instructors would be harder on you and push you more. You were fair game to be harassed unmercifully. But as long as you didn't quit, they wouldn't wash you out.

And harass you they would. The instructors were on our asses continually to quit. "*YOU PUKE! QUIT, YOU PUKE! YOU AIN'T GONNA MAKE IT—WE'RE GOING TO GRADUATE THIS CLASS IN A TELEPHONE BOOTH!*" And they almost did.

It was only the second day of training when the first guy quit. He was soon followed by others. It was hard to understand how some of these people could not have known what they were getting into. On average there is a 60 percent loss rate in UDT/SEAL training from men quitting. In our class, the loss rate was 86 percent.

At the beginning, I had only cared about getting myself through the course. That changed a lot. Later on, just before Hell Week, the twenty-five or so of us that were left were pretty close and starting to work like the team we had to be.

There is no physical standard of what a UDT or SEAL man should be besides passing training. If there is a common physical type of person who graduates it is a guy of average build, medium height and weight, who just will not quit. No matter what it takes, this guy will just keep going until the objective is accomplished.

In our class we had this one skinny guy, Heinz, who at the end of every day would stand in front of the mirror in the head, flex whatever muscles he had, sore as they were, and say, "The big hairy bastards are gone, but I'm still here!" He did that for sixteen weeks. His picture is in my office today along with the other graduates of Class 23 East Coast.

I suppose that now is the time to tell the secret I have been hiding for years. Some suspected it. Yes, I had an easy class. We didn't go over the Death Trap, a rather famous obstacle that would-be frogmen face on their way through Hell Week. You try to cross two ropes suspended fifteen feet above a pond while explosions shower you with mud and instructors move the ropes. No one has ever made it all the way across the Death Trap. But when I trained it was being repaired.

Instead of the Death Trap, my class had the Around the World. And before I hear comments from other UDTR graduates out there, yes, you had the Around the World, only my class had to do it *twice*! Personally, I would rather have had the Death Trap.

Up to this point, we had been doing all of the usual exercises for UDT training. Today, in training, they have log drills. The students do exercises holding a large chunk of telephone pole besides also doing boat exercises. We didn't do log PT, but the instructors made up for it with the rubber boats.

If we hated those red helmets, we despised the IBS (Inflatable Boat, Small). Already, our class had been taking the IBS everywhere we went. We would run with it carried on top of our heads, sometimes with an instructor bouncing along inside it just for fun. Calisthenics would be done with our feet propped up on the boat's sides, and arm lifts holding it in our hands. The IBS is twelve feet long and six feet wide and weighs about three hundred pounds. And we hated every ounce of it.

The instructors wanted our class to do a traditional Around the World at Little Creek and again when we went down to Puerto Rico. What the instructors want, they usually get, so off we went.

Around the World is a scheduled problem which each seven-man boat crew had to complete with its IBL (Inflatable Boat, Large). The IBL is over fourteen feet long and almost eight feet wide and weighs over four hundred pounds, just a little something extra for the boat crew. Along with the boat, we were given a handout chart showing the route we would take. The uniform was fatigues, boondocker boots, helmets, and heavy kapok life vests worn over inflatable UDT vests. The kapok vests weighed six pounds dry and about twenty-six pounds wet, a condition they were in most of the time. And on top of all this was the IBL. A staggering load for seven men to carry in normal conditions, and the conditions were anything but normal.

For this Around the World evolution we would take our IBLs through hundreds of yards of swamp and muck, pulling, carrying, or paddling as the need arose, always protecting our boat from harm and checking in along the way at instructor-manned checkpoints.

After the swamp and mud flats, we would cross over a seawall jetty bordering a channel entrance from Chesapeake Bay. The seawall was riprap, mostly just a big pile of large loose stones constantly doused with salt water, very slippery and difficult to move over. After crossing one wall we would paddle cross the channel and cross another identical seawall. Next we would paddle our boats over a long stretch of open water along the bay, guiding by landmarks we could barely see in the darkness. Then we were back on land and moving farther along, all the time guiding over obstacles, barbed wire, mud flats, open ditches, and canals and then to the final checkpoint.

An instructor would be on top of Mount Suribachi, that big sand dune on Beach Seven, to check us through this last obstacle. Being made of loose sand, Mount Suribachi was too yielding to crawl up dragging our IBL, and too steep to walk up carrying the IBL on our heads. You had to negotiate the sand with a kind of half-crawling walk with the IBL on your head. If you didn't cooperate and work as a team, a boat crew could not complete the course. If you managed to win, be the first crew to complete the evolution, you were supposed to get a "reward," an extra thirty minutes of sleep. I never knew of anyone in our class actually receiving that blessed extra sleep.

Our instructors were an interesting bunch of guys. Among them were Shelby Jones, Fat Rat Sutherland, John Parrish, and Henry Spiegle. Parrish and Spiegle I had seen before, though I hadn't known it. They both had parts in the movie *The Frogmen*. When the UDT helped make the film back in the early 1950s, John Parrish played the part of a Japanese diver who attacked Richard Widmark's character underwater. Henry Spiegle acted as Richard Widmark's double on most of the underwater scenes in the movie. In fact it was Spiegle who fought Parrish in the big underwater fight toward the end of the film. These were the men who were training us, and they all wanted us to be capable of cheating on the rules. That was the name of the game—break the rules and bend the situation to your advantage, but do not get caught!

At three o'clock in the morning, we had been doing the paddle trip across part of the Chesapeake. All of us had a pretty good glow on and were singing while paddling our IBL. That told our instructors that we had been drinking. They knew we had booze, but couldn't find it in the boat. And that made them proud of us. It didn't take much, but they couldn't find it; it had been smuggled to us and hidden.

Almost all of the boat crews tried to sneak booze along on the evolution. The instructors knew this and almost always found it when it was there. Even Waddell was searching our gear and came up empty-handed. The instructors as a group checked our boat while we just stood there with our inflatable rubber UDT vests worn underneath our kapok vests.

The UDT vest is very useful in part because it gives you additional buoyancy while taking up little space. It can be inflated as needed through an oral tube as well as with a CO_2 cartridge. Liquids can be poured through the oral inflation tube if you use a small funnel made from a piece of paper. Those liquids can later be drawn out through that same tube. The instructors never did find our booze, and we continued with our Around the World.

Yeah, we had booze, but not everyone drank. Some of the finest UDT and SEAL operators I've known never took a drink, never touched a cigarette, never swore. A later friend of mine, Gene Tin-nin, one of the finest SEALs I knew, was like that. Swearing, drinking, and smoking are not what make a man a man, and UDTR training showed us that.

Some instructors were real hard-core pushers, drove us to the limit and past it. Other instructors were the "trainee's friend" and would help guys through difficult sections and guide them the right way. This was something like the good-cop-bad-cop, Mutt-and-Jeff routine they show in the movies and on television, and there weren't many trainee's friends, maybe one or two per class. The system worked to increase the number of men graduating training without lowering the quality of the end product.

Bernie Waddell was one of the hard-core instructors we had, and a damn good one. Waddell was the master-at-arms of all the instructors. Waddell ran us through PT and the obstacle course, but didn't train us in swimming. I knew then that Waddell and another instructor, Bill Goines, were the only two black men in UDT 21. Waddell wouldn't swim us, but man, would he run us into the ground on PT and the o-course.

We had three black students in my class when we started. One, Thomas, made it to graduation. Another quit right away, and the third guy thought he had a way of getting by when his work started getting weak. He walked up to Waddell and started laying out a line on him about brothers and how they had to look out for each other against the rest of us. Was that ever a mistake. The guys who had quit and left the day before could have heard Waddell tell this man off.

"BOY," Waddell boomed, "YOU ARE NO BROTHER OF MINE TILL THE DAY YOU COME TO UDT, AND I'M GOING TO RUN YOUR ASS OUT!"

The man quit before the day was over. We all thought it would be a very good idea not to piss Waddell off, especially now that we had seen the difference between his normal shouting and what happened when he was really mad.

Waddell was the man who introduced us to one of the well-known pieces of UDTR training, the obstacle course. Our o-course was a series of twenty-six obstacles, none of them easy. The easiest one was a zigzag line of elevated logs you had to run across, the Log Walk. There were three of the logs, each successive one higher, and the ends of the logs were attached to trees. You couldn't step from one log to the other—it was too high, and the tree got in the way. You had to jump and keep your balance to complete the obstacle.

Other fun things were on the course to keep us occupied and happy. The High Net, a cargo net going fifty feet straight up; you climbed up one side and down the other. The Belly Robber, a chest-high series of logs you had to jump into, on your stomach, and weave over and under. And the Wall Climb, a wooden wall you were supposed to walk up, using a hanging rope, and climb over. I never did get the Wall Climb right; I always had to shinny up the rope.

The one obstacle that always gave me the willies was the Slide for Life. This was a tall wooden tower that had two ropes angling down from one side. Below the ropes was a long pool of deep muddy water. The objective was to climb onto the rope, which had about a thirty-degree downslant, and slide down to the ground on your chest, straddling the top of the rope.

I had never liked high places. Climbing out on that rope, hanging fifty feet above the water, was a real bitch, but I did do it. We learned very quickly that you had to keep your eyes glued on that rope as you slid down it. Looking down or to the right or left could cause you to lose your balance and fall into the water.

When we were first introduced to the o-course, it took me forty-five minutes to get through it. To graduate, you had to complete the course in under fifteen minutes. I did my final completion in just under twelve minutes.

The first four weeks of training were heavy, and I mean *heavy*, into physical training. There was very little classroom training; they were not going to waste any time teaching someone who couldn't make the grade where it really counted. They came up with a real ass-buster in the form of PT that the instructors would use as a form of punishment. A "circus" would be awarded by any instructor who thought we had earned one.

A circus was simply burnout PT. We would be run through calisthenics until we dropped, literally, from exhaustion. You would get to the point where you couldn't do any more—in boxing they would call it a technical knockout. For a variation, they could choose to give us a circus in the surf zone. The surf zone is that active area of the beach where the waves come crashing onto the shore, and onto any luckless trainee who happens to be doing push-ups.

While the class was still large, I would try to stay in the middle of the group when running or doing PT. The instructors would harass us, but the harassment was directed at the group rather than at individuals. As the class got smaller, everyone received individual attention from the instructors.

When our class got small, there was no middle of the group, and I received my fair share of attention. The two instructors who gave me their particular attention were Dave Casey and Jim Tipton. Dave Casey was also a quartermaster, and his line with me was that he didn't want any more quartermasters in UDT and was going to drive me out.

"WATSON," Casey would shout at me, "YOU ARE LOWER THAN WHALE SHIT, AND WHALE SHIT IS AT THE BOTTOM OF THE OCEAN. YOU AREN'T GOING TO MAKE IT—I'M GOING TO MAKE IT MY PERSONAL BUSINESS TO DRIVE YOU OUT."

Jim Tipton was the same way, only he had a slightly different line. Tipton was a torpedoman second class, and he didn't want any more second classes in the Teams. He would really get on me. When I was down doing push-ups, Tipton would be right there bent over and shouting in my face.

"QUIT, PUKE!" Tipton would bellow. "YOU'RE NOT GONNA MAKE IT! QUIT, YOU PUKE, YOU USELESS PIECE OF SHIT! QUIT!"

Tip, as I later called him, became one of my very close friends and was a fellow plankowner of SEAL Team Two. Plankowners, according to Navy tradition, are all the members of a ship's, or unit's, original crew on the day of her commissioning. They are said to own a plank of the ship's hull and are usually a very close-knit group. But while he was an instructor, Tip acted as if he wanted to break me up and flush me down the head.

The instructors would remind us all of our standing in their world twenty-six hours a day, with constant reference to our ranking against different varieties of fish manure. This started well before Hell Week and continued all through training.

Because the class was scheduled to go to Puerto Rico for further training, including Hell Week, the instructors felt we shouldn't miss out on some of the fun back at Little Creek. To send us on our way properly they gave us that Around the World party. But the day finally came and we were moving out.

The first week of February, the whole class, all twenty-some of us, went down to Roosevelt Roads, Puerto Rico, for eight weeks of training. Ours was the first class to go to Puerto Rico at this stage in our training. We departed on the USS *Pymouth Rock* (LSD-29) on February 6.

On board the *Rock* for three days traveling to Roosevelt Roads, all they did was burn us out with PT—something of a break for us, there being no sand runs aboard a ship. We did get some classroom training, and something they don't teach as much now, the history of the Teams. We learned about Admiral Kauffman, the father of the UDTs, who landed the NCDUs (Naval Combat Demolition Units) at Normandy. Later the name was changed to UDT. Some of this history was being taught to us while we were steaming past Fort Pierce, where it had all started during World War II and where the UDT/SEAL Museum stands today.

From day one of our arrival in Puerto Rico we were kept separated from the rest of the base. We had our own little barracks complex on top of a hill with a swimming pool behind the building. All of this was away from the rest of the base, right off one of the airstrips.

They started burning us right away with constant PT, circuses, running, and IBS drills. Not all of the instructors treated us the same way all of the time. It was quickly noticed that if Tipton or Shelby had gone out the night before, the next day wouldn't be quite as hard. For example, if Tipton had been out drinking the night before, he didn't really want to run. Since we had to run, Tipton would just stand in the middle, and we would run in circles around him.

Some people can stand heat better than other people. With others, it's cold that they can handle better. It depends on what you prefer, sweltering in the heat or freezing your butt off. Our class had both. We faced the full Hell Week in the heat of Puerto Rico.

You really sweated your ass off during Hell Week. A few of the guys fell victim to heat exhaustion, and I think I was one of them. I don't remember going out, but I was told I did. One night, during Hell Week, we were ending a long run and going uphill, approaching our barracks. There was a ditch between the road and the grassy PT area in front of our barracks. As we made the left turn to go to the barracks, I ran straight into the ditch.

The next thing I remembered was coming to with Tipton and the corpsman working over me. I must have been going on automatic, because I don't remember running into the ditch. Tipton, of course, treated me with all the concern the instructors uniformly showed for our well-being.

"YOU'RE GOING TO QUIT, WATSON. I TOLD YOU YOU WEREN'T GOING TO MAKE IT, YOU USELESS PIECE OF SHIT." All of this while he was expertly treating me for heat exhaustion, preventing it from becoming life-threatening.

Jumping to my feet—or at least I think I made it to my feet—I snapped out, "Let's go."

"YOU ARE NOT ONLY A USELESS PIECE OF SHIT, YOU ARE THE DUMBEST TRAINEE IN THE NAVY. COME ON, WATSON, ALL YOU HAVE TO DO IS QUIT, AND YOU WON'T HAVE TO DO THIS ANYMORE. YOU'RE NOT GOING TO MAKE IT ANYWAY."

"No, no, let's go, I'm ready for more," I croaked as loudly as I could. Tipton finally relented and moved the class on.

During Hell Week we carried our IBLs almost everywhere with us. Bouncing along on the top of our pointy little heads was that miserable rubber boat, crushing down on our red helmets.

Fat Rat Sutherland, who acted as our "trainee's friend," was the man who pushed the team aspect for us during our Hell Week. The boat crews were seven men, but when a man quit, the instructors wouldn't immediately rearrange the crews evenly. It could come to only three or four guys struggling with their boat.

It was when this happened that the trainee's friend would talk to the man who might be just about to quit and tell him, "Come on, hang in there. You're part of a team—you don't want to leave your buddies carrying this boat all by themselves, do you?" Sometimes just those few words of encouragement could keep a man going.

Of course, the instructors also had ways of holding a crew back if they thought it was getting too far ahead of the pack. An instructor would leap up into the boat you were carrying and jump around, sometimes jumping from boat to boat. And *don't* drop that instructor—the earth would open up and swallow you whole, or at least you'd want it to.

The lack of sleep and constant strain took its toll of us. Many of the guys would go into automatic on some of the long runs and swims. Automatic is where you don't want to quit but you can't seem to keep going. You shut off everything but the muscles it takes to keep functioning and literally go to sleep on your feet.

One thing you learned quickly was not to look too far ahead and wonder if you were going to get some sleep. Instead you would just focus on the task at hand, and concentrate on completion of that one task. Sometimes, it helped to tell yourself, "If I can just get this evolution over with, maybe the instructors will give us some time to rest." We didn't often receive a break, but if you let that get to you, you were finished.

One evolution would immediately follow another, whether it was running, rubber boat drill, or a circus. All you would have in your mind was to get this evolution over with and maybe you would get a reward. There were always rewards for doing well, and punishments for doing badly.

During Hell Week they came up with some pool evolutions unique to the UDT. They would put a bucket of rocks on the bottom of the deep end of the pool. Trainees had to swim down to the bucket and move it to the other end of the pool. The only way to complete the evolution was to pick up the bucket and walk along the bottom to the other end of the pool.

Another fun pool game was to swim the length of the pool holding an empty bucket in your hands. If you pulled the bucket tight up against your butt you could seal off its mouth and then just flutter- or frog-kick to the end of the pool. Upper-arm strength was not ignored either. The instructors would tie heavy towels to a swimmer's wrists and into the pool with him. Swimming with two water-soaked towels tied to the arms is not to be missed by anyone who really likes torturing himself.

Breath-holding was another thing carefully built up by the instructors. The normal evolution would be to swim back and forth the length of the pool underwater without coming to the surface. If you did surface, you would have to go back half the distance already covered and start again. To win that game you had to stay down and make your lungs almost burst, but not surface. I didn't make it the first time I tried, but I got better fast.

I was determined to make it. Sitting way in the back of my head were those words from my orders to UDTR, "Report to the USS *Frigate Bird* for duty." I was not going to quit. They were going to have to kill me to make me quit. And they couldn't kill me—that was against regulations, wasn't it?

Bill Brumuller was a UDT man on Temporary Additional Duty from St. Thomas, where UDT 21 was. Here was another UDT man who really impressed me. If I could get through all this training, I would be able to work with men like Brumuller, Tipton, and Tinnin. Later on, these men would all become my close friends, with Tip and Bill both being fellow plankowners of Team Two. But first I had to finish training, and there was one more day of Hell Week to go.

Our last day of Hell Week was So Solly Day on Piñeros Island at the eastern tip of Puerto Rico. Piñeros is a little chunk of land that nobody would miss if it was blown off the map, and our instructors tried to blow it off with us on it. Making you crawl through surf and sand with explosions rocking the earth around you is the way the UDT asks, "Just how badly do you want to be a frogman?" After a week of little sleep and maximum output, So Solly Day comes as close to taking you into the confusion, noise, and terror of combat as a peacetime Navy can supply.

Let me tell you it is one very proud group of dirty, exhausted, water-soaked, sand-covered sailors who are still standing at the end of Hell Week. There is still a lot of training yet to do, but the instructors seem to respect the trainees just a little bit.

Swimming is, of course, a large part of the training. Starting off with simple pool swims of only a few hundred yards back at Little Creek, the swims gradually get longer and much harder.

When we had completed a mile-long swim, they awarded us our first pair of swim fins. The fins used then were hard, stiff rubber models called "duck feet" and were made by Voit Sporting Goods. The fins would almost always give you a cramp in your instep until you became used to them.

We were first introduced to the face mask while in the pool down in Puerto Rico. The instructors would run us ragged, but they always kept a careful watch on safety. When we were learning how to clear a mask underwater, the instructors would first make us fill the face mask half full of water and then continue swimming. The idea behind this exercise was to teach us to breathe only through the mouth when swimming. That way if later, when we were using a diving lung, we lost the mask, we could continue swimming and complete the mission.

A number of us had trouble using the half-full face mask and had our own method of getting extra practice. At night we would take our face masks with us into the shower. We would fill our masks with water and take our showers with our masks on. Bob Stamey and I had the most trouble with our masks, and we ended up taking a lot of showers.

For some reason Bob Stamey quit, but he came back in the next class and graduated. Sometimes if the instructors felt that the reason for a man's dropping out was legitimate, and that the man was worth it, they would let him into a later class to try again. The man who graduated as the honor man from my class had dropped out from an earlier class. His name was Bill Daugherty.

We were in the water every day. Once our mile swim had been completed and we had our fins, it was open-water swimming in the ocean. Our final qualifying swim was from Vieques Island to Puerto Rico, a distance of about ten miles. The currents, waves, and other factors add up to make that swim effectively much longer than it appears on a chart. We were in the water swimming constantly for fourteen hours.

The currents were the real killers on this swim. At one point my swim buddy, Heinz, and I were looking down at the same piece of sea floor for an hour and a half. We had to swim hard just to hold our own, but eventually we completed the evolution.

Tough situations like the current on that qualifying swim happen to everyone at one point or another during training. And the fact that the person has completed training tells all the men that serve with him that whether or not he's the best at everything, he's game for everything. An example is Bernard Waddell. UDT operators would comment that Waddell couldn't swim, and perhaps that was true, relative to the swimming abilities of others in the Teams. But Waddell completed that qualifying swim, and therefore I can attest that the man can swim.

There's a real high point during training for almost everyone who passes through UDTR. For me it took place down at Roosy (Roosevelt) Roads during cast and recovery. We were the last UDTR class to use the old LCPRs from World War II. The LCPR—

Landing Craft, Personnel, Ramped—is the old Higgins boat with the small bow ramp and the two forward gun tubs. These were the boats they showed in the movie *The Frogmen*, and for all I knew, ours were the actual boats that had been used in the film.

Cast and recovery is the oldest UDT technique for getting men into and out of the water fast. An IBS is made fast to the side of the LCPR and the boat makes its casting run with the IBS on the side facing away from the shore. The men get into the IBS, either singly or in pairs, and at a signal from the controller, roll off into the water while the boat maintains speed. During demolition swims, another man is in the stern of the boat throwing demolition packs over the landward side as each man hits the water.

After the team completes its mission, the men line up at the rendezvous point, spaced out evenly. As the LCPR makes its recovery run, each swimmer puts up his left arm as the boat bears down on him. A snare man in the middle of the IBS, straddling the outboard side and bracing against a seat, has a figure-eight loop in his hands. The figure-eight loop is called a snare, and the snare man hooks it over each swimmer's upheld arm. As the snare hits the swimmer's arm, the swimmer clamps down on it and is hauled into the IBS by the snare man. The swimmer scrambles out of the IBS and into the LCPR to make room for the next recovery.

This procedure actually takes longer to describe than it does to do, and doing it is a real blast. Everyone has a point in training where he personally feels that he has made it, and cast and recovery was mine.

We were just off the coast of Vieques doing cast and recovery for the first time. There wasn't any real swimming involved—the instructors just wanted us to tread water until they came about and picked us up. I will always remember that first time I rolled off into the water from that speeding boat and I thought, This is where it's at.

Then the LCPR had turned around and was making its pickup run. That snare hit my arm and I was snatched out of the water, and the next thing I knew I was in the rubber boat scrambling into the LCPR. The thought that went through my head was: I'm a frogman now—I've done it. That is the Hollywood frogman, rolling off a speeding boat and then getting snatched out of the water. Richard Widmark, move over.

I still had a lot of training to go, but my attitude was just a little bit different. One of the instructors saw to it that just a bit of the air was let out of my sails before I got too full of myself.

We were on the return trip from some cast-and-recovery practice off Vieques, and the sea was starting to get pretty choppy. We were on our way back to the old dry dock where the LCPRs were kept. The flat bottom on the LCPRs gives them a real rough ride in a rising sea. Gene Tinnin was one of our instructors riding in the LCPR that day. I cannot remember ever having heard Gene curse or swear, but he could really let his opinion be known, especially to a trainee.

The boat took a real hard swell, and everyone inside the craft was being tossed about. I saw Tinnin take a hard fall onto the deck and slam against a bulkhead. Without thinking I immediately grabbed his arm and snatched him up before he got bounced around too much. While pulling him to his feet I asked, "Are you all right, buddy?"

Gene just about came unglued when I said that. "Don't you ever call me buddy, you stinking trainee," Gene shouted. "You're not going to make it to the Teams, and the *only* time you could ever call me buddy is if you ever walked through the doors of UDT 21." I logged that statement for later consideration.

That little incident cost me a number of push-ups and really set me back in my place. Tinnin wasn't too bad about it, though. He did wait until we were back at the dock before he made me do those push-ups.

We trained in demolitions in Puerto Rico after we had passed Hell Week. There we were, enthusiastically attempting to blow poor Piñeros Island off the charts again. We would conduct a hydrographic reconnaissance of a beach, making note of the obstacles that had been placed there for us. After the recon had been completed and we were evaluated, the class would return to the same area and conduct a demolition swim, blasting the obstacles out of the water.

There was a great deal more to the process than simply placing explosives on targets and tying them together with primacord. The instructors kept a tight rein on us, and for this subject we received a lot of classroom training. Careful consideration was given to safety long before we were ever allowed near live explosives. We were taught how to calculate charges for many different types of obstacles as well as how to tie them together for simultaneous detonation.

It was the classroom work that was almost my downfall. We would have loved to overload a target and blow it out of existence, but that wasn't the way it was supposed to be done. Formulas had been designed to calculate exactly how much of what kind of explosive was needed to do the job. As long as we were in a hands-on training evolution, I was okay. But the mathematics almost took me out.

Fat Rat Sutherland was very good at math and would spend extra hours coaching me through the formulas. Again the trainee's friend came to the rescue of a foundering trainee. In the UDT, and later the SEALs, you couldn't always just bull your way through a situation; you had to be able to think. There were a certain number of exams you had to pass to graduate training, and demolitions especially had some regular written tests.

Later on when I was with the SEALs in Vietnam, Fat Rat's time with me proved very useful. You would often think about a target and figure if two pounds would do the job, twenty pounds would guarantee it. But when you had to carry everything with you slogging through a swamp, every pound counted, and so you had to calculate for a known target.

But finally we were finished with training in Puerto Rico and we went back to Little Creek, again by ship. Aboard the ship, Gene Tinnin again demonstrated to us the caliber of instructors we had in UDTR training.

Tinnin had been leading our class in PT aboard ship on the way back to Little Creek one morning when he made a suggestion to us. "Why don't you hamburgers try and set some sort of record for your class," he said. After some discussion and suggestions, not all of them printable, practical, or even legal, we decided on doing jumping jacks. Gene agreed to this, and he laid down the ground rules.

"Okay," Gene said, "when the first man stops, that's when we all stop. The goal is two thousand two hundred and twenty-three. Ready! Exercise!" And we were off.

Well, we did it. Each individual in my class did 2,223 consecutive jumping jacks there aboard ship, and Gene followed along on each one. Tinnin was wearing one of the old-style loose canvas bathing suits, and it rubbed his crotch and privates raw. We all could see this because blood was actually running down his legs. But as long as we were going, he wasn't going to quit either.

We walked up to Tinnin after the exercise and said that we had the record now. Gene told us that it would be so recorded and for us to fall out. He stood there on the deck until we were all out of sight. He wasn't even going to try to walk while we could still see him. That was the caliber of the instructors we had, and we respected them all the more for what Gene did. I think our class's record still is standing, especially now that they no longer run UDTR at Little Creek.

Back at the Creek we still had some training yet to go before graduation. We were all in pretty good shape and were now able to do things we wouldn't have thought possible only a few weeks before. We still had IBS drill and evolutions to complete, and they had become even longer and harder.

We hadn't been the sharpest class in the world, but we had completed training by pulling together as a team and were due to graduate soon. The day before graduation, two instructors, Shelby Jones and Jim Tipton, decided we still had one more lesson to learn. They ordered the class out and gave us a circus in the surf zone.

Burnout PT the last day! What had we done? They said it was to prove to us that we hadn't graduated yet. As we worked out with the cold April waves pounding down on us we decided that this was bullshit! We were standing there busting our humps when one of us said, "Wait just a damn minute—there are eighteen of us and just one of him." Tipton had already left. All eighteen of us stood up and just defied that instructor. Discipline be damned, we had done nothing to deserve the treatment we were getting and we were not going to stand for it. We were all in good shape, better even than some of the instructors, and were starting to feel a little froggy about it.

In fact, the class got together, our officers included, picked up Shelby Jones bodily, and threw him into the Chesapeake. We stood there and just laughed! Then we walked back to our barracks.

Walking was a real no-no for trainees, and we hadn't done much of it in the last several months.

That's what they had wanted to see! Our class was working as a team and bucking the system. The system said one instructor could tell twenty guys what to do, and they had better do it. But we had gotten to the point where the instructors wanted to see the entire class pull together as a team, and we did.

I hope that it is the same today in the SEAL Teams—that the team is a unified group working together to get the job done, without any individuals standing outside the whole. There is no room for movie-type Rambos in the Teams.

Our graduating class had fourteen enlisted men, two American officers, and two foreign officers. Quite a comedown from the 126 men who had started four months earlier. For some of the men, the training had come fairly easily; others had had to work full out almost to graduation day. I was going to learn years later, when my friend Rick Marcinko was assembling SEAL Team Six, that it was the man who had to work hardest to get what he wanted that you could depend on the most.

For our graduation we were in the auditorium of the Amphibious School building. It was four bells—that's 1000 hours for the military and ten o'clock for the civilians, and for the Marines, Mickey's big hand is pointing to the 12 and his little hand is pointing to the 10—when I graduated UDTR with my family watching. The award didn't appear to be very much—a paper diploma showing you had graduated UDTR and a small blue cloth tab for the shoulder of the uniform. The tab read "UDT 21" where the rest of the Navy would have the name of a ship. There is very little in this world that can mean as much in as simple a package.

The instructors had lined up at the back of the auditorium so that the graduating students could walk past them to shake their hands. After the graduation announcements had been read, how we had been through the toughest training in the military, the officers shook our hands and gave us our diplomas, and we were dismissed. We had the day off and could report to UDT 21 the next day.

When I approached Gene Tinnin in the instructors' row he put his hand out to me and I grabbed it with a smile. "How's that, buddy?" I said.

Gene snapped back at me, "You're not through the doors of Team 21 yet."

Why, you sonofabitch, I thought. But I wasn't the kind of guy to react immediately. I put my annoyance away and logged it for later consideration. Paybacks are a bitch.

Besides, I had something important to do. After leaving the formalities I quickly had my UDT 21 tab sewn onto my dress blues. I had a lunch date and I was not going to be out of uniform.

The *Limpkin* was in port the day I graduated, and I was going aboard for lunch. I don't think there was another man in the Navy as proud of that UDT 21 tab as I was when I went aboard the *Limpkin*. I was there to tell them that this quartermaster had made it and he was not coming back. After lunch I went aboard the other ships in the division, the *Hummingbird*, the *Jacana*, and the *Frigate Bird*. I even stopped off in the commodore's office for a moment, and he was in. I pointed to the tab on my shoulder and said, "I'm not coming back." A lot of the men, including the commodore, congratulated me and said that they never believed I would make it. But I had, and now I was a UDT man!

A new expression had entered my vocabulary, "clausty." Claustrophobia, the fear of enclosed spaces, was something you were tested for in UDTR. "Clausty" was the UDT term for being not really afraid, but hesitant to do something. My entire class was a bit clausty about reporting to UDT 21, so we did what had gotten us through training—we went as a group.

Quickly, we were assigned to platoons and initiated into the Teams routine. Deployments were available for us to go all over the world, and I soon found myself north of the Arctic Circle. After that duty, I found myself just a little famous. A picture of me made the cover of the January 1962 issue of *All Hands* magazine. Our whole detachment had been jumping from a helicopter into the water near Thule, Greenland. A Navy photographer snapped a shot of me just as I left the bird heading for the water.

But I was going to do a lot more than just jump out of helicopters into the water. When the chance came up, I worked hard and won a place in a UDT group going to Airborne School. That training led to a lifelong love of sky diving. Later, Diving School helped round out my UDT training.

At Diving School, I became proficient at using open-circuit

scuba, like an earlier version of the sport diving rigs of today, and was taught the safe use of the dangerous closed-circuit rebreathers, the Draeger, Mark V Emerson, and mixed-gas Mark VI Emerson. Now I was a fully trained UDT man, able to jump out of planes or boats and move on top of or underneath the water. But my biggest challenge would come after the UDT.

SEALs!

It was on January 8, 1962, that UDT 21 was called to a muster that was to change my life forever. It was a nice sunny day with the temperature in the low sixties, not cold even for Norfolk in the winter. We had gathered behind UDT 21 headquarters, in front of Sub Ops, at 1300 hours EST. An officer in front of the formation called out, "The following named men fall out and go into the classroom." Here is the original roster of SEAL Team Two, nicknames and all:

OFFICERS

Gordon Ablitt
Roy H. Boehm—"Boss"
John F. Callahan—"Skipper"
Joseph DiMartino—"Joe D"
David H. Graveson
Tex Hager
William Painter
Dante M. (Stephensen) Shapiro
Charles C. Wiggins

CHIEFS

James C. Andrews—"Hoot"
Rudolph E. Boesh—"Uncle Rudy"
Donald Stone*—"Doc Stone"

MEN

Harry M. Beal—"Short Meat"
B. Benzschawel—"Bennie"
Pierre Birtz
Wayne Boles—"Kahuna"
Ron Brozak—"Bro"
William Brumuller—"Panda Bear"
Charles Bump
William E. Burbank, Sr.—"Billy"
A. D. Clark—"AD"
John W. Dearmon
George W. Doran
James F. Finley
Samuel R. Fournier
Ronald G. Fox
William H. Goines
William T. Green
Tom Iwaszczuk
Stanley S. Janecka
Charles W. Jessie—"Jess"
Rex W. Johnson
Michael D. Kelly
Claudius H. Kratky—"Kraut"
Louis A. Kucinski—"Hoss"
James P. MacLean—"Scotty"
Richard D. Martin*—"Leg Martin"
Frederick McCarty*
Mike McKeawn
Melvin F. Melochick
Tom Murphy
Richard Nixon*—"Doc Nixon"

------

* Assigned as corpsmen, not UDT-qualified.

Bob Peterson—"RW"
John Ritter
Paul T. Schwartz*—"PT"
Bobby G. Stamey
Joseph Taylor—"Jerry"
John D. Tegg
James C. Tipton—"Tip," "JC"
James T. Tolison—"JP," "Jess"
Robert A. Tolison—"RA," "Trash Mouth"
Per Erik Tornblom—"Swede"
Jim Wallace, Jr.
James D. Watson—"Patches," "Mrs. Watson's little boy"
Leonard A. Waugh
Harry R. Williams—"Lump Lump"

Some of the men were still in training or were unable to get away from their units or UDT platoons until replacements had been trained. They all arrived later to fill out the initial complement of fifty officers and enlisted men. Roy Boehm had asked for extra men to be assigned to Team Two because some of the initial complement were taken out for assignments before they ever reached Little Creek.

But we didn't know anything about the SEALs and Team Two yet. As they were calling the names we looked at each other and noticed some things about the people they were calling. All of us were qualified for open-circuit, closed-circuit, and mixed-gas diving gear, and we were all parachute jumpers. Something was obviously going on, and we wanted to know what it was. We walked over to the classroom and took our seats.

Scuttlebutt had been traveling around for several months about Roy Boehm and a special unit. As the rumors went, Roy was putting together a unit to go down to Cuba and mess with Uncle Fidel. "Boss" was something of a legend in UDT even then, and there wasn't a man I knew who wouldn't follow him down into hell to plant charges on the boilers.

After we'd all arrived in the classroom, a number of blue-suited civilian types from D.C. started to explain what was going on. They had a regular spiel they were putting out about how fortunate we were to have been chosen. After a thorough screening lasting more than a year and a half, we had been selected from the ranks of UDT 21 as the best men to be part of a new unit that the Navy was putting together. The unit was to be known as the Navy SEALs, for SEa, Air, and Land, the three environments we would operate in. Oh, really, we thought. We were told that the unit for which we'd been selected was a voluntary outfit and we had twenty-four hours to decide if we wanted to be a part of it. The new organization was also classified Secret and we were not to discuss it except among ourselves.

There were twenty-seven enlisted men and five officers in that room. Not all of the men were available when their names were called off, and Callahan hadn't arrived yet. One of the officers, a young ensign fairly new in UDT, immediately started to complain that it was a suicide outfit they were putting together and he wanted no part of it.

Roy snatched that kid up and snarled in his face, "Boy, where there's a way in, there's a way out. And don't you ever forget it!"

It was the next day that Roy found out that officers didn't have a choice—they were assigned to the new unit. Roy didn't want that young officer. If he didn't want to be with us, we sure as hell didn't want him along. But we were stuck with him. That ensign ended up being permanently assigned to the Med (Mediterranean) platoon and never operated in the field with us.

We walked out of there that day a little stunned. Louie, Tip, JP, RA, Lump Lump, and I just stood there looking at each other and wondering if all this was for real. Someone asked, "Well, what do you think?"

It was Louie, I remember, who answered for all of us. "Well, we never backed down before, there ain't no sense in starting now."

So we said, "That's it—we're in."

A few of us went down to the beach to party. Eventually, Tip, Louie, and I ended up in a place called Penny's just outside of Gate Five. Louie's wife, Tiger, was on his ass not to stay out all night, so Louie was the first to leave for home. Tip and I had been drinking for a while when I noticed a young woman over in the corner. She was with a fleet sailor. Still, I started making my move, figuring I could blow him out of the saddle, which I proceeded to do. Fleet sailors' or officers' wives and girl friends were fair game.

It had turned cold that night and started snowing. Her place was out in Ocean View, and I followed her along out there. We went into her house and closed the door. As soon as we put the lights out, the vice squad came in through the windows and doors; I think one guy even came down the chimney.

"You're under arrest!" they said.

What the hell, I thought, trying to figure out what was going on. This little adventure had resulted in my being the first SEAL arrested. Not exactly the distinction I had been hoping for.

There were four or five cops, one of them an older veteran. The older cop took me into a back room and asked for my identification. Back then we still had liberty cards for being off base. I handed the officer my ID and liberty card. "Oh," he said. "You're with UDT."

"Yes sir," I answered. Right then was not the time to be a smart-mouth. Then the officer started to hand me back my ID and card. When the civilian police were going to take you into custody, they kept your papers. This guy was going to let me go.

But some young officer who had the woman out in the living room could see what was going on through the door. He called, "He made his bed, now he's going to sleep in it. I've got the paddy wagon coming."

That officer wasn't fooling. Within a short time the police had arrived and I was on my way downtown. Now it was about two-thirty in the morning. What was going through my head at the time was part of the briefing we had been given earlier that day.

In the screening that was done of us they had learned that we were all sly and cunning and bore watching at all times. But none of the men chosen had a bad record. I had managed to keep my record clean, and it had paid off. Now here my dumb ass was in jail, and the Team wasn't fifteen hours old yet.

The officers asked me, since I was in the military, did I want to be turned over to the shore patrol? No, I answered. And the last thing I wanted to do was call the house. I did not want to make my wife come down and bail me out of jail. This was not the first time that thinking with my pants had gotten me into trouble, nor would it be the last.

The police wanted $38.50 for bail. I didn't have $38.50 on me, so they put me into a cell. My cellmate was a drunk they had picked up earlier in the evening. A couple of hours later, someone came in

and bailed the drunk out. As he was leaving, the drunk handed me a candy bar and said, "They don't feed you in here."

Boy, have I gotten myself into a situation, I thought. What do I do now? I knew I had Quarters in the morning, I didn't have any money to get out, and I didn't want to call home. There wasn't anything else to do, so I called "Uncle Roy," Roy Boehm. Since I was already in the shithouse, I might as well do it big-time.

They let me call Roy, and I told him where I was and what was going on. He said he was on his way, and that ended the conversation. They put me back in my cell. Now it was about five-thirty.

A little later, I heard people coming down the cell block and another guy laughing. I went over to the bars and I looked down the hall, and there was Roy, laughing his ass off. Oh, man, I thought. I can't be in too much shit—he's laughing.

The turnkey let me out of my cell, and Roy put his arm around me. "Come on, son," he said. "Let's get out of here."

It was only two years earlier that I had joined UDT, and Roy couldn't have known me that well. But right then if he had said he needed someone to swim up the Baltic and blow up Leningrad, I would have volunteered in a heartbeat. Instead, I just looked at Roy and asked, "You're not pissed at me, Boss?"

"Young man," he said, "the day you get caught doing something I never did, then you're in a world of shit. Between now and then, let's get out of here." So we left.

We climbed into Roy's car and left the station. As we rolled up Oceanview, Roy asked, "You got any clothes in your locker at the Team?" I answered that I did. "Well, there isn't any sense in going home," Roy said. "We might as well head in to the Team. We'll stop and get something to eat on the way in."

We walked into the restaurant and stopped. Playing on the jukebox was a popular song, "You're the Reason I Don't Sleep at Night." We both cracked up. The other patrons must have thought we were crazy.

Later on I found out that that night's adventure never got into my service jacket (military records). Whenever something would come in from the shore patrol or downtown regarding the case, I'd be told to report to the skipper's office. Roy would just hand me the unopened envelope and say, "You want to take care of this?"

Because he never opened the envelope—he just looked at the return address—Roy could honestly say he didn't know anything about it.

Within a few weeks of the founding of the SEALs we were put on alert for possible action. Cuba was heating up, and it looked like the United States might get involved. We had no equipment or weapons—not much more than the uniforms we were wearing at that first muster. Allowance lists were being made up, but nothing had arrived yet.

The commitment for Cuba was given to the West Coast, SEAL Team One, as well as to us. Team One was in the same situation as we. The time difference between the East and West Coast made Team Two three hours older than Team One, but it hadn't received any equipment either. Roy's answer was, "Send them over here, I'll equip them." Roy always had a positive attitude.

"Hoot" Andrews, a storekeeper chief, was now at the Team. Hoot, Roy Boehm, Billy Burbank, Bill Goines, and others were all in supply trying to solve the equipment problem, begging, borrowing, or stealing anything they could get their hands on. Sears Roebuck, GEX, and Army/Navy surplus stores were among our sources of supply. Roy had an open purchase order to buy anything he felt we needed, and we needed everything.

Roy had his crew moving up and down Virginia Boulevard hitting stores for what we needed. They bought .38 revolvers from Sears, camouflage uniforms from the Army/Navy store. Holsters, belts, and ammo holders came from a police supply company. An initial phone call to ArmaLite in California resulted in sixty-six AR-15 rifles, selective-fire versions, arriving at Little Creek for Team Two. Those AR-15s were probably the very first weapons of their kind used by the U.S. Navy.

Everyone in the Team was issued a warbag, and we were ordered to keep them at the ready. While the alert was active, the only way we could leave the base was if we could be back in thirty minutes, standing next to our equipment. We even had what we called a "ding-dong alert." A phone list was set up where one man would call others who would call others and so on until everyone was notified. Roy thought it was just a matter of time before we were called up to head for Cuba.

Men who were briefed to go in by air kept their T-10 parachutes packed with their gear. Guys who were swimming or going in by boat had their breathing rigs or boat-crew gear at the ready. Ammo, loaded magazines, weapons, everything was in our small building stacked in corners, lockers, or on the floor. If the trucks showed up, all we would have to do was grab our stuff and we could be on our way within minutes. The building we were in was right around the corner from the disbursing building for the base. Those yeomen in disbursing with all that money around were a bit uncomfortable with us so close.

They tested us on response time every few days. A very few men disappeared on operations, but I was not a part of it and the operations were never discussed. Roy was very serious about the alert, and he let us know it the first day.

Roy liked to drink as much as any of us, but he put the word out with no room for error. "I tell you, guys," Roy said the first day, "this is going to be the name of the game from now on. If I need you, goddammit, I'm going to need you sober. If I can stay sober, so can you bastards!"

The alert and the occasional drills went on for weeks. The constant tension was starting to get to us, but we continued to do our jobs and build up SEAL Team Two. There were special request chits you could fill out for some time off if you had a reason. But you did not want to say that you needed to take your wife or kids somewhere. As far as Roy was concerned, you didn't have a wife issued in your seabag and you had joined the Navy. The needs of the service came first.

Another family point that Roy made very early in the Team's life was that there would *not* be a Team Two wives' club. Roy said that he had seen that sort of thing disrupt units like ours before and he was not going to let it happen to Team Two. A wives' club could be a detriment to morale and a source of possible security leaks. Being a SEAL has always been very hard on a man's personal and family life. There is a bill to be paid for being one of the best.

But the constant drills and security checks were starting to get us all down, and we needed a break to boost morale. I think it was Tip who started it one day. Tip, Louie, and I had picked up some request chits one day at Morning Quarters. As a joke, Tip filled out his chit requesting permission "to go out and get drunk."

That looked good to me, so I filled mine out requesting permission "to go out and get drunk with Tip." Louie was requesting permission "to go out and get drunk with Tip and Jim." This whole thing just mushroomed, and it seemed everyone was filling out a chit with the same request, only the list of names was getting longer. Bill Green was shocked by what we were doing. "You guys are going to get in trouble," he kept saying.

Finally we turned in the requests to Rudy, who was the chief of the Team. Rudy looked at the chits, and then he filled one out requesting permission "to go and get drunk with his men." At Quarters, Rudy turned the whole mess over to Roy. Roy read the requests and said, "If you guys have the balls to ask this, so do I." He turned around and asked the yeomen for a chit and filled it out the same way as Rudy.

Across the athletic field from the Team Two building was the headquarters for UDU2. At the time, UDU2 (Underwater Demolition Unit 2) was the command that UDT 21 and SEAL Team Two came under. An officer named Hodge was COMUDU2 (Commander UDU2), and Roy had to report our status to him every morning after Quarters. Taking the pile of requests with him, Roy walked over to UDU2 headquarters.

Roy walked into Hodge's office and put the pile of requests on his desk. Commodore Hodge looked at the requests and told Roy, "Okay, you have until eight o'clock tomorrow morning."

When Roy came back all he said was, "That's it, Rudy. Liberty's down. I'll see you guys at the Redbird." The Redbird was our local hangout over on Shore Drive.

The first one running for his locker was Bill Green. Rudy pulled Green up short. "No, you dumb shit," Rudy said. "You didn't fill out a chit. You've got the duty for the day." With Bill standing there, the rest of us took off.

Team Two's initial skipper was Roy Boehm, but he remained as the CO only for a short while. Lieutenant John Callahan, an officer from the West Coast UDT, was to be the official CO of Team Two. It was something of a joke among the men that we were getting a "West Coast puke" as a skipper. "West Coast puke" was a common expression back then. To the Coronado crowd, we were "East Coast pukes."

It took a long time for Callahan to arrive. Between delays in coming from the West Coast and meetings he had to attend in Washington, Callahan didn't actually arrive at Team Two until several months after its commissioning. When he did, Roy Boehm went up to him and said, "Boy, am I glad to see you."

"No, you're not," answered Callahan. "You're doing a great job running the Team, and you still have the job. I have to go down to Fort Bragg for a month or so." After checking out the Team and our area for a couple of days, off Callahan went for training at Bragg.

Callahan made a speech to us that first day he was there. He told us what he thought of our beginning the SEALs and what would happen in the future. "Men," he said, "you are very lucky to have been selected to form such a unit. I advise you to set your aims high, because with every year, and every new commanding officer, a little bit of what we create here today will be lost. The day will come where the only difference between the SEAL Team and being aboard ship will be that the building won't rock and roll."

We only had first and second class petty officers in the Team at that time. Rudy, Doc Stone, and Hoot were our only chiefs, with Rudy being the keel that the new Team was building around.

Doc Stone had been assigned by the Navy's BuMed and had never gone through training. There was a real handicap that Callahan had to operate under as the CO of Team Two. Coming in as an outsider and stepping all over Roy's toes—or so we thought as enlisted men—and being a complete unknown to boot did not make things easy for Callahan. But being the kind of leader he was, he soon earned our confidence and trust. And he respected us in turn.

The skipper would work with us, and he would party with us. He believed in working hard and playing hard, and if you couldn't work hard and play hard, you had better quit playing. At the Team you were expected to work hard first. And that's the way it always was—you could raise hell, but the job had to be done first.

Other officers, especially those outside the Teams, had different opinions of us. Captain Watkins, the commander of the Amphibious Base when we were first put together, had no use for UDT, let alone this new bunch of animals called SEALs. There were all kinds of little regulations and requirements Watkins would pile on us as we tried to do our jobs. We couldn't do PT without wearing T-shirts, because all those naked chests would upset the officer's wives. All kinds of little bits of bullshit like that.

As far as we were concerned, if you were on a military base you should expect to see men performing their duties, not being showpieces. As far as Watkins was concerned, we were nothing but a bunch of misfits the Navy had placed under his watchful eye. Rudy would be constantly running interference between the base personnel and us. But that was all right with him, as long as we were getting the job done. It was to be years later in Vietnam that Rudy finally had the last word with Captain Watkins.

But long before we were to arrive in Vietnam we had to build up this new unit called SEALs. The allowance lists were the items of equipment that we were to receive from government stores. Roy Boehm had bought the minimum materials to operate with government funds when it looked as though we were going to Cuba at almost any minute. Now we had the time to assemble the catalog of supplies that we would normally keep in stock.

We were told by the higher-ups that we could have anything we felt a need for. Cost was not considered a major objection. Instead of purchasing materials from outside suppliers, the Navy would issue us everything it could. We sat down as a group over a beer and Roy asked us, "What do you want for weapons?" As a handgun, we asked for the Smith & Wesson Model 19 Combat Magnum, a .357 magnum revolver. Since that was what we all decided we wanted, Roy said, "That's what I'll order."

What we finally received were Smith & Wesson Model 15 Combat Masterpieces, a .38 Special revolver. The .357 is a much more powerful cartridge than the .38 Special, and there is no mistaking the difference between the two calibers, or at least so we thought. When Roy Boehm started tracing the order to find where the change had been made, his trail ended in Washington, D.C.

There was a Navy commander supply officer somewhere in D.C. who had changed the order from the .357s to the less expensive .38s. As it turned out, this officer had been at a pistol range firing a .357 magnum revolver but the range officials had issued him .38 Special ammunition to use. The weaker .38 Special is often fired in .357 Magnums, especially for initial training or practice, as the .38 is more easily controlled. But putting the .357 Magnum cartridge into a .38 Special weapon, if you could get it to fit, would usually result in the destruction of the weapon.

This officer was convinced that he could save the government money by issuing us the regulation .38 Special Combat Master-piece. When questioned on the subject, the commander stated that he "had fired the .38 in a .357 and could see no difference in the weapon." It was armchair commandos and headquarters guerril-las like that rear-echelon commander who really made our lives interesting, and a lot harder than they needed to be.

And things were already pretty hard for some of the guys. Billy Burbank was down in supply with Hoot, trying to make some sense out of the chaos of requests he was getting. Those of us ordering items for the allowance list would put down the things we wanted. Hoot, Billy, and their crew would look up the numbers and do the ordering.

It seemed that the magic number was sixty-six—if you wanted anything for the allowance list, Hoot and Roy said, you were sup-posed to order sixty-six of them. This was to ensure there would be enough equipment including spares for Team Two when we reached our intended initial strength of sixty men without making out an entire new allotment list. Much of the listed equipment was based on needs we had seen in UDT, especially for things like underwater gear. But the SEALs were going to be involved in a lot of land combat and guerrilla warfare, and the equipment you need for that is a lot different from what we had in UDT.

Most of the time we would get what we wanted. The first weap-ons that we received were some .45 caliber M3 greasegun subma-chine guns that the Navy sent us and the AR-15 rifles. The greaseguns we considered too heavy for our purposes, especially the loaded magazines. Though we kept some around, no one I knew really wanted the greasegun. The best package of firepower and weight we had was the new AR-15. This was several years before the Army adopted the AR-15 as the M16. But Roy had used his open-purchase system and gotten us sixty-six brand-new AR-15s fresh from the Colt factory.

Roy had ordered 136 AR-15s, the selective-fire models with green stocks. Half of the weapons were sent to Team One, along with instructions, magazines, and spare parts. Wanting to examine the AR-15 himself before making his purchase, Roy took some Team Two men up to Baltimore with him to check out the weapons the dealer had available. Roy and the guys shot the AR and fully tested it. They even tossed the weapon into the surf zone, covering it with sand, silt, and salt water, and it continued operating. With proper care, the AR-15 was able to withstand any abuse Roy gave it. Team Two now could issue one of the newest weapons available on the market.

We didn't have facilities for shooting the AR-15s at Little Creek, so we ended up using a range at Dam Neck. There we were assigned a number of Marines, a couple of sergeants and one second lieutenant, to run the range for us. Since it was their range, the Marines were in charge. They split up into two groups, half downrange behind the butts pulling targets and the other half on the firing line.

The Marines we were assigned to had never seen an AR-15—they were used to M14s and M1s—but they did know the weapon had a selector switch. We got ready to fire. Louie, Tip, Jess, and I were in the first line to shoot. As we were getting down into the firing position, the lieutenant sounded off. "There will be no automatic fire on this range," he said. "Everything will be semiautomatic fire only.

"Lock and load one magazine. Ready on the left? Ready on the right? Ready on the firing line! Shooters, you may commence fire!" We all just raised our heads a little bit and looked up and down at each other. At the command "Commence fire," all of us switched over to automatic and let that magazine rip. The lieutenant immediately confiscated all of the weapons and threw us off the base.

We thought we had pushed it too far and were all in a world of shit. Roy Boehm wasn't with us, and Rudy was our Chief in charge. Rudy was plenty worried about what would happen when we got back to the base. The next morning at Quarters, all Roy wanted to know was what took us so long to piss the Marines off. He also wanted us to know that this was an ass-chewing and our penalty was to meet later at the Redbird.

During the very early days of Team Two, we worked long, hard hours, but it all paid off. Pulling jokes on each other, the Marines, and the whole Navy in general seemed to be the order of the day. Even so, we found time to do things that helped bring us a little closer together as a Team. Time I had spent in the chart shop back with the Fifth Platoon in UDT 21 now came in handy. I sketched out some ideas for a unit patch and got together with Fat Rat Sutherland over at the UDT 21 chart shop to help me iron them out.

The final design we came up with is a circle holding a large number 2. Over the center of the 2 is a barking seal. Below the seal is a face mask and fins sitting on top and behind the canopy of an open parachute. Sitting over the shroud lines of the chute is an M3A1 submachine gun (greasegun). Above this whole mess, but still inside the border circle, are the words "SEAL TEAM." The border and the 2 are white, the seal brown with white patches. The mask and fins are light green and the parachute white. The lettering and gun are black and the background inside the border is blue.

The design became popular with the guys, and Callahan signed an order to have it considered the official emblem of Team Two. The Navy approved it, and in May 1962, my idea became our official patch. Fat Rat and I used to make an extra dollar or two painting plaster plaques of the patch and selling them to teammates.

Training was, of course, our major occupation in the early days. The schools and qualifications a man needed to operate as a SEAL were still to be developed. During our initial briefing we had been told that the mission of the SEALs would be to "develop a specialized capability for sabotage, demolition, and other clandestine activities conducted in and from restricted waters, rivers, and canals and to conduct training of selected U.S., Allied, and indigenous personnel in a wide variety of skills for use in naval clandestine operations."

The training for our "specialized capability" was going to come from many sources and schools, both civilian and military. The initial SEALs, myself included, would go to these schools and training to help evaluate them for further use. Since we didn't have a complete picture of what training we would need, we tried out schools that were recommended to us by others, such as the Army Special Forces.

Within a few months of commissioning, a group of SEALs, myself included, found ourselves on a flight south. We were headed for Panama and the U.S. Army Jungle Warfare Training Center at Fort Sherman in the Canal Zone.

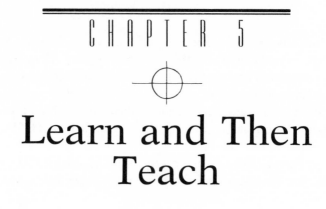

Learn and Then Teach

The U.S. Army Jungle Operations Course 900-D-F6 is given deep in the tropics of Central America and is intended to give the student an understanding of what it means to operate effectively and survive in a jungle environment. If the student graduates with a score above 85, he will receive a uniform patch and certificate proclaiming him to be a trained Jungle Expert. Welcome to Tarzan School.

Harry Beal particularly enjoyed himself down in Panama. The first day we were there, a group of us were standing outside the mess hall shooting the breeze when suddenly we heard someone cry out from inside the hall, "Hey, Short Meat!" No, it couldn't be. It sounded like Harry's voice, but who the hell could he be calling Short Meat? Harry had to be the shortest man who was ever in UDT and was certainly the shortest SEAL. Where other trainees might have to put a can on their helmets to carry their share of the boat in training, Harry practically had to wear a stovepipe hat.

We charged into the mess hall, and there was Harry at the head of the line, talking to the servers and grinning from ear to ear. The local Indians the Army had hired to work in the mess hall were damn near pygmies, and Harry towered over the tallest of them.

Beal never wanted to leave Fort Sherman—he had finally found a place where he was "bigger'n everybody."

We managed to make a few bucks from the Army while we were down at Fort Sherman. There was a small beach there that wasn't considered open unless there was a lifeguard on duty. Most of the young men down there weren't able to swim real well, certainly not as well as we could. When the people there finally learned a little more about us, most of the guys were able to work as lifeguards at the beach on their off-duty time and got paid for doing it.

The first night operation—I'll call it Boheo Night—we again demonstrated the difference between Army and Navy training. After a class during the earlier part of the day, the whole group of us had to build a boheo—a stick and grass lean-to—to spend the night in. A proper boheo has a raised platform to keep the sleeping occupants off the ground and a slanted thatch roof to, supposedly, keep the jungle rains off.

We were shown the various materials the jungle provided, how to assemble them and why. After this period of instruction, we broke down into small groups to put the theory into practice. Not only did we have an edge as SEALs, the need for proper teamwork having been beaten into us from Day One, but as Navy men we also could tie a knot that wouldn't slip.

Most civilians are likely to think of a jungle as a flat area filled with brush, trees, and active animals. Well, the brush and trees are there, but the jungle, especially in Panama, is anything but flat. They have jungle-covered mountains down there. It was on the side of one of these mountains that the class had to build their boheos.

Using cut poles and vines for lashings, we were soon able to put up the base platform of our boheo. Sleeping on the ground in the jungle will quickly make you suffer from the damp as well as from the insects and other critters that are all over the place. The thatch roof was easily made from leaves and fronds, first shaken to dislodge any unwelcome wildlife. Working as a team, we were able to move into our boheo and sleep just as it hit 0-dark-30.

Some of the Army teams were still trying to finish their boheos as darkness hit. And in the tropics, night falls like a heavy blanket. It was so dark you couldn't tell if your eyes were open or shut. We just lay there and listened to the sounds of the jungle.

The jungle in Central America is noisy at night—the grunting cough of the jaguar, the scream of the jaguarundi as it makes a kill, the crashing of a boar running from one of the many hunting predators, and always the sounds of millions of insects. But that's not what we listened to that night. About eleven or twelve o'clock what we heard was the creeeaaakkk, snap, snap, snap . . . "Aaawww, shit!" . . . CRASH! of Army boheos falling.

Later, after the crashing was over, there were the sounds of homeless soldiers looking for a place to sleep.

"You got room enough for one more?" a plaintive voice would come out of the darkness.

"Get the hell out of here, soldier!" would be the blunt SEAL answer.

Survival of the fittest, the law of the jungle. No one really knew who we were. We all had "SEAL 2," or in one case "SEAL 1," on our chests, but nobody asked us what that meant. And we didn't volunteer. We were supposed to be a somewhat secret organization.

Another course in jungle survival introduced us to preparing a meal from something that could be caught or found in the local jungle. Some of the vegetables, like the watercress and potato substitutes, were actually quite good. Where things got a little queasy was in the meat department.

Eating the monkeys and the snakes was a big deal, according to the instructors. As SEALs we didn't have any particular trouble with the food. Monkey tastes a lot like chicken, and snake is okay. Most of the soldiers, however, were squeamish and had a lot of trouble with the monkey and the snake. A field-dressed monkey without its fur looks a lot like a newborn baby. A rumor had it that the instructors would have the students eat bugs, and some of the beetles down there are *big*.

Classes were taught in all aspects of jungle operations and survival. We learned how to conduct ambushes and how to counter them. Small-boat operations, communications, the effects of heat on the body, guerrilla operations, and jungle navigation were all in the curriculum.

Our last major exercise was a big E&E (escape and evasion) operation through the jungle. We were to stay ahead of our instructors and cross a long course to reach safety. Much of the training we had received would be used to help us find our way through the jungle and to stay ahead of the instructors who would be hunting us.

We SEALs would always try to find a way to cheat on a problem, or not really cheat but bend the odds in our favor. The instructors would set up checkpoints to try to capture unwary students on the E&E course. All of the checkpoints were close to trails or minor roads that the instructors would travel on to get ahead of the evading students. Foreknowledge of these procedures helped us in planning our path through the jungle so that we had the least chance of getting caught.

We spent the night preparing for the next morning's problem. Using a file and a whetstone, I honed my machete to a razor's edge, as did each of our group. One of the lessons we received during training was in the importance of the machete in jungle warfare. Properly sharpened and used, a machete can chop through a branch or sapling with a single stroke. And our machetes were very well sharpened.

The E&E test was to be a thirty-six-hour practical exercise requiring our movement (infiltration) through eight thousand meters of "enemy-dominated" jungle to friendly territory. Though eight thousand meters doesn't sound like much—it's only about five miles—those meters are through valleys and over mountains thickly covered with jungle. This was going to be one tough course.

The directions the next day were simple. It was about one-thirty in the afternoon when we were told that a smoke grenade was about to be set off. During the time the grenade was burning, we were all to disappear into the jungle. When the smoke cleared, the instructors would start after us.

When they popped that smoke, we took off. Our plan was to haul ass through this nearby thicket, and I mean just burrow a hole through it. Moving at almost a dead run, I was taking point with my previously prepared machete. Holding that machete vertically in front of me, I ran through the brush letting that razor-sharp steel cut through the vegetation like the bow of a ship moving through water. As the point man's machete became dull, one of the other men would exchange his sharp one for it. Our intention was to reach the camp, friendly territory, by dark.

After we had gotten through the thicket, we stopped for a moment to get our bearings. Looking to our rear, we could see several squads of soldiers, the other students, just walking up our trail! Jess faced the soldiers and snarled, "If you don't quit following our trail and go find your own way, we're gonna pound your asses, tie you to a tree, and leave you for the instructors to find. Go play you're own damn game!" The soldiers decided that perhaps there might be an alternate route they could take.

The major part of our plan was to get ahead of the instructors before they set up their checkpoints. We figured that if we got ahead of them, the instructors would be too busy messing with the rest of the class to notice that we were ahead of their schedule. Once we had gotten through a couple of hundred yards of thicket, they weren't going to come through it after us. Though we managed to get ahead of the instructors, or so we thought, we did not make it to the camp by dark. When it got to be 0-dark-30, night fell, and we had been told, "Do not move through the jungle at night." Bullshit—we were big hairy frogmen and we could do what the Army couldn't.

Thinking we could again stay ahead of the game, we continued to move after dark. Harry Beal had the point, and we were all moving along close behind him. It was so dark that the luminous tape on the back of our hats couldn't be seen. So that we could see enough of each other to stay in line, we hung our Rolex watches from the backs of our necks. At least the glowing radium face of the watch could be seen by the guy following you.

Harry was checking the ground in front of him with a long kubesa stick. It amused us how the Army had these odd names for everything. The kubesa was a six-to-eight-foot walking stick you would make from a straight sapling. With the kubesa you could check your footing on treacherous ground and make enough of a disturbance in front of you to chase most snakes and critters away.

Suddenly Harry stopped. Bang, bump, thud; we all walked into one another. "What the hell?"

"We ain't going no further tonight," Harry whispered.

"What do you mean, you ain't going no further? Get a move on."

"I can't find the bottom!"

"What in the hell are you . . ."

"Here, you try," and Harry handed me his stick. Waving the stick around and pushing it down in front of me, the only thing I could feel was empty air. Someone picked up a rock and threw it. We never heard the bitch hit bottom.

That was it. We just sat down right where we were and went to sleep. After Hell Week, you can sleep anywhere, no problem. The next morning when it was light enough to see, there wasn't anything to see in front of us. We had spent the night on the edge of an eighty-foot cliff with a straight drop. If we had moved forward one more foot, we would have followed each other right over the edge.

About three hours after dawn, we reached friendly territory. We had accomplished the exercise in record time. The next group to come in was five hours behind us. The instructors asked us how we had gotten through the area so fast without being noticed by the "enemy." "We never saw any of you moving through the area," they said. "You couldn't have had time to snoop and poop"—that is, reconnoiter—"before you got here."

"All we did was bust ass to get past that first checkpoint," we told them, "and the rest was simple." They had never looked at the problem like that before.

We finally graduated from Jungle School and all went back to the Creek as Jungle Experts. Our travel plans became all fouled up from lack of proper communication, so we split up and found our own ways back home. Buster Brown headed back to Coronado and I bummed a ride on a navigation training flight headed for Little Creek. There was enough room on the plane so all of us from Team Two ended up on a Navy flight headed for Norfolk.

When we got back to the Team, they asked us to rate the Jungle Operations Course. I personally didn't think it was worth the time. We had plenty of instructors ourselves who could take the course and teach it back at the Creek. We did learn a good deal of useful information at Fort Sherman, but I just felt we would do well to teach the subjects ourselves, bringing in the necessary materials to our own classrooms.

We had been at the Creek for less than a month when it was back to the field again. The Team was going to join in several exercises, including LANTPHIBTREX 1-62 and QUICK KICK 1-62. Operating from the submarine *Sea Lion*, we were going to conduct operations off Vieques, Puerto Rico, with a contingent of Marine Force Recon personnel led by a Captain Woziniac. The Force Recon people would be taught lock-out and lock-in techniques by those of us aboard the sub and then conduct their own operations during the exercises.

We were supposed to be playing games with the Marines and the Amphibious Forces, acting as infiltrators and guerrilla forces. This was the first time the SEALs were conducting operations like this, and we had quite a bit yet to learn. But then so did the "enemy" have a lot to learn about SEALs.

While offshore before the operations were scheduled to start, we gave the Force Recon personnel some training. Using the *Sea Lion*'s escape trunk, we taught the Marines lock-out and lock-in techniques as well as a little underwater swimming. Launchings were practiced as well, since we were going to operate from a submarine using rubber boats.

That first night a group of us left the *Sea Lion* to paddle in to Vieques. Tip, Louie, Scotty MacLean, Swede, Jess, RA, Leg Martin, and I left the submarine with the decks awash. We were going in big-time for a sneak and peek, paddling in with rubber boats, no outboard, as we would in a wartime situation. Tip and I were the number one and number two men in the boat, which meant we were designated as the scout swimmers.

When you are a scout swimmer you strongly hope that you don't have a by-the-hook coxswain. According to the manual, the combat swimmers would get out of the rubber boat two to three hundred yards offshore and conduct a reconnaissance swim before calling in the main party. While we were paddling in, Tip and I were looking at each other wondering when we would be told to swim in. As the beach was getting closer, we started wondering just what was going on.

Louie, being the coxswain, wasn't saying a word but just guiding the boat in. Just as the rubber boat grounded on the beach, Louie quietly said, "Scout swimmers out."

Right! I thought. This is going to be a fun operation. And Tip and I stepped out into about four inches of water for our "recon swim." So we moved up on the beach to unload our rubber boat. We had with us a load of chemical time pencils, M-80 firecrackers, and smoke grenades, along with rations and other supplies. The time pencils would be attached to the firecrackers, which they would fire after a delay.

If the spoon—the safety lever—of the smoke grenade was taped down, the pin could be pulled and the grenade wouldn't fire until the tape broke. Putting the firecracker underneath the tape would cause the smoke grenade to go off when the cracker fired, giving us noise and smoke. These were going to be the fake demolition charges that we were to place on strategic targets around the area. Tip and I didn't think a single cracker would give enough noise to be immediately noticed, so on our "charges" we put a string of M-80s together. Briefings were to be put out to the Marine forces not to mess with any of the charges if they were discovered.

We hid the rubber boat, gathered up our supplies, and moved inland to a spot we had earlier picked out on a map. Reaching our rendezvous point, a large tree next to a clearing, we secured our gear and went to sleep for the rest of the night. We were scheduled for three days of operations and then would return to the *Sea Lion*. The Marine Force Recon team we had been training on the *Sea Lion* also went in to the beach in rubber boats at another location. They had their own targets to hit, and we wouldn't be operating together during the exercises.

No one on the island knew we were there, so we had an easy night. The next morning was anything but easy, at least for Louie. When we woke up, there was Louie, getting his face licked by a cow that was standing over him. We had spent the night in a pasture, and come the morning, this cow must have thought Louie was her lost calf. And Louie wasn't going anywhere. Even though he is a big man, Louie just lay there. When a cow in standing on you, you wait until the cow goes away before you get up.

After Louie's morning wakeup call had left, we remained in the pasture area. While we were there, Louie asked me for my weapon. I trust Louie more than a brother, so not thinking anything of it, I handed him my weapon. We had been issued pistols for this operation, .380 automatics. No ammunition, instructions, or anything had come with the little mothers. How we ended up with these miserable weapons nobody would say, or at least nobody ever owned up to it. When we asked them for instructions, the issuers said, "Don't worry, you'll figure them out." Yeah, right.

The pistols were small Colt Pocket Automatics. To take them apart for cleaning you would pull the slide partway back and give the barrel a half turn and the weapon would come apart when the slide went forward. Louie had just managed to figure this out when Tip came running up to us. Tip must have seen someone coming, because all he said was. "Let's go! Let's get out of here!"

"Here, the enemy's coming," said Louie, as he handed me back my pistol, in about nine pieces.

According to our plan, we were supposed to hide out during the day while the Marines looked for us. We hid, all right, on a public beach down the road from the Marine camp. Disguising ourselves to blend in with the indigenous natives, we stripped to our shorts and moved in with the civilians on the beach. To extend our combat rations we foraged for sustenance among the natives. We were trading K-Bar knives and other items for bottles of rum. We had buried the C rations we had brought with us, so the patrols had nothing to recognize us by. Helicopters were flying overhead looking for us while we were splashing in the surf with all the pretty young things. "Oh look, it's a Marine helicopter! Let's all wave to the poor working soldier boys!" Fuck 'em—we were playing the game our way.

Taking things a bit further one night, we attended a Marine movie! Putting our uniforms back on, we just walked right into the Marine camp and attended an outdoor movie they were showing. It was not all bravado—we were scoping out the camp for possible targets. The film was less fun than listening and talking to the Marines all around us.

The men were all talking about this new outfit the Navy had on the island that was going to be the "enemy." "Oh, really," we would answer, trying to keep a straight face. I don't even remember what the movie was, we were having so much fun jerking those Marines around. After the film we just walked right back out, and they never even knew we had been there. At least they didn't know until later when some of our charges started going off.

There were all sorts of targets available for our attentions. Ammunition dumps, POL (petroleum, oil, lubricants) storage sites, supply dumps—we visited all of them, leaving our little packages behind. Tip and I left our little overloaded charges among a few of our points of interest. Later on, while back on the submarine, Tip and I thought, What if some Marine picks up one of our charges just as the pencil is going to blow? It was a moment's worry, and then we remembered the Marines were supposed to have been briefed not to handle foreign objects. As it turned out, our fears were justified.

One Marine, not paying attention to what he was doing, picked up one of our charges just as it was going to blow. The bang cost the man two of his fingers. That Marine was the first unofficial SEAL "enemy" casualty, Vieques 1962.

Now with our missions completed, we had to get back aboard the sub. At first light on the last day of our mission, we were to meet the submarine and exfiltrate from the island. The submarine was to come up to periscope depth and look for us in the rubber boat. We returned to where we had hidden the boat. We had no trouble locating it and launching from the beach. No one had found the boat, and we were all feeling pretty good. Our operations had gone well, we had completed a good sneak and peek, and it looked like we were going to get away free. After paddling near the rendezvous site we could see the periscope of the submarine cutting through the water. Everything was going well—and then everything seemed to hit the fan all at once.

It was just dawn, and we could see the submarine's periscope coming. Just past the sub, running a parallel course, was a waterspout! A waterspout is a whirling funnel-shaped column of wind and water, like a wet tornado. They are a relatively rare weather effect, but we had found one. The wind-driven water would eat our rubber boat the way a shark would swallow a rubber duck. Paddling madly, we had that IBS moving as if it had a ten-horsepower outboard motor on it. We wanted no part of that waterspout.

As if dealing with Mother Nature wasn't enough, another problem popped up. This may have started as a fun op, but it wasn't ending as one. Swede suddenly started going apeshit on us.

Swede was the biggest man in the boat, and he suddenly started screaming, "They're all over me, they're crawling on my skin!" He was swatting and scratching at himself, damn near flipping the boat over in the process.

Louie was cool, as always. He was looking at Swede, lifting up his uniform to help him. "What the fuck are you talking about, Swede? There ain't nothing on you."

"No, no, they're there, I can feel 'em crawling all over me."

"Well, jump in the water and drown them."

So Swede jumped in the water. The rest of us were trying to decide which was better to watch, the Louie and Swede Show or that waterspout. The Louie and Swede Show won out.

Louie called over the side to Swede, "Everything all right now?"

Swede screamed up to Louie, "No. They're all over my head now."

Well, Louie decided to simplify matters a little bit and be helpful as only he could. It looked like we might beat the waterspout to the sub, but we still had to land on the deck. There was no way we could control the boat with Swede holding on and struggling in the water. Louie said, "Come on over here, I'll get 'em," and he started hitting Swede over the head with his paddle.

Now, here's the situation. Swede is starting to get pissed off at Louie for smacking him with the paddle. We're still trying to get to the submarine before that waterspout changes direction and comes over to us. And we weren't letting Swede back into the boat. Whatever it is he had, we didn't want it.

Things somehow ended up all right. We managed to land on the submarine and avoid the waterspout. As soon as we were on the deck, Leg Martin ran down into the sub's sick bay. Leg came back and gave Swede a shot that took away all the "bugs" that were crawling on him and it was all over. Leg later told us that Swede had come into contact with something, I never did find out what, and had had a severe allergic reaction.

The mission was over, and we now had some time to relax. We picked up the Marine Force Recon personnel and started to learn about their adventures on Vieques. There was a cook on the sub who really thought a lot of us. The operations went on over Easter, and the cook, whose name was Candy, took to calling us his Easter Seals.

On the cruise back, the Marines were going to leave the sub at Moorehead and we were going to go on to Little Creek. While we were coming up around Cape Hatteras our luck with the weather ran out. Running along at snorkel depth as we were, we could feel the effects of the heavy storm we ran into. It was beginning to look like Cape Hatteras was going to live up to its nickname, the Graveyard of the Atlantic.

The waves were tossing the sub around. The crew was handling everything, and all we could do was stay in our bunks, out of the way. That is one helpless feeling for a sailor. Suddenly, over the intercom, we heard an announcement that makes a submariner's blood run cold. "Water down the main induction line! Fire in main control!"

All of our training wasn't going to do us one bit of good in a sinking submarine and heavy seas. We all came flying out of our bunks, and most of us looked to Tip for leadership. Jim Tipton was submarine-qualified, and we figured he could tell us what to do.

"All of you just get back in your bunks," Tip shouted. "Stay out of the crew's way and let them handle it. They know what they're doing."

We reluctantly crawled back into our bunks. Since we were up in the forward torpedo room, just about all of us had our eyes on that escape trunk in the overhead. If things got bad enough, some of us were willing to take our chances with the Atlantic rather than suffocate in a burning sub. A good UDT man always goes to the water in tight situations.

We did get through that storm, thanks to a good skipper and crew. We never learned what had caused the fire, but later on we found out just how close we had come to going to the bottom. If it hadn't been for the skill of the crew, the boat would have been lost, and all of us along with it.

Earlier in training, Roy Boehm had explained to us what it was like doing a swimmer attack against a submarine. He told us about all the voids, ballast tanks, and fittings that would trap an unwary diver. Roy wanted us to have confidence that we could handle a sub if we needed to, and he had talked the skipper into heaving to off the Carolina coast. Working in teams, we were all going to conduct a sneak attack on the *Sea Lion.*

One Lump—Arthur Williams—had previously been in the Army Special Forces. Since we already had a Harry Williams, Lump Lump, in the Team, Arthur Williams quickly became known as "One Lump." While undergoing diver training in St. Thomas with UDT 21, One Lump had been my swim buddy. Since he had left the Army and enlisted in the Navy, One Lump had passed UDTR and now was with us in Team Two. Again, being my swim buddy, One Lump was paired with me for the sneak attack on the sub.

They had given us wooden clamps to use in place of our normal limpet mines. The plan was for us to go upcurrent of the *Sea Lion* in our rubber boats. Once we were in position, the first group would swim underwater with their Draegers and place the clamps on the sub's bottom. The second group of swimmers would then come in and search the bottom of the sub, removing the clamps. It was figured that this operation would give everyone good experience in working underneath a submarine.

Per our normal procedure, we tried to bend the rules in our favor. As we were getting into position for the swim, which was taking place at night, the first group told the second group where they would attach the clamps. This way Roy would be happy that we got all the clamps on our first try and we wouldn't have to crawl all around underneath a submarine in the dark. The section of the sub that Lump and I had to search, up near the bow, we knew didn't have any clamps on it. Neither of us really wanted to get underneath that hull in the dark anyway. Under the sub it was full of obstacles; pipes and fittings projected out that you could easily become entangled with, damaging your breathing gear or even tearing out your mouthpiece. Along with all the projections were hollows and openings that you could accidentally enter. Once inside, your compass would just spin around from all the steel.

When we swam up to the submarine, on the bow, Lump and I surfaced and let the current take us right down along the side. According to plan, when we got down to where the screw guards were, we would climb onto the sub and the exercise would be over. Tex Hager was one of the observers aboard. So when we got to the stern of the sub, Tex asked us, "Well, what did you find?"

"Nothing—the hull's clean," we answered.

"How could you two have searched the bottom when you kept your heads above the water? Neither of you went down from the time you hit the bow till now!"

"We're telling you there are no clamps there. We searched it."

Tex couldn't call us liars, since there weren't any clamps in the area we had been assigned to search. He didn't know that we knew where the clamps would be before the attack.

The word did get back to Roy that there might be a problem. It was suspected that One Lump and I might be a little clausty about working underwater in tight places. It was noticed that neither of us wanted to go under that sub at night.

We got back to Norfolk, and about a week went by. Tip and Roy had been through a lot together, including some pretty tight operations. Most of what I knew was second- or thirdhand at best, but all of us in the Team had a world of respect for the both of them. Tip and I had become the best of friends over time as well.

Another nighttime sneak attack exercise was scheduled. Tip and I had been assigned as swim buddies. As we were getting our Draegers on in the boat, Tip talked to me on the side away from anyone else.

"You know I think the world of you, Jim," Tip said—a big change from when he was my instructor at UDTR. "I don't give a damn if a herd of horses comes after you down there. Don't surface. You hear me? *Don't surface!* If you want to stay in the Team, I don't give a fuck what happens—don't you surface."

With his advice echoing in my ears, Tip and I went on the swim. Tip was real cool underwater. I didn't particularly like diving. Whenever you swim with a new buddy, you have to learn about each other. Never having swum with Tip before, I learned things right away. Jumping into the water, we went down to about twenty, twenty-five feet, and Tip set the course. As we were swimming along, I could swear I heard music of some kind. Now just what the hell was going on? First Tip warns me, and then this?

Was Tip singing? Climbing up along the buddy line that connected Tip and me, I put my ear next to his mouthpiece. "Laa la laa, dee dum dum dum." He was humming to himself! Later on I learned that humming to himself was how Tip passed the time on a swim.

Afterward, we came out of the water, and everything had gone fine. It was then that Tip told me what had been going on. "I was to check you out tonight, Jim," Tip said to me. "Roy is considering shitcanning you from the Team. After that song and dance on the *Sea Lion* he figured that you might be too clausty for this outfit. I'm going to be glad to tell him that I think you're fine and I'd swim with you anytime."

I found out later that One Lump had also been tested. Roy wanted to keep us in the Team, but only if we could pass the tests.

Years later, after I had returned from my first tour in Vietnam, Roy Boehm was officer in charge of the SERE (Survival, Escape, Resistance, and Evasion) School in Little Creek. Being pretty proud of the little bit I had done on my first tour, I went to see Roy wearing my decorations. He just carried me around that SERE School showing me to his students and trainers. "Here's one of my men," Roy said. "Look at this chest. That's one of my boys, one of my men. A hunter."

Calling a teammate a hunter was the greatest compliment you could give. The term had come out of Vietnam. Being a hunter meant that you did much more than what was asked of you. If there wasn't a target, you would go out and look for the enemy. Rather than wait for the enemy to come by or for someone to just hand you a mission, you would go out and hunt Charlie down in his own backyard.

To this day I keep saying to Roy, "Yeah, but you were the one who gave me a second chance. You were ready to shitcan me, and you had every right to, because I didn't like that kind of swimming."

"It's okay," Roy would answer, "You worked out all right. I knew you had what it takes to be a SEAL."

CHAPTER 6

School Was Never Like This

In the SEALs we consider ourselves physically tough, but there was one Marine school some of us attended that made UDTR actually seem easy. The Marine Corps Cold Weather Training Center in Bridgeport, California, had an evasion, escape, and survival course. In its day, this 163-hour course was one of the roughest programs of military instruction that anyone could take in the U.S. Armed Forces. UDTR was harder in the sense that you could quit at any time and walk away—it took determination to stay. You couldn't quit the Marine E&E course, but my God did you want to.

Force Recon Marines, combat pilots, and Special Warfare personnel like the SEALs all might be students at the school. Man's greatest fear is that of the unknown, and that was the thought that led to the creation of the E&E course.

The basic purpose of the POW portion of the course was to give you a taste of what to expect in a POW camp, especially a camp run by Asian Communists. Many of the instructors at the camp had been prisoners themselves during the Korean War. These men brought their own experiences to the course. Called "brainwashing school" by many of its graduates, the place was shut down after a congressional investigation, not long after my class passed through.

Some SEALs and UDT men had already completed the course before I got there. And those wonderful people left 201 files* on the SEALs who were scheduled to attend the course later. Being one of those lucky people, I had some idea of what was coming, but that wasn't enough to prepare for the reality of the course.

The school was in a very mountainous and cold part of California. The only reason the water in the creeks wasn't frozen was that it was moving too fast. Jess Tolison and I were attending the course together with Charlie Bump and a young SEAL who had only been out of training a few months. Both Jess and I were second class, but he was a bosun's mate while I was a quartermaster. In the Navy at that time, bosun's mates still had rate precedence, so even though I had been a second class longer than Jess, he had rank over me.

When the instructors had us first report, Jess and I managed to have a little fun with them. It was June 19, and the sergeant was standing in front of the student formation preparing us for our equipment issue. "Awright, do I have any E6s?" the sergeant called out. No one answered so he just moved down the ranks. "How many E5s do I have?" A whole bunch of hands went up, including Jess's and mine, since second classes are in pay grade E5. "Anybody prior to such-and-such a date?" The sergeant went on like this until he found the man who had been an E5 the longest, and that man happened to be me.

"Awright, sailor, get out here in front of the formation. You are going to be the NCOIC"—noncommissioned officer in charge—"of this group. I want you to march the class over to that building and get them their issue. Any questions?"

I just stood there and let the sergeant drive on until he stopped for breath. Then I said, "Excuse me, Sergeant, but do you see that man over there? The one looking excited? That's Jess. He's a bosun's mate and he's senior to me."

"What the hell are you talking about, sailor?"

---

* The 201 file is the complete history of an individual in the military. His family history, military career, posts assigned to, and schools attended are all contained in the file.

"He's a bosun's mate, so he's senior to me," I repeated.

The sergeant called over to Jess and asked him his date of rank, which was more recent than mine. "No, he hasn't got rank over you," the sergeant said. "You've been an E5 much longer than him."

Now was the time to play with this Marine. "But, Sergeant," I said, "the Navy doesn't work that way. You're a Marine—you should know that. He's a bosun's mate. I'm a quartermaster, he has rate precedence over me."

"Well, shit! Come here, you." And the sergeant proceeded to give Jess the same line he had just been giving me about what he expected of the class and Jess in particular. Since we had been messing with this Marine sergeant, he decided to get back at Jess.

"Awright, sailor, the quickest way you know how. Get the class from here over to the warehouse for their issue." The sergeant was expecting Jess to do the usual military thing and march the class over to the building. Jess did not do things in the formal military way.

"Class! Ten-hut! Fall out, fall in over there, and get your gear." And the students trotted over to the warehouse to draw their equipment. Jess and I walked over, leaving that Marine sergeant standing there with his mouth hanging open.

The next day we were scheduled to be captured and taken to a prison camp. Sometime during the day, instructors acting like enemy soldiers would enter wherever we were, a classroom or the grounds and physically capture us. We were not supposed to know this but we were still trying to play the game by our rules.

Bump, Jess, the new kid, and I were sitting in the barracks that night talking about what was to come. "Hey, guys," I said, "as long as we stick together we can handle it. The freezing water, stripping us naked in the cold, no clothes, and all the other shit they're going to put us through—we can do that. As long as you keep in the back of your mind that it's against regulations to kill us, you'll make it. Just like UDT training, they can't kill us. We don't care what they do, we can handle it. Let's just stick together."

The next day, they captured us. Just walking from one class to another, *bam*, we were ambushed. And these guys played the game. They were all wearing foreign uniforms, carrying foreign weapons, and would not speak English. Acting like they couldn't even un-

derstand English, they physically threw us to the ground and secured us.

There was no question that we were now prisoners. "Keep your
face down, you American pig!" they shouted at us. They would
speak a little English when they wanted something. But if you
asked them a question, they didn't understand. If you insisted, a
fast kick would usually be your only answer.

On the first day we had signed a document giving the trainers
permission to use physical force with us, to the extent that they
deemed fit for the training. That document was already causing
some regrets.

Jess and I were secured alongside each other, lying in the dirt.
He quietly spoke to me. "Hey, Jim!"

"Uh huh," I answered.

"Guess what!"

"What?"

"We're in the wrong place."

"Uh huh." Then the fun really started.

Right away we realized that they were going to play the game
big-time. These people knew their stuff and were going to see to it
that we learned what could be expected in a real prison camp.
UDTR takes a week to create the confusion of battle you could face
on an enemy beach. These guys showed us the very worst face of
war, and did it very quickly. After only six hours in the camp, we
started to wonder what country we were in. It's hard to believe
they could do that to professional military men like us. But they
did, and they did it well.

Even though we knew that this was training, a game, as we
called it, they had us shook real fast. The instructors kept to their
roles so tightly and so realistically that they caused us to start
wondering where we actually were. The camp they put us in and
the flags they were flying had no relationship with the United
States whatsoever. They quickly removed even our individual
identities.

You were given a number and expected to answer to it, and not
your name. Comrade 120 or Comrade 37 would be called out by the
guards, and you had better answer to it damned fast. These instructors had no reluctance to use their hands, feet, or fists to
punctuate their orders.

One of the first things they did when we were "captured" was find out who was the senior officer. In our case it was a Marine pilot. This one man stood up and the guards just flat up and knocked him out. While the first man was lying there, they asked who the next senior officer was, and boom! By the time they got to the third and fourth senior officers, no one wanted to stand up. Very quickly and efficiently, the guards had eliminated any effective leadership among the prisoners.

The camp itself looked like pictures of prison camps in Korea or Vietnam that have been published. There were guard towers made of bamboo and trees all around, with men manning guns up in them. Surrounding the camp was a fence wall with double concertina (coiled barbed wire) at the top and bottom. There were some thin-walled little shacks we were to stay in, but we didn't spend much time in them.

There was a north gate and an east gate in the camp. When your number was called out, you had to go to one of the gates quickly. Once at the gate, things became real hard, real fast. They would put you into a black wooden box, not large enough for a full-sized American to sit in. You would have to kneel in the box while they closed the lid on you. Then they would start piling rocks on the lid, forcing it even more closed down onto your back.

With the suffocating weight of the lid pressing down on you, you would swear you couldn't breathe. But the instructors had carefully planned things out earlier. There would be just enough room, but no more, and just enough weight, but no less, for you to crouch there in the box for hours, sucking in the darkness.

Later on it was explained that the North Koreans had used such boxes in their prison camps. Only the North Koreans hadn't been quite as careful about the weights as our instructors had. Another diversion they had for us at the camp was two fifty-five-gallon oil drums buried in the ground. The drums were welded end to end, making a long tank. Two or three guys would be secured in the drum and then it would be filled with water. And that mountain weather was cold!

One thing the guards particularly liked was to strip and secure a redneck rebel type and a black man together in the drum. Enforced integration, Korean Communist style. They also liked to string a man up in a parachute harness. This wouldn't have been so bad except that they kept swinging and spinning you around until you were completely disoriented and vomiting on yourself.

And all during these little exercises, the guards would be asking you questions. Little simple things like "What is your blood type?" or "What is your religion?" And that information was on your dogtags. But you couldn't tell them. That was the one thing you could not do—give them any information they asked for. We were to follow the Code of Conduct to the letter.

Article V of the Code of Conduct stated that "I am required to give name, rate or rank, and service number," and nothing else. Article V has been revised today to read that "I will evade answering further questions to the best of my ability." People will break eventually, as was brought home during the Vietnam War. But when we were taking training, a prisoner was expected to give out no information, period.

There was a Force Recon Marine there in the camp with us taking the course. That Marine was an example of how different people have different breaking points and the ways those points can be reached. The guards never even touched the Marine, but he broke, spilling his guts out. He never went in the pool or the box or any of the other little fun things they had for us to do. Every ten minutes, the guards would call out that Marine's number to go to one of the gates.

"Comrade 22, come to the north gate." And that Marine would run to the gate. "We're going to let you go this time, comrade, but when we call you back, be prepared to suffer."

They continued with this for hours, running that Marine around and keeping him twitching over when the interrogation would start. It finally got to the point where that Marine just said, "That's it, I'm gonna spill the beans."

We tried to talk him out of it. "What are you talking about? They haven't touched you yet!"

"Yeah, but they said they're gonna!"

"But they haven't done it yet, goddammit!"

But that was it—he had reached his breaking point. The next time Comrade 22 was called to the gate, he told the guards anything they wanted to know. That Marine had orders out of Force Recon before he left Bridgeport.

The SEALs weren't immune to the actions of the guards either, or at least one of us wasn't. The young SEAL was one of the people who can make it through UDTR but really shouldn't have. There seems to be a 10 percent rule in military training—some people, about 10 percent, manage to slip by the filtering process that is supposed to winnow out those who aren't really up to it. Graduating classes from UDTR were so small that it was very hard to catch these 10 percenters, there were so few of them. But there were some in the Teams.

That little SEAL—and he was physically small—just couldn't take the punishment they handed out in the POW camp, and he broke. Told them everything they wanted to know.

A real sophisticated trick they showed us was the court-martial routine. The guards would say that they were going to court-martial your buddy for "crimes against the people" and ask if you wanted to defend him or be a witness in his favor. If you answered yes, they said, "Do you want to swear in on your Bible or our rule book?" Almost always the answer would be "On my Bible."

Put your hand on the Bible and your other hand in the air and *click*, they had a picture of you in front of the Russian flag swearing allegiance to the Communist Party. Pictures like this would be used as propaganda. The instructors showed us how all these things worked.

But they didn't work on Jess and me. We were tight. The instructors would have had to kill us to get what they wanted. We were too proud of the Teams and ourselves to let this stuff get to us. Maybe if Jess had said, "The hell with this, I'm going to talk," I would have broken. But I was not going to be the first. And I think Jess was thinking the same thing about me. We leaned on each other, and that helped get us through. Except for that young kid, who was gone from the Teams a few months later, none of the SEALs broke. But some of the Marines and a lot of the pilots did.

They did feed us in the camp. We had potato soup. There was a large fifteen- or twenty-gallon pot of boiling water with one potato in it for all of us. They fed us twice in three days. In spite of all that, we managed to get back at them just a little bit.

While I was stuck in the box one night about three o'clock in the morning, I had the guard watching me telling me how he hated the

Marine Corps and what he was going to do when he got out. I'd turned it around on them—I had the guard spilling his guts. And Jess managed to get a guard to do the same thing with him.

None of the prisoners, including us, had any idea how long the exercise would go on. One morning, about eleven o'clock, the guards just stood us up and told us it was over. "All right," they said. "This part of the program is over. We're taking you back to main camp. You'll get something to eat and a couple more classes. Get a good night's sleep. Tomorrow you will start the E&E exercise."

Some of the students looked pretty shocked, some even close to tears. We wanted to go out and find some beer, which we did.

That course taught us some real lessons. Every man has his breaking point, and there are people in this world who know how to find that point. An Air Force man told me what was probably the best answer. "Just tell them anything, as long as it isn't classified. Spill your guts, sign anything they put in front of you. Babble at them. As long as the rest of the world knows that if you capture our guys, this is what they'll do, it has no propaganda value. They'll have nothing. Somebody ought to wake up and make that the policy."

That POW camp had changed my ideas about resisting questioning. This officer's proposal wasn't the most appealing, but it did make sense. Unfortunately, the policies aren't put out by the men who will have to live up to them. They're written down by protected, high-ranking officers and civilians who sit behind desks and never have to worry about being captured. Being a big, rough, tough American who refuses to say anything against God and country doesn't help. It's when tough men like that finally break that the bastards get something from it.

Later in the day, after we had returned to the main camp, we had some more classroom instruction on the survival aspects of being in the field as well as methods of evading searching enemy troops. The next day we began the survival and evasion field exercises. The class was spread out in small groups over a fairly wide area to survive for several days while living off the land.

As SEALs we stayed together in a group. To make sure we would not be hungry again—the memory of potato soup at the POW camp was going to stick with each of us for a long time—I had smuggled my snub-nosed .38 revolver into the field. We weren't sure we could get away with using the pistol on the exercise, but we were not going to starve anymore. There were cows in those hills, and we were going to eat well.

The issue equipment was considerably less powerful than a handgun. They had issued us an Air Force survival knife, a fire starter (flint), some fishhooks, a parachute canopy with all of its suspension lines, and our field clothes. The parachute was to be used to make a shelter, fishing lines, nets, whatever might be needed to enhance survival. The instructors had told us in what area to set up and to camouflage our camp as best we could. Though they would not be "looking" for us during the survival portion of the exercise, we were to practice good fieldcraft the same as if we were in enemy-held territory.

There were not going to be any enemy patrols in our area, or so the instructors thought, but we were to remain as inconspicuous as possible while eating as well as we could. If enemy forces did show up, the instructors would act as partisans and help get us back to friendly territory.

As near as we could tell, the hint was that if we managed not to be too obvious during our little camping trip, the "enemy" wouldn't come out and raid our party. This was not going to be a problem. We had all gotten our fill of the "enemy" back at the POW camp. The SEALs were going to be good little frogs and set up a regular hidden homestead, maybe.

Setting up our camp, we built a reasonably hidden shelter, much like the boheos at Jungle School. Food was our primary thought, and like all good sailors, we looked to the water to supply our needs. Charlie, Jess, and I proceeded to start fishing in the stream nearby. The stream held some really beautiful trout that were quite happy to take our baited hooks.

Charlie and I were having a good time hauling in fish. Jess, on the other hand, standing right between us, couldn't have caught a fish if he'd been using a shotgun and a half-pound Dupont lure (explosive charge). Finally Jess just said, "Screw it, I'll go dig some worms." It seemed that day he was just one of those guys who could not catch a fish. But Bump and I were doing well. The trout ate our worms and we ate the trout.

For two days we stayed near our stream and ate fish. One time we found a bird nest with a number of baby birds in it. Off went their heads and into the pot with them. We tried to make a fish soup, but that didn't taste very good.

There were plenty of fish, but we finally wanted something different. We thought of snaring a deer but that didn't work. So what else could we hunt? During the classroom training we had been told about the porcupine and how it could be caught easily and was edible as long as you boiled it long enough. This sounded like something we could handle, so one afternoon we organized a porcupine hunt.

The group of us formed a skirmish line going up the side of the mountain we were on. In a skirmish line, you line up all facing in the same direction. Usually, the maneuver is used to concentrate your firepower forward. For now, it would help us cover the widest possible area on our hunt. We had already been on the exercise three days and the prison camp before that hadn't exactly been a picnic, so our strength was starting to wear a little thin. Walking up the side of a mountain in the thin air and cold takes a lot out of you anyway.

We had gotten only about halfway up the side before Jess called out to me, "Hey, Jim!"

"What?"

"What's a porcupine look like?"

"I dunno. Wait a minute. Hey, Charlie!"

"What?"

"Do you know what a porcupine looks like?"

"How should I know?"

None of us had ever seen a porcupine—we were all raised in the city and had no idea what one really looked like or where it lived. We had been told that there were porkies all over the area we were in but not how to find one.

"Hey, Jess!" I called out.

"What?"

"Let's go fishing."

"Right!"

So back down the mountain we went.

The thought of something a little more filling than fish kept going through our minds. We could see cattle moving around some of the pastures nearby. We thought we might wrap layers of parachute canopy material around my little .38 pistol to muffle a shot. Going up to one of these cows would be easy, and a quick shot to the head would give us hundreds of pounds of fresh beef.

It was the amount of beef we would end up with that made us think. There was no way that we could eat all that meat in just a few days. Not only would the leftovers draw vultures and coyotes, they would be an obvious sign that we had done something we really weren't supposed to do. Back to the fishing hole we went.

By the last day of the exercise, the instructors had become impressed with the way we were handling ourselves. It had gotten to the point that the instructors were telling us what was going on with the rest of the class on the exercise. It seemed that the pilots, who were in their own group, were mostly just sitting in the little campsite they had made pissing and moaning about their situation. The instructor we were talking to found it almost unbelievable that men would give in to a bad situation so easily.

It was now time for the evasion portion of the exercise. The instructors, acting as partisans, informed us that the dreaded enemy was sending out patrols. Enemy forces had heard that we were in the area and were searching for us. It was time to break camp and move on to friendlier regions.

"I'll give you a direction and what to look for to find the next friendly partisan," our instructor said. And with that we were off on a cross-country chase.

The instructions we had been given were not the normal military directions. In a foreign country, partisans would not speak in terms of compass headings, klicks (kilometers), or pace counts. "Go east toward the pointed mountain until you come to the tree that splits as a fork," a partisan might say. Distances would be given in odd units such as "half a day's travel." Things like this would get us used to accepting unusual instructions.

Half of the class seemed to get lost right away. We knew that once we got to "friendly territory" the exercise would be over, and that was something to look forward to.

Every time we came to a partisan we were expected to ask for any food or drink that the man might have available. One partisan thought he had really had us, but he just didn't know Charlie Bump or Jess Tolison. When asked if he had any food, the partisan broke out a jar of jalapeño peppers, thinking that he was about to put one over on these rough, tough SEALs. That partisan's jaw bounced off the ground when Jess and Bump ate the whole jar and asked for more!

The last partisan pointed out our final objective. "See those trucks over there?" he said. There was a line of trucks we could still see as the sun was setting. "If you can reach those trucks, you will have passed the last checkpoint," our partisan said. "That is friendly territory, and the enemy cannot fire in that direction. Once you reach those trucks, you will have passed over the border. The exercise will be over and you'll be safe. But first you must get past the border guards."

"Oh, really."

So that was it—all we had to do was get past the border guards and we could relax. It was getting dark, and we were by far the first people to the border. Those few guards we could see were not allowed to shoot us, and they were between us and a hot meal and beer.

Taking a page from my jungle warfare training, we cut and trimmed some heavy sticks. Sneaking and peeking to find the weakest point in the guards' line, we found where only two guards were between us and the trucks. Quickly, we got into a short skirmish line. When Jess called "Go," we went. Charging to the border we actually knocked down and ran over the two guards.

Those two guards wanted to play the game, and we accommodated them. When they got in our way to stop us, we plowed right through them. If they had actually been armed guards willing to use their weapons, we would have come up with a very different plan. But what we did worked, and when we reached the trucks, we were in safe territory. The other guards didn't come after us, and the trucks took us back to the main camp.

"Okay, you guys," the instructor at the camp told us. "We have the mess hall all set up for you. There's soup and sandwiches. Eat some soup and have just one sandwich. You guys haven't been eating too well recently, and if you eat too much now, you'll just get sick. Eat slow and everything will be fine."

"Yeah, just take us to the mess hall," we answered. While we were on the exercise, Captain Woziniac, who was the CO of the Marines' Second Force Recon, arrived on the scene at the main camp. We knew the Captain from our early days with the *Sea Lion* when we trained the Marines down at Vieques, Puerto Rico. Captain Woziniac had known we were in the field. When we finally got to the mess hall, it was chow time for the SEALs. We charged into the food like a group of hungry bears, and the instructors at the hall were worried that we'd get sick. "Hell," Jess said, "We been eatin' all right. There just ain't been enough of it. Besides, this ain't fish."

"Okay then, that's it," the instructor said, "Get a good night's sleep—there's no reveille in the morning. Get some rest, and we'll see you about noon."

We headed over to our barracks, intending to sack out. When we entered the building, there was Captain Woziniac sitting on several cases of beer. "Well, it's about time you showed up," he said. "I expected you guys much earlier than this. What's the matter, some Marines beat you?"

"No sir, no Marines beat us here, sir. You want to get up off the beer now, Captain?"

"Captain Ski" took our joking in good fun. Here we were again. We had been advised not to do any drinking because it would probably make us ill. I don't know what was expected of us, but we downed all the beer and nobody got sick. By the time we finally left the camp, we had all of the instructors' respect.

That was probably the hardest individual school I had except for UDTR training. The guards at the POW camp really knew how to get whatever they wanted from a man. In a later class, Jim Tipton was taking the course. By that time the instructors at the camp knew who SEALs were and what they could expect of them. Because Jim had smacked a guard, they made an example of him. They put Tipton into a straitjacket and lowered him into the drum headfirst.

Jim figured they would take him out if they thought he was drowning. Although the camp had doctors all over just to be sure the trainers didn't go too far with anyone, the guards would leave a man in the drum until he quit thrashing around and then they would pull him out just short of sucking in water. Figuring that he could hold his breath longer than they would expect, Tipton just went limp in the drum. The guards left him in the drum until he almost drowned. When they finally pulled Jim out, he was barely conscious and his lungs were filling with water.

Since the school was finally closed, it's hard for me to say whether the training was worth it, but it taught all of us who took the course one thing. That lesson was to save the last grenade for yourself—don't ever get caught. I don't know if a man can actually do that to himself, but I do know that every man has a breaking point. There are people in this world who know how to find that point and go past it.

To the best of my knowledge, which is considerable, no SEAL was ever taken prisoner in Vietnam. No SEAL casualty was ever left behind, either. During World War II a small handful of UDT men were taken by the Japanese during one operation. Those men never broke and only told the Japanese what they were supposed to tell them.

In September, the entire Team, with Roy Boehm at the head, went down to Fort Bragg, North Carolina, home of the Army Special Forces. The Team was going to take some of the unconventional warfare training offered to us by the Army Special Forces.

One thing that happened on the way down to Bragg illustrates the way the Team thought and worked together. After men had completed UDTR training and joined the Teams, they seemed to lose all of the earlier prejudices that they brought with them into the Navy. Training didn't have any kind of magic wand that the instructors would wave over a redneck and suddenly he would be more tolerant of his fellow man. It was more that after having been through so much together as trainees, men in the Teams were color-blind toward their fellow Teammates.

On the trip to Bragg that first time with the whole Team, we were driving down in civilian vehicles in sort of a loose convoy. In North Carolina the convoy stopped to get breakfast at a small truck-stop restaurant. The twenty or so of us going to Bragg were sitting at the little four-person tables scattered around the room. We were all dressed in green fatigues with bloused, spit-shined jump boots, so the staff thought we were Army troops from one of the local bases. JP, Goines, Louie, and I were sitting together at a table. Some time had passed before we noticed that the other guys were getting their food and we hadn't even had our orders taken yet.

The cooks in the back were real busy; the Team just about filled the place. A waitress went by, and I stopped her and asked, "Just

what is going on? Can we please have some service? No one has taken our orders yet."

Looking at me like I was some kind of bug, the waitress answered, "I'm sorry, sir, but you're in North Carolina now. I won't serve this table as long as he is sitting here." And she indicated Bill Goines. There were maybe two black men in the Teams then, and Bill was the only black SEAL in Team Two. While I just kind of sat there stunned with my mouth hanging open, JP handled the situation with proper SEAL diplomacy.

Standing up, JP announced, "Hey, guys! This place won't serve a teammate!"

Looking over at our table, the rest of the Team could see what the problem was. Without another word, the entire Team got up and walked out the door. Plates were left at the tables, and complaints about our orders being almost done were just ignored. You do *not* treat one of our own like that. If a man had the intestinal fortitude and physical ability to pass the training that it took to enter the Teams, then he was a SEAL or UDT man. Things like race, color, religion, and personal taste simply didn't matter.

We arrived at Bragg without any further incident. Most of us were looking forward to the classes we had been told about. The course was a two-week block of instruction in foreign small-arms familiarization, firing, field stripping, unconventional warfare, and kitchen-table demolitions (improvised munitions). We not only got to play with some of the Army's toys, but also managed to spend some time messing with our counterparts in the Army, the Green Berets.

Kitchen demolitions was probably the most interesting instruction they gave down at Bragg. The instructors taught us how to make incendiaries and explosives using materials you would find in the average kitchen. This was fun, even for those of us who couldn't cook. The morning was spent whipping up different things in the Special Forces devil's kitchen. That afternoon we were going to go to the demolition range and fire what we had made.

Bill Green was beating away at his table, and nobody else wanted to be within three tables of him. Bill had a reputation for being a little drifty on occasion and would let his enthusiasm get the better of him. This normally didn't bother us very much. But while watching Bill bang away at his mixtures, the mad scientist at work, none of us really wanted to share table space with him.

We had a good time. Most of what we made were incendiaries, but the variety of things you could crank out from commonly available materials was amazing. After chow we packed up and headed down to the range with our stuff. Some of us were making bets on whether these things we had made would go bang, burn, or just sit there spitting and smoking.

Most of the men who were instructing us had been up at Little Creek while I was still at UDT. One of the things our instructors pointed out was that the range procedures we would follow in the Navy were different from those of the Army. "On an Army range," the instructor said, "one big difference is that you holler 'Fire in the hole!' three times before you fire your charge." In the Navy we would holler "Fire in the hole" only once, check the range guards on either side, and, if the range was clear, let go the charge.

The Army regulations didn't seem to be any kind of problem, so we prepared to fire our stuff. Bill Green wanted to be the first, and we all just let him. It was common knowledge in the Team that Bill liked to overload his targets, so we took this into account on the range. When Bill went out to set his charge, we all moved out to the proper safety distance, plus about half a mile.

Then Bill got down into position with the hell box (detonator). Looking to the right and then the left, Bill hollered, "Fire in the hole! Three times!" and twisted the firing handle.

It was hard to tell which was more exciting to watch, Bill's incendiary burning or the sergeant chewing his ass off. "I did what you told me, Sarge," was Bill's only answer to the range NCO. Those Beanies just didn't have a good sense of humor, and they just about tossed the entire Team off the post.

But things settled down rather quickly. The rest of us set off our materials and were impressed with the results. Further classes taught us how to make pipe bombs with improvised explosives and even how to build a firearm with a piece of pipe and matches. There was a question of where you would get all the wooden matches needed when you were out in Bumfuck, Egypt, but we didn't let that ruin our fun.

There was a slight problem with UDT tradition of overloading a target whenever possible. It seemed that those pipe shotguns just didn't accept what we considered a proper charge without exploding when they were fired. Some of the guys would play by the rules, and their improvised weapons did fire properly. The idea behind launching a charge of broken glass with a bunch of matchheads was to kill an enemy soldier and take his weapon. Looking at the results of remote-firing most of our pipe guns, a number of us figured a big rock might be a safer way to work that particular source of supply.

Besides teaching us how to make our own version of the zip gun, the instructors gave us a complete course of instruction in U.S. and foreign weapons. The French MAT-49, British Sten Mark II, German MP-40 (Schmeisser), and Swedish K were among the submachine guns taught to us, along with the American M3 greasegun and M1928A1 Thompson. Before then we had had almost no experience with submachine guns. But once the instructors showed us how to load the weapons and which end the bullets came out of, we had little trouble qualifying as experts on the Army ranges.

There was one large, black Special Forces sergeant who was giving most of the mechanical weapons classes, teaching us how to field-strip and maintain all the different weapons we were firing. When we were assembling the weapons, that sergeant always said the same thing. "Don't fouse [force] it. Don't fouse it. It'll come out awright if you don't fouse it."

"All right, we won't fouse it."

One time on the ranges we did have a small bit of trouble with the instructor. While we were firing the M2HB .50 caliber machine guns, a deer walked across the range. The range NCO called out a cease-fire. That was not the time to tell these SEALs, who couldn't hear him very well anyway, to stop shooting. Scratch one deer. The only real problem was that there was so much unexploded ordnance downrange they wouldn't let us go and get the deer.

It was while at the weapons course at Bragg that Team Two used automatic weapons properly for the first time. UDT men really didn't use much in the way of small arms, and we SEALs were still learning what it would take for us to complete our mission. Before arriving at Bragg I didn't know the difference between a Schmeisser and a Sten gun. It was during the course that I first developed my interest in weapons, which later guided me to working in Ordnance.

To some of the SEALs, this was just another course to learn and absorb. Others of us really got our cookies off firing the different kinds of weapons. Louie also enjoyed working with the weapons, but he seemed to lean toward the heavier machine guns. He was one of the guys trying for that deer.

Tradition held that the Navy and the Army would mess with each other whenever possible as long as it wasn't in the middle of a battle. Being good upstanding sailors, we tried to follow the traditions of our service, especially when we were at Bragg.

The Special Forces Jump Club was where the Team liked to spend off-duty time when we were at Bragg. The club was a place we could relax and have a beer. It was also near the hospital and the nurses' quarters, so we all found it very convenient. We all hung out at the Jump Club rather than the larger base NCO Club, since we really didn't get along with the large Airborne units at the base or the "legs"(non-Airborne soldiers). The Jump Club was where the Special Forces guys had their own bar, along with pin-ball machines and pool tables.

A group of about a dozen British SAS (Special Air Service) troopers were at Bragg, having recently served in Malaysia. The Brits were teaching the Berets, and ourselves, some of the lessons they had learned while fighting the Communist insurgents.

The British had a very distinct line drawn between the officers and the enlisted men. SAS officers just did not mingle with the men during their off-duty time. The Special Forces and SEALs, on the other hand, were much more relaxed, and there was camaraderie between officers and men. Roy Boehm and John Callahan both liked to go out drinking and carousing with all of us on liberty.

There was a popular joke making the rounds of the Team while we were down at Bragg. It seems there was this drunk standing on a corner watching this other man talking to the women walking by. Every time a woman walked by, this one guy would speak to her and wind up in a conversation with her. The drunk finally walked up to the other man and asked, "Hey, buddy, what are you doing?"

The other man answered, "I stop the women and talk to them. Some I get their phone numbers and others I don't."

"How do you get the phone numbers from the ones that are interested?" the drunk asked.

"Well," the man answered, "I go up to the women and say, 'Tickle your ass with a feather.' If they get upset and say, 'What did you say?', I answer, 'Particularly nasty weather.'"

The drunk continues watching him and the man seems to be doing quite well with the ladies. "I gotta try that," says the drunk to himself. As the next lady walks by him the drunk calls out, "Hey, lady, stick a feather up your ass?"

The astonished woman turns on the drunk. "What did you say!"

"Raining like a fuck out, ain't it?"

For that era in the service, that was the joke of jokes. So there we were, sitting at the club laughing our heads off. The Limey Captain from the SAS unit was just sitting at a table with Roy and some other officers while we were raising hell. "I don't know," said the Captain. "That isn't how we behave back in England." He had been making snide comments about us and the Berets all evening, and Roy Boehm had had just about enough of that officer's attitude.

Roy picked up a pitcher of beer from the table and poured the entire thing over the man's head. "I can't believe it. I can't believe it," sputtered the SAS captain.

"Raining like a fuck out, ain't it?" said Roy as he set the pitcher back down.

After Roy had dumped that beer on the SAS Captain, the British boys kept trying to even the score. It was during one of the impromptu challenges that would crop up at the club, after a sufficient number of beers, that the SEALs were initiated into the Dance of the Flaming Assholes.

Arthur Williams (One Lump) had been an NCO with the Special Forces before he came over to the SEALs. I knew One Lump wouldn't back down from anything. The SAS men asked if anyone wanted to challenge them to the Dance of the Flaming Assholes. They had come up with this "entertainment" in Malaysia just for something to do to keep from going crazy.

"What's the Dance of the Flaming Assholes?" we asked. The Special Forces men were keeping quiet, so either they knew what was going on and were suckering us in or they had already wised up to these SAS troopers and their games.

The idea was to take equal lengths of toilet tissue and twist them up into short ropes. One man from each command would drop his drawers and spread his cheeks. The toilet paper would be strategically located and clamped in place when the man let go of his cheeks. On the word go, the paper would be lit. The guy who dropped his paper first was the loser. The two contestants would dance around with this burning paper; this is how the dance got its name.

Being former Special Forces, One Lump was going to stand up for the Team in front of all his old cohorts. One Lump was sitting carefully for a week, but he won and seriously impressed the SAS men. You could've burned One Lump inside and out, but once he had taken it on himself to represent us, he wasn't gong to let any Limey outdo him. Personally, this was something I wasn't really interested in trying. I may have done some stupid things but that was not one of them.

That was the kind of camaraderie we had then. And it was stunts like the dance that helped give the SEALs a reputation for doing almost anything. But I learned that all of the Special Warfare people in the world were much the same. It didn't matter if you were a SEAL, Special Forces, SAS, or a French combat swimmer, we all shared the dangers that came with being elite forces. And that seemed to make us think a lot along the same lines, whether in combat or on liberty.

Later that year, things took on a much more serious tone. On October 22, 1962, President Kennedy announced that the Soviet Union had placed offensive nuclear weapons on Cuban soil. By October 24, the U.S. Navy had a blockade in place in the Caribbean. The blockade was to turn back any ships carrying offensive weapons to Cuba. The world moved very close to all-out nuclear war.

The military had been put on full alert, but the SEALs and the Special Forces had already been preparing. SEAL Team Two was ready to go into Cuba within hours of receiving the orders. We would go in by water and parachute, with the Army Special Forces doing much the same.

We sat at Little Creek for days waiting for the order committing us to Cuba. President Kennedy was having a stare-down with Soviet Premier Nikita Khrushchev. Khrushchev blinked first. He sent a letter to the United States stating that the missile launch sites were going to be dismantled and the missiles returned to the Soviet Union. The crisis was over and the alert called off. It was both a big relief and a big letdown for all of us at the Creek.

All of our training was to prepare us for the kind of operation that Cuba would have been. Not getting the go-ahead signal was something of a letdown. But the relief at not having a nuclear war was much greater than any disappointment we had at not having Uncle Fidel to play with.

Roy Boehm finally left the Team in November after the crisis was over. Roy's methods for getting us outfitted in the shortest possible time had rankled some of the higher-ups in Washington. The next assignment for Roy was to help set up the LDNN training course in South Vietnam. The LDNN (Lien Doc Nquoi Nhia, "soldiers who fight under the sea") personnel were going to be the South Vietnamese version of the SEALs. Having started Team Two, Roy was now going to continue the job overseas.

For the next several years, the SEALs trained and developed their capabilities. For almost half a year, I was part of MTT 1-63, a Mobile Training Team sent by Team Two to help establish a UDT course in Turkey. For months we trained members of the Turkish military in demolitions, weapons handling, parachuting, diving, and all the other skills we had developed for our own operations. The graduates of our training went on to become instructors at the Turkish UDT school. Other MTTs were doing much the same training with the Greeks, Norwegians, and others.

Our own training wasn't cut short either. Mine included Army Ranger School, Instructors School, judo instructor training, jumpmaster training, HALO (high altitude, low opening) training, parachute packing, training in maintaining the Mercury outboard motor, and even the UDT/SEAL Nuclear Weapons course. That last training resulted in my being one of the first SEALs qualified on the baby atomic bomb, the SADM, or Small Atomic Demolition Munition.

All of my school and qualification patches were sewn on the jumpsuit that I wore when visiting outside parachute jump clubs. Tom N. Tarbox (TNT), Team Two's skipper in 1964, loved hassling me about the number of patches on my suit. One day, TNT had the men over in Air Ops sew rifle-bore cleaning patches all over my jumpsuit. TNT figured I needed a few more patches. It was Tarbox, through this incident, who gave me the nickname "Patches."

During all this time, Rudy Boesch put us through PT and long-distance runs almost every day. It became something of a challenge to come up with different ways to sneak out on Rudy's runs. As the men qualified to operate, more and more mission requirements were placed on us. We had to be physically fit to perform what was expected of us. And for all our trying, Rudy Boesch made sure that we stayed in condition.

Other training and testing was done. Louie Kucinski almost single-handedly tested the Pegasus underwater vehicle for the SEALs. After Louie wrecked—that is, tested—it twice, the Teams decided against the Pegasus. While diving in St. Thomas, Ron Brozak, Swede, and One Lump discovered an old boat anchor off the docks. They raised it and brought it back to Little Creek, intending to sell that old chunk of iron for big bucks. After months went by, that anchor became a kind of mascot to Team Two. To this day, every time the Team has moved to a new building, the anchor has been taken along. It stands in front of the headquarters of Team Two today.

President Kennedy visited the Team in June 1963. He was very impressed with the unit that he helped to make. When Kennedy was assassinated, some SEALs who were deployed to schools were put on alert. The thought was that there might be an attempt to take over the government in the confusion after Kennedy's death, so the alert went out to most of the military. After the funeral, things returned to normal, but most of us would never quite be the same again.

Men from Team Two were sent to the Dominican Republic during the emergency there. Other SEALs went to Central America, Europe, and Asia. But it was to be in Southeast Asia, in a little country called Vietnam, that the SEALs were to receive their baptism of fire.

CHAPTER 7

1966

1966 was going to prove to be a very interesting year for Team Two. The action in South Vietnam was starting to heat up. Team One on the West Coast had the major commitment for any SEAL actions in Vietnam. Team Two had already sent some people as part of Mobile Training Teams, and Roy Boehm had helped set up the training school for the South Vietnamese counterparts to the SEALs, the LDNNs, after he left Team Two.

Team One had only a small contingent of SEALs incountry, along with several detachments from the West Coast's UDT 11. Team Two was hoping to have some detachments of its own operating in Vietnam, but that wasn't going to happen until later in the year. For now, SEALs in Team Two would continue training and operating as they had been doing.

In January, Team Two was having an interteam judo tournament. The contest was a process of elimination, and Jess Tolison and I had made it all the way to the finals. Jess and I cared for each other like brothers, but the rivalry of competition would make each of us work hard to defeat the other. This kind of competition helped keep us sharp and develop our skills. "Exercising the young lions," and some not so young, the officers called it.

Judo is also called "the gentle way," but this competition proved anything but gentle. Our bout had been going on for some time without either of us winning any points over the other. I knew Jess as well as I knew myself and he was coming in at me left-handed. Aha, I thought, he's going to feint with his left and actually come at me right-handed. I'll counter for the right hand and beat him before he's even started. I was wrong.

Jess never did switch to right-handed, and the next thing I knew I was six feet into the air and heading for the mat. Because I was so wide open, Jess lost his balance during the throw and he was going to "maki-komi" me. During a real combat, you would maki-komi—drop down hard onto your thrown adversary—and end the fight. In sport competition you don't do that, lest you seriously injure your opponent. Before we even hit the mat, Jess was calling out, "I'm sorry!"

We smacked into the mat with Jess on top. I heard the snap, crackle, and pop of my shoulder as it ground into the mat with our combined weight on it. I had an A/C (axio/clavicular) separation. My left shoulder was all bent out of shape, with a bone pressing up against the skin. When I turned my head I hit the bone that was sticking up with my chin. And *pain!* Oh Lordy, this thing hurt.

The corpsman at the match immediately checked me out and immobilized my arm. Jess took me to sick bay on the base. The doctors just took one look at me and said, "We can't do anything for him here. Take him over to Portsmouth." During the drive to the naval hospital at Portsmouth, Jess couldn't stop telling me how sorry he was. I wasn't in the best of moods—I absolutely could not get into a comfortable position—but I didn't blame Jess for the incident.

We were both dressed in our judo uniforms when we walked into the emergency room at Portsmouth. After a short examination, the doctors wanted to admit me to the hospital. The doctor said that there was nothing they could do in the emergency room, that I would have to be scheduled for an operating room when one became available.

"Wait a minute," I said. "Since you can't do anything until you have an OR available, why do you want to admit me to the hospital?"

"We want to help make you comfortable and give you medication for the pain."

"Just give me the pills and tell me when you want me back. I'll be a lot more comfortable waiting in my own home and bed."

This disturbed them a bit; they weren't used to dealing with SEALs. They gave me the medication and Jess drove me home. Jess also went into the house first and explained to Marlene what had happened. Jess was hurting worse over the accident than I was, if that was possible. We were close. Back then, everyone on the Team was close and we looked out for each other.

The next day, Jess picked me up and drove me to Portsmouth. An operating room had been scheduled, and I was prepped and wheeled into the room. When I woke up later, I was in a cast from my waist to my neck with my left arm strapped in place inside the cast. There was a hole in the cast up near my neck where there was an incision in my shoulder. Well, I thought, at least this is going to get me out of PT with Rudy for a while.

The day after the operation, a doctor came into my room with the X-rays of my shoulder. Showing me what they had done, the doctor pointed out where two screws had been put into the bone to hold my shoulder together until it healed. "Boy, I hope somebody kissed me," I said. The doctor looked bewildered. "You see, Doc," I said, "I'm used to being kissed whenever somebody screws me." The nurse in the room broke up laughing.

"Can I go home or on liberty, Doc?" I asked.

"When you can get a uniform on, you can go on liberty," the doctor said. And with that he and the nurse left the room.

I called Marlene at the house. "Bring the oldest jumper I have to the hospital," I said. "The one with a zipper in it. And bring a needle and thread and a razor blade."

Marlene brought the things I asked for and helped me fit a uniform over my cast. After we'd cut the sleeve of the left arm all the way open, I could get the uniform over the cast. Once I got my arm into the other sleeve and zipped up the jumper, I was in uniform.

Walking out to the doctor's office, I asked, "Permission to go ashore, sir." The uniform was a little misshapen, but it was a uniform.

Shaking his head, the doctor said, "You've got it," and he signed me out of the hospital on liberty. I still had to go back and spend time in a hospital bed for treatment, but at least I was able to go out on liberty now and then.

While I was on the ward in the hospital, Captain Kane's son was in the bed next to me. Captain Kane had been in the UDT back in World War II and was now the group commander at the Underwater Demolition Unit, what the Underwater Demolition Command had evolved into. Kane's son was a Marine and had been injured in combat while in Vietnam. While Captain Kane was visiting his son, he and I developed a nodding acquaintance.

Whenever anybody from the Team was in the hospital, guys could get the afternoon off to go visit him just by asking for it. I know some of the guys just wanted to get the afternoon off, but Gene Tinnin was not one of them. Gene was about as far my opposite as anyone in the Team, which was somehow why we became such close friends. I was a drinker and a hellraiser, hardheaded, arrogant, and a pretty bad womanizer. Gene was the opposite; he never drank or swore and was a great family man. The Tinnins had the ugliest basset hound I had ever seen. I normally love that kind of animal, but Chigger was about three dogs long, two dogs wide, and only half a dog high. She had to have a roller skate under her belly, it dragged so much.

Whenever Gene wanted to take his wife and two sons on leave, my family would take care of Chigger. It was little things like that which showed who you were really close to. Gene would come and see me in the hospital with a six-pack of Cokes in his hand every day or so. This was before there were twist-off caps on bottles. Gene had carefully taken off the caps, poured out about a quarter of the soda, filled the bottles up with rum, and carefully fitted the caps back on the bottles, manufacturing a six-pack of rum-and-Cokes.

One night, a whole bunch of the guys from the Team, Louie, Tipton, John Dearmon, and others, came in drunk on their asses. The guys had been drinking at the club when one of them said, "Let's go see Jimbo. He's gotta be feeling bad just lying there in the hospital." Before showing up, they stopped at a package store and bought me a fifth of rum. They were almost immediately thrown out of the hospital for being too rowdy.

So between Gene's premixed rum-and-Cokes and the guys bringing me a bottle, I was pretty well set for my stay. A couple of the nurses knew what was going on, but since I was not on any medication and didn't abuse the privilege, they turned a blind eye. A few of the guys from the Team had been in Portsmouth over the years, and some of the staff had a world of respect for the SEALs. Comments were made that we healed almost twice as fast as an average fleet sailor. A few of the doctors attributed that to the SEALs' very high level of physical fitness.

Sometimes we just ignored an injury. One SEAL had broken his leg and was in a cast. To make a demonstration parachute jump with his teammates, that SEAL cut the cast off his leg and made the jump. Later he got in trouble for it, but the story was already making the rounds of the fleet.

Captain Kane came in one night and by mistake opened my bedside table rather than his son's. He eyeballed my bottle of rum, then just closed the door and continued with his visit. The captain had been in the UDT, the skipper of UDT 21, and through World War II as well. Kane knew how we played the game in the Teams. After his visit, Captain Kane quietly said to me, "I hope you're using your head with that bottle, Jim."

"Yes sir," I answered. "Neither one of us is on medication, and the staff knows we have it. We don't overdo it. In fact, most of the time when the other patients are asleep, we get a nurse or corpsman to get us Coke to mix a drink with." That satisfied the captain, and I never heard another word about it.

We always made sure not to get anyone else in trouble. And we tried to keep ourselves out of trouble as well. We were young and very full of ourselves in the Teams. The word "can't" just wasn't in our vocabulary. We were all on a bit of an ego trip. Nobody could do anything we wouldn't do, and we would do a lot of things other people wouldn't even try. There was a very strong "can-do" spirit in the Teams.

We would always try to keep our heads whatever we did. It was an unwritten rule in the Teams to know your limitations. But we could still get in over our heads, especially when drinking. Gene was probably the Team's first designated driver when we did our carousing as a group. There were enough risks we took every day just doing our duties; we didn't have to add to them by driving drunk.

Many, many times, such as when we were at Fort Bragg, Gene would pick up the gang and drive them back to the barracks. A finer SEAL, or man, I never knew. When he made warrant officer, Gene was transferred to Team One. He was killed in Vietnam in 1968 while leading his men. I miss him to this day.

By late May I was in good health and was increasing my duties. A group of us traveled down to Eglin Air Force Base in Florida to train some of the Air Commandos in scuba operations. While at Eglin we were also testing out the AN/GRC 109 radio, most commonly called the Angry-109.

A number of the higher-ups were real enthused about the Angry-109. Jake Rhinebolt was one of the real pushers for us to have our own long-range communications. The 109 is CW (continuous-wave) only and requires the operator to be able to send and receive Morse code. Several of us had gone to CW school at the Amphibious Forces base and were able to send and receive eight to ten words a minute by the time we went to Eglin. As a quartermaster, I was trained to read Morse code by blinker lamp aboard ship. But watching Morse and listening to it are very different things.

Kratky was pretty sharp on the radio and acted as the primary radio operator. Little Creek had a base station, and we had arranged to send and receive messages on a fixed schedule. The setup for our radio operations was complicated. The first day we were out in the woods at Eglin with the antenna set up and the radio all cranked up. And the Angry-109 really was cranked up. The radio had a large hand-cranked generator to supply the power, and one guy would sit and operate the two hand cranks, much like giant bicycle pedals, while the radio was being used.

At the Angry-109 station, we also had a PRC-25 short-range radio so we could talk to the barracks at the main camp. In the barracks we had another PRC-25 and a man on the phone talking to the Team at Little Creek. At Little Creek, Kratky had set up his Angry-109 on the golf course so he could try to talk to us. After much trying, and cranking that damned generator, the only person to have contact with the Creek was the guy in the barracks using the phone. We never did have much luck with the Angry-109. We even jumped the system in on practice parachute drops. But the rig just never did work out for us and the idea was eventually dropped.

When we all got back to the Creek, it didn't take long before things really started looking up. In June, Rick Marcinko arrived at Team Two as a shiny new ensign. I had known Rick only slightly earlier when he was a second class radioman in UDT 22. One day he seemed to just disappear only to show up later as an OCS graduate and mustang officer.

Rick was a hard-nosed officer who pushed himself and his men as far as they could go and beyond. We respected Rick for what he had accomplished, and he respected us for our skills and experience. Unlike some other officers, Rick knew he hadn't been in the Teams very long and he didn't have the attitude that just because he was an officer he had the answers to everything. When he didn't know the best way to do something, Rick would ask one of us who had dealt with the problem before.

Though he would always make his own decisions, Rick listened to what his men said and took the advice seriously. When the results were good, Rick would share the glory with us. When things went bad, he would protect his men and take the blame. Rick Marcinko also had the habit of always saying exactly what was on his mind. If he didn't agree with something, Rick would speak right up against it. He wasn't the most political officer in the world, but he never let his men go into a situation that he thought was bad right from the get-go.

They say that people who are a lot alike don't normally get along, but Rick and I hit it off right away. I don't really know what it was—maybe it had something to do with us both being loudmouthed, arrogant, and bullheaded. We would work together sometimes during the summer and spent some off-duty time together. But I really didn't start operating with Rick until September.

In late June I managed to pass another training course that was a little different from the rest. Every so often a modification would be made to an earlier device and, when it was important enough, we would take further courses to learn the new wrinkles.

Course J-00-919 was a special Nuclear Warfare Course (SEAL and UDT) taught at NUWPNTRACENLANT (Nuclear Weapon Training Center, Atlantic). There were some new modifications made to the SADM (Small Atomic Demolition Munition), and it was important that those of us trained on the earlier system learn the new weapon. Primarily, it had been made a lot harder for us to blow ourselves away and take a large chunk of the surrounding real estate with us. Nukes gave me the willies, even itty-bitty ones; I really didn't like them. Besides, they were a bitch to go fishing with.

Rick had been settling into the routine at Team Two while I was at school. He soon learned of the Team Two tradition of trying to skip out on Rudy's PT. Both Rick and I had managed to slip out from Rudy's run one morning. We were supposed to be doing something in Supply but instead were enjoying the morning in Rick's new station wagon. While driving down Virginia Beach Boulevard we had the radio tuned to WCMS, a local country-music station that was popular at the Team.

WCMS had a promotional contest going on involving its mobile station. The trailer would be parked at different locations around the area during the day. The announcer would say, "Our mobile truck is at such-and-such a location. The next five people who pull in and say 'I listen to WCMS' will win a prize."

When the contest announcement went out on the radio, Rick suddenly shouted, "Shit! That's right over there," and turned the car.

"We listen to WCMS"—and Rick won a free paint job for a car. The man in the truck wanted to put us both on the air and interview us. "No, no, no, we're not supposed to be on liberty right now." We were both dressed in fatigues and were not supposed to be off base. Everybody back at the Team listened to WCMS, and Rudy would have us running for a week if he found out where we had been.

Leaving the station, we continued on our way. Rick's car was a brand-new station wagon and did not need a paint job. He sold the prize to Ronnie Rodger for around twenty-five dollars. Ronnie drove a beat-up piece of shit that needed a good paint job.

During the early part of the summer, Team Two was hosting some French combat swimmers from Toulon. The exchange was part of a hands-across-the-sea cross-training agreement we had with the French military. The French detachment was under the command of a French lieutenant who had lost his left hand at the wrist in some kind of accident. The loss of a hand certainly didn't slow down that lieutenant, and his men weren't any slouches when it came to being operators either.

Second Platoon was working with the Frenchmen during their visit. Each of us in the platoon was assigned a French swimmer as a swim buddy. Anything we did, whether it was jumping, diving, or training in the bush, those Frenchmen stayed right alongside. By the time the French swimmers returned to France, they had picked up a good many new techniques and operating methods from us. Now it was time to send a SEAL platoon over to France to train there.

Since Second Platoon had hosted the Frenchmen when they were here, we were chosen to go to France. Jake Rhinebolt was in charge of the platoon when we set out for France. We were going to leave from the Washington, D.C., area, and there was a little side trip the Navy wanted a few platoon members to take before we left.

There were fourteen SEALs going on the exchange, two officers and twelve enlisted men. Jake Rhinebolt, who was in charge of the detachment, Pat Patterson, Bob Gallagher, and I were called in to the Pentagon for a special assignment and briefing. We were first warned about the need for strict security on the detachment's operations. Then we were told why. The higher-ups wanted the four of us to conduct a reconnaissance mission while we were in France. Without our hosts knowing, we were to recon selected beaches in the Toulon area, conducting hydrographic reconnaissances as completely as possible, for some "unnamed" government agencies. The base at Toulon where we were going to be training was the major missile-testing site for France's submarine missile program. We were to obtain as much information as we could about the base, things like the thickness of the concrete around the testing beds where the missiles were fired out over the water, the dimensions of test facilities, and the times of any launches we might witness. In general, they wanted any information we could get on the base.

It felt a little funny, the idea of spying on people who were supposed to be our allies. But orders are to be carried out, and these were no exception. Without letting the other team members know what we were doing, and especially hiding our sneak-and-peek from the French, we would gather the information as we had been asked to. What we didn't know was that the higher-ups already had all the information they wanted on the beaches and sites we were to examine. The planners on the Navy staff wanted to compare what we could get with what they already knew. That way they would have a very good idea of what the clandestine espionage capabilities of the SEALs were in case they really needed to send us out at later times.

The rest of the platoon was not to know about the operation. Later, while in France, Pat and Jake decided to let Harry Humphries in on what was going on when we needed another man. Harry was a sharp, cool-headed, aggressive operator and was a real asset during our spy operations.

The platoon flew in to Orly Field near Paris on August 4, and we were to continue on to Toulon by train on August 7. After all, we had to spend some time in Paris to get familiar with the countryside. For a few days we were just tourists, living in a hotel and visiting the Eiffel Tower and all the other famous sights. Paris really surprised me; it was different from what I had heard back in the States. It is a very clean city and very pleasant to walk around in.

During one of our wanderings in the city we stopped by a very interesting shop. Sam Fournier, Scotty MacLean, and I all play the guitar at different levels of skill. Just as we were passing a music store, a man set a handmade six-string banjo in the window. The banjo had a real big body and a guitar neck, a very custom instrument. Sam already played the mandolin and the guitar, but he had said that he wanted to learn to play the banjo someday. Since this custom banjo had a guitar neck, Sam could play it like a guitar and it would sound like a banjo.

Sam went into the shop and started tinkering with the banjo. It sounded pretty good and Sam was impressed, but he wanted to compare it to his own guitar. We went back to the hotel, picked up our guitars, and went back to the shop. I had a Gibson and Sam had a Martin, two of the best guitars you could buy at the time. Back at the shop, Sam just fell in love with that banjo. We spent the afternoon playing country-western music. The owner of the store thought we were just fine, because he had a crowd in the place all the time we were there playing. He even had wine brought in for us.

With a bunch of kids back home, there was no way Sam felt he could afford several hundred dollars for the banjo. But Sam was going to retire out of the Team inside of about a year. We all chipped in and bought the banjo for Sam as sort of an early going-away present. The deal was set up so that Sam thought I'd bought the banjo for myself, but it was the platoon who really wanted him to have it later as a retirement present.

Though I wasn't there, the guys all told me about a great gag they pulled on Scotty MacLean while at a restaurant. Within the Team, if you didn't have any money and the crowd was going someplace, you were welcome to come along. There would come a time when somebody else wouldn't have any funds and you would help cover for him. This would go round and round through the Team. The situation did make for a common joke inside the Team. If somebody with the group didn't have any money, it was common practice to try to slip out on the guy and stick him with the bill. The rest of the gang would be nearby to keep an eye on things and have a good laugh watching the "stickee" trying to get out of the bill.

While we were in Paris, a bunch of the guys were out entertaining a few Parisiennes, with Scotty as one of the group. Scotty was broke and the other guys at the table knew it. Without Scotty noticing, the rest of the guys slipped away from the table. The group had been sitting on a terrace on the second floor of this restaurant. After they had slipped away, the guys waited across the street where they could still see Scotty at the table.

Now Scotty was in a fix—he had to either keep ordering or pay the bill. And he didn't have any money to pay the bill. At the main door of the restaurant was this very big black man acting as sort of a combination maître d' and bouncer. The main door was just below the terrace where Scotty was sitting, and the guys could see Scotty looking over the sill of this short iron railing at the bouncer below. Later on, Scotty told us what had been going through his mind.

Scotty's plan was to jump over the rail to the ground below. What he was wondering was whether he could recover from a PLF (parachute landing fall) fast enough to be able to smack the bouncer out before the guy could get his hands on him.

When he finally made his move, Scotty never laid a hand on the bouncer. As Scotty smacked into the ground right behind the bouncer, the bouncer just took off running. Seeing that the bouncer was running the other way, Scotty just took off in the opposite direction.

Not all the time we spent in Paris was just sight-seeing. Jake, Bob, Pat, and I had to spend some time getting briefings at the American embassy on what to look for and examine during our stay. It was at this time that we brought Harry Humphries in with us. The man who was briefing us was some white-shirt Agency man. I didn't know who he was and I didn't want to know. If something went wrong, I wouldn't be able to say who had told me to do what. All I would say was that I had felt like looking around at the time. We knew who the Agency people were in general and we acknowledged that what they did was valuable, but we really didn't have much of a taste for the espionage end of things.

The platoon would continue on to Toulon by train. To keep from standing out too much, we all studied the customs of France in the pamphlets we had been supplied with. According to our information, the custom in France was to bring wine, cheese, and bread in a string bag aboard the train for meals during the trip. Since we didn't want to stand out, we all went and bought string bags and did the same.

Once we were aboard the train we discovered all the passengers did bring their own food—sandwiches and regular lunches in brown paper bags just like the working-class stiffs back home. The only people on the whole train with the traditional string bags were us. We might as well each have been wearing a big sign saying "American Tourists." So much for the blending in inconspicuously.

But one of the Team's Don Juans got along quite well with the French whether he understood the local customs or not. He had not let cultural differences stand in his way but was working hard on improving Franco-American relations in his top bunk in the sleeper car, even before we left the Paris railroad station.

The trip to Toulon was uneventful, but arriving at the base we had a bit of a surprise. The French combat swimmers had their own base, separate from the main naval base at Toulon. "Wow, just like Coronado and the West Coast Team," we said. Back at Little Creek, Team Two was just off in one corner of the main base. Out West in Coronado, Team One had its own compound across the street from the Amphibious Forces base. The commando base was out on a small peninsula separate and secure from the rest of the installation.

The French combat swimmers treated us very well while we were there. The French military have wine served with the meal. A rough red wine is the standard-issue table wine, but there was a small window in the NCO club where, for a few francs, you could purchase a better wine to have with your meal. The commandos were always buying us the better wine. They just didn't want us to drink what they considered the inferior issue wine.

I considered the French diving rig much better than the system we were using in the SEALs. The French Mark 57 closed-circuit was a good swimming rig that I felt had some real advantages. The whole system fitted on your chest, leaving your back free to carry other gear. The oxygen bottle and baralyme canister were where you could easily reach everything, but the rig didn't have a breathing bag like the American systems. The exhaled air went into the baralyme can, which absorbed the CO_2 as soon as you breathed out, so you never worried about a CO_2 buildup as you had to with some of the earlier rigs I had swum. In general, I found the Mark 57 to be the most comfortable system I ever swam with. The Draeger rigs that the Teams are using today are very much like an improved version of that French Mark 57 I swam with so long ago.

On arrival at the base, I began preparations for our intelligence-gathering assignment. While we were walking around the base, Bob Gallagher had told me, "We've got to get some pictures of this. This place is hot shit for those guys back home." I immediately took to wearing one of the Team's 35mm cameras around my neck anywhere I went, just being Joe Tourist. After a while, nobody even noticed the camera; it was just part of me.

Bob and I had just decided to go balls-to-the-wall on our assignment. Rather than just give the people in Washington measurements, we would photograph the installation. Since Bob was the senior man, I would be doing the riskier act of taking pictures. As just a dumb first class, I would have a better chance of bluffing my way out if I was caught. For three days we just walked around taking pictures of different things and of Bob standing nearby. We had previously measured and made note of different measurements of Bob and his uniform—how far apart the buttons were, how long the sleeve was, things like that. With Bob standing next to the end of a bunker wall, it was real easy to measure the thickness of the concrete by comparing it to Bob's measurements.

One day the lieutenant who had been at Little Creek came up to me and said, "Excuse me, maybe we didn't tell you clearly enough, but cameras are not allowed here."

"Oh, well, excuse me, sir," I answered, "I didn't know. I'll put it away. I just like France and wanted some pictures for the family to show them where we've been." Just play big and stupid, which was easy, and act deferential. So now it was time to quit using the camera. Besides, we had shot several rolls of film already. Harry had been doing exactly the same thing that I was on different portions of the base. But once I was caught, that was it, no more cameras. If you act as if you belong there, you can get away with all kinds of stuff on the average military base, no matter what country it's in. But if you play people for a fool and get greedy, you'll get caught every time.

The beach recons were even easier. Every weekend we would go to the targeted beaches. Paddle boats, operated with foot pedals, were for rent all over the place, since these were public beaches. Putting small slate boards in our pockets, we would rent a paddle boat and pedal around the water like tourists. With wrist compasses, we would take bearings and sound the waters with little lead lines made of fishing line and sinkers. Nobody suspected anything. We were just two guys in a paddle boat drinking beer and playing at fishing with a handline. We surveyed miles of beach that way.

Since we were away from the Creek, and Rudy, we didn't do PT. But our French counterparts did. All except this one young second class petty officer equivalent Bob and I noticed. That second class didn't do anything he didn't want to—he was the king of the roost on that base. If somebody told him to do something, he would just tell him to go to hell, if he was being polite, and walk away. I finally asked my French swim buddy, John, what the story was behind this guy.

It seemed that the second class had gotten his rank by a presidential appointment from Charles de Gaulle himself. During the French-Algerian war, the man had taken out an enemy machine-gun nest, by himself, with a bayonet when he was just a seaman. Only the president himself could bust this guy in rank, but he was probably never going to see another promotion. No wonder the man was so cocky, and more than a little weird. But it takes all kinds to make a unit, and the French combat swimmers were a very good unit.

Not all combat swimmers were as strange as that little second class. John, my swim buddy, was a really straight-shooter, and would have made a great SEAL operator. One night, John and I were to go out on a sneak attack. We would use a two-man kayak to get within swimming range of the target. Hiding the boat on shore, we would put on our closed-circuit rigs and swim to the ship. After the attack, we would go back to where we had hidden our kayak and paddle away.

Earlier in the day, John and I had packed our kayak for the evening's operation. Without telling John I had placed a jug and a couple of beers in my part of the boat. I didn't know it, but John had done the same thing at his end of the boat. Later that night, after the swim, each of us grabbed his bottles and offered the other a drink. We both had a good laugh about how great minds must think the same.

It wasn't that drinking was a real part of being a SEAL or a commando. It was just that there were a lot of hard drinkers in the various units. Besides, "splicing the mainbrace" helps warm you up after a cold swim, and some of those French swims were real cold.

It almost seemed that the French got back at me for my spying with one operation they put us on. A general briefing told us that the next day we would meet with a submarine to practice getting on and off the sub while underwater. This didn't particularly faze me—lock-ins and lock-outs were old hat back in the Team. So with John as my swim buddy, we met the sub the next morning.

While moving forward to the torpedo room, I kept looking at the overhead for the escape trunk. We reached the forward bulkhead and no escape trunk. How the hell were we getting out of this boat? It was about then that I saw the crew working on one of the torpedo tubes.

Turning to John, I asked him a dumb question. "I know I shouldn't ask this, but how are we getting out of here?" He just pointed at the open torpedo tube. "You have got to be shitting me," I said as a cold knot settled into my stomach.

Years before, the Teams had experimented with getting men out of a sub by using the torpedo tubes. Information was that the procedure had never worked out and had been dropped by the Navy. Here I was about to do something the Navy had decided against using. I was not a happy puppy.

They gave us an open-circuit mini-lung for breathing, a small hammer, and a flashlight. An American torpedo tube is twenty-one inches in diameter. I don't know how big a French torpedo is, but that tube looked way too small for getting on and off a submarine through. John went into the tube feet first. Then I entered the same tube head first. We were lying there head to head, John looking up at me and me looking down at him, when they closed the inner door of the tube.

Darkness, and the sound of our breathing going through the regulators. The closeness of the tube threatened to overwhelm me. I couldn't help thinking that a coffin was about the same width as that torpedo tube. You could feel the steel of the sub and sense the cold waters beyond. It was supposed to take eight minutes to flood the torpedo tube and open the outer doors. I now know how long eternity is. It's eight minutes.

We could see each other's eyes with the light of our single flashlight. The hammer was to be used to signal the submarine crew if something went wrong. Submariners don't like people to mark up their boats, so I was not going to use that hammer. But it was a struggle. I had never really liked diving, but this was something else. We had absolutely no control over what was going to happen to us; we could only wait until the tube was full. And that slowly rising cold water threatened to panic me. First the water covered John so that I couldn't see his face anymore. All I could see was the water bubbling from his exhalations. Then it was my turn. As the water closed over my head, I had to keep thinking that the next step was for them to open the outer doors, and then we could leave this tube. The water rose higher, and my head was already pressed against the unyielding steel of the tube. As the water closed over my face mask, I was practically giving myself a concussion pushing against the top of that tube.

There was a sudden sliver of daylight at the end of that black tunnel as the outer door slowly opened. John was a bigger man than I was and was ahead of me in the tube. When that outer door was open, I was outside waiting for John to catch up. Somehow I had gotten past him in the tube. There are not enough men in the Teams to make me voluntarily do that again. I don't think that I'm really clausty, but I do diving because it's required, not because I like it. That tube exit was really too much. None of the platoon thought much of leaving a submarine through the torpedo tube. Even Bob Gallagher, and they do not come any bigger, badder, or braver than Bob, didn't enjoy that exercise. Scotty MacLean, God bless him, was voicing all our opinions in no uncertain terms. Scotty did not want to get into that tube. We all relaxed a bit ribbing Scotty about his upcoming adventure. Finally even Scotty got into the tube and exited the sub. SEALs do the job, but we don't have to like it.

A safety boat was waiting on the surface to pick us up as we left the sub. After the whole platoon was out, through the same tube, the boat surfaced and took us aboard for the trip in to shore. The Frenchmen had my respect for their ability to use the torpedo tubes as we use an escape trunk. And the combat swimmers will even reenter a submerged submarine through the torpedo tubes, something we didn't have to do.

We were getting ready to leave when the commandos sprang one last surprise on a few of us. Bob Gallagher, Pat Patterson, and I were issued French combat swimmer badges. The badges were the symbols of the combat swimmers and were issued by serial number. Even Rhinebolt hadn't received one, and he was the officer in charge of the platoon. Receiving the badge was quite an honor, but my swim buddy John had a special gift for me.

When they were in Little Creek, we had shown the combat swimmers everything that we were allowed to. And the same thing had been done by the commandos when we visited them. But some things are supposed to remain confidential, and where a Team is being deployed is one of these. All of the older combat swimmers had been to Vietnam back when France was fighting the Viet Minh in Indochina. While I was packing, John came into my room and handed me a set of tigerstripe camouflage coveralls and then just looked at me.

"Here," he said. "I know where you are going, and these blend well."

"Oh," I said, taken a little aback.

"And do like I did."

"What's that, John?"

"You'll notice that there are no holes in them."

I corresponded with John for a few years after that, but finally lost contact with him. While I was in Vietnam I did try to follow John's advice and I avoided getting any holes in the coveralls.

Now it was time for us to return to Paris for the first leg of our trip home. When we rode the train this time we didn't have our little string bags. We carried our chow in paper bags just as everybody else did. There was only a one-day layover in Paris while we waited for our plane, so we didn't get the chance to go out on the town much. Jake Rhinebolt and Pat Patterson went over to the American embassy, but we didn't have any kind of formal debriefing. When we did get back to D.C. and showed the intelligence people our pictures, they only asked, "How on earth did you get those?"

"Just walked in with a camera and took them," we answered. "How did you want us to get them?" That just blew their minds.

It was a good trip and we enjoyed it, learned a lot too. Now the Teams often cross-train with other combat swimmer groups. The Germans, Canadians, Italians, Greeks, British, and French are all working with the SEALs today.

Besides the stories, we all brought another souvenir back with us. While we were in France, all of the French combat swimmers wore men's bikini swimsuits, and we all had a pair. Bob Gallagher, for all his hard-core attitude, had a good sense of humor. He got those of us who had bikini suits to wear them under our UDT swimsuits. The UDT suit was a tan canvas pair of shorts that we wore when the Team did PT. When Rudy called us out for the morning run, he would always run at the front of the formation. When Rudy called "Forward, double-time," all of us who had been in the French detachment dropped our UDT swimsuits and ran in our bikinis.

The shit hit the fan on that one. Rudy took it as it was intended, just a big joke, but somebody else didn't think it was very funny. Some captain's wife saw us running in those little tiny suits and almost had a heart attack. Her complaints to her husband resulted in the Team having to wear full sweat suits on runs for a while. We'd thought a Navy base was for military personnel. If somebody's wife didn't like what they saw, she shouldn't go where the

men were. But things were changing, and not all of them for the better.

While Second Platoon had been over in France, there had been some changes at Team Two. Lieutenant Joseph DiMartino had temporarily taken over command from Lieutenant Commander Thomas Tarbox on August 5, 1966. Then shortly after our return from France, on September 2, Lieutenant Commander William Early took over command from Joe D. Second Platoon also had some new officers arrive in September. Lieutenant Fred Kochey was our platoon leader and ran Alfa Squad. Ensign Rick Marcinko would be Second Platoon's assistant platoon leader, which would put him in charge of Bravo Squad, where I was.

Rick had been spending the summer getting his qualifications behind him and he was now fully qualified to operate. Team Two was now committed to sending two platoons to Vietnam for combat duty beginning in January 1967. Second Platoon had been picked as one of the first two platoons to go. We had all been training for years, and now it looked like we were finally going to put that training to the test. But before we left for Vietnam, we would all have to go through a whole new training program.

Most of us in the platoon were excited about the prospect of going to Vietnam. There is always some reservation about what could happen, but Vietnam was the kind of war the SEALs were intended for. Not all the SEALs were enthused about the idea of going to war. These men wanted the prestige of being one of the best but didn't want to pay the bill. As soon as Team Two received its Vietnam commitment, two people immediately put in their requests for transfer. They said they'd had enough of Team Two for a while and wanted to be instructors at UDTR. As soon as the war was over, a number of people like those first two were allowed to come back to the Team.

Bob Gallagher and I were pretty disgusted by the requests for transfer. If there were men who didn't like the idea of going into combat, they shouldn't have been in the service to begin with. As Bob put it, "They want to wear the name but they won't play the game." What I said about them was a little less polite than that.

But we had little time to waste on people who didn't want to go. There were ten enlisted men and two officers who were definitely going to Vietnam, and they had better be ready! A whole new

training program had to be devised to help us develop the skills we thought we would need in the jungles and swamps of Southeast Asia.

Bob Gallagher was going to be our platoon chief in Vietnam. They don't come much better than Bob. We called him the Eagle, partly because of his bald head and hell-raising attitude. Bob had a very shrewd mind and would carefully analyze a situation to come up with a solution. Building things with his hands came very easily to Bob, almost as easily as taking things, and men, apart with those same hands. Helping to develop our training regimen was something Bob gave a great deal of thought to.

Mr. Rick was also a real asset to our squad. Rick was as tough and sharp as a forged knife, and ground just about as thin too. But that toughness was mated to an intelligent mind. Though he had as big an ego as any of us in the Team, Rick could put his own opinions aside and listen closely to what more experienced, but lower-ranked, men would tell him. Besides just listening to advice, Rick would act on it.

The squad fell into place fairly quickly. Bob Gallagher was also the assistant squad leader, second in command to Rick. Bob's position in a patrol would be the rear man, covering our avenue of escape and discouraging any pursuers. Ronnie Rodger would be the automatic weapons man and pack our M60 machine gun. Ronnie was a big, strong operator able to shoot or punch his way through just about anything. Joe Camp was the radioman and would actually be the squad's big gun. Joe would be able to call in anything that was out there with guns on it to come help us. Protecting Joe and the radio was a high priority, even if he did win the poker pots a little too often. Jim Finley was a real gladhander who could get along with just about everybody. Since Jim was so flexible with people, he was made the squad's rifleman/utility man, filling in as the mission required. And then there was Mrs. Watson's little boy, Jimmy.

It was during one of our group discussions—or bitch sessions—that I received my assignment in the squad. In the other services, squads would assign a man to point on a rotating basis, not giving enough thought to experience or training. A point man's job was to seek out the safest route for his squad to follow, while still staying on track to the objective. Along the way, point men were supposed

to detect booby traps, ambushes, and any enemy forces who might be in the way of the approaching squad. And all of this was supposed to be done without the point man being detected himself. The life expectancy of the average Vietnam infantry point man was not very long. I was going to be Bravo Squad's point man.

The argument I had put forward to Rick was simple. Why not post our most experienced and trained man on point? Instead of accepting a fast turnover of point men, we would use the one who had the skills to keep himself, and the squad, out of trouble from the start. I thought the second-best-trained man should have the job of rear security and cover the squad from the back. But the squad's next-most-trained man, and most experienced, already had that job. Seeing the obvious advantages to the squad, Rick agreed, and I became the point man. When on operations, Joe Camp would rotate point with me on a regular basis. In the original squad layout, it was Camp who would have been the primary point man.

Now the squad had to train how to act as a team in the Vietnam environment. On top of that was the need to develop SOPs (standard operating procedures) for different situations before we got into them. Everything available from all the services was studied to give us the best chance of coming home again after accomplishing our objectives. And as far as we were concerned, our main objective was to take the war to the enemy, not to just sit and wait to react to Charlie's actions.

Instruction would be given at the Creek on whatever subject we considered necessary. If there was somebody in the squad who knew the subject well enough, he would share his knowledge with the rest of the men. Jake Rhinebolt had decided we should all learn rappelling from helicopters. Jake figured there would be times in Vietnam when we had to get into an area and a helicopter wouldn't be able to set down. Gene Tinnin and I were the only men in Team Two at that time who had rappelled from helicopters, and Gene was unavailable. So it was up to me to teach the other platoons. Whenever a class was going to be taught, you had to make a lesson plan and training schedule. This made sure that a record was kept of all the training so it could be repeated later for other classes. After putting together all of the paperwork, I was ready to begin.

The men had experience in rappelling down cliffs using a

double-rope system, but in descending from a helicopter, you only use a single rope. The only place on the base suitable for the introductory ground training was the eighty-foot water tower. We were all set to go and start training there when somebody raised a question that I didn't have an answer for.

A first class petty officer did not have the authority to set up the kind of training I was about to conduct. Regulations were that you had to have a qualified officer as the OIC. Rick got wind of this and went to Jake Rhinebolt and said that he was sufficiently qualified and that he would be in charge of the class. That satisfied Jake and the regulation, so we began. After the classroom work of showing the men how you put on a Swiss seat and use a double loop on the braking caribiner, off we went to the water tower.

Climbing up that metal ladder on the water tower was harder than the rappelling. Besides just getting up on the bitch, when you rappelled from the tower you had another problem. The base of the tower was wider than the top and you had to pass through the support structure on the way down. The situation didn't look too bad, and I rigged out a pair of lines. By standing between the two lines, I could watch both students going down the rope, helping where necessary.

Since Rick was the OIC, he wanted to be the first one down, demonstrating the technique to the other men. Rick wanted me, as the instructor, to stay on the tower and make sure each man had his rope properly hooked up. No problem. After I made sure he was ready, over the side Rick went. Sliding down the rope in a nicely controlled descent, Rick didn't have any trouble getting to the ground.

As the rest of the class were sliding down on their own ropes, Rick came bounding back up the ladder with a big grin on his face. Slapping me on the shoulder, he said, "I like that. It's neat!"

"What are you talking about, Rick? You said you've done this before."

"No, I haven't. I listened to your lecture, but I've never done it before. I just said that because you needed an officer to back you up and you're my kind of guy."

The class went very well, and I liked Rick's backing me. That was just the kind of officer he was—he backed his people, they were

what he believed in. The Eagle didn't particularly like my class, though. Bob Gallagher is a man among men; he just doesn't like sliding along a rope to get to the ground. But he took my class along with twenty-two other men and did what was necessary.

The next step in the rappelling training was to use a helicopter. This was another time when some headquarters guerrilla figured he knew what we wanted better than we did. The helicopter I asked for was an HC-43, which was a new, single-rotor, turbine-powered bird that could hover well and would provide a good training platform. Someone up in higher headquarters figured I had made some kind of mistake. There are officers who think that just because they have gold on their shoulders instead of stripes on their arms, they must automatically know more than any lowly first class. Some staff officer hadn't heard of the HC-43, just the HC-34, so he figured I must have made a mistake and really wanted the latter.

The old HC-34 is a piston-engine helicopter that doesn't have enough power to hover. If you tried to hold the bird still long enough for rappelling, the engine would blow up. "Aw, shit!" I said when I saw that old piston-pumper land on the pad. After some argument with the higher-ups, I finally ended up with the proper helicopter.

As rappelling class became more advanced, we started doing the things we thought would be necessary for Vietnam. We rappelled at night, from a helicopter, through trees! Bob really didn't think much of that class. Neither did the crew chief of the helicopter. To anchor the rappelling lines for our exit out the rear ramp we tied them off to the rear transmission housing. This helicopter was an HC-46, a long bird with twin blades, one set fore and one set aft. The transmission housing was the only thing we could find that looked strong enough to support our ropes. It worked, but later we found out the transmission housing in an HC-46 is made out of aluminum and isn't as strong as it looks.

One of the reasons for learning the rappelling was to give us a quick system to get into inland waters. Using the bigger HC-46, we could carry a fully equipped STAB (SEAL Team Assault Boat) on a cargo sling and have the crew inside the same chopper. By cutting loose the boat and rappelling down on board, we could get a heavily armed squad into places where the VC wouldn't be expecting us.

Since the STABs were such short-range boats, the idea of transporting SEALs and a boat by chopper appeared to have some real merit. We had four of the STABs, some of them brand-new. Bob Gallagher, along with Lieutenant Blackjack Macione and Lieutenant Larry Bailey, had completed modifications to the original trimaran boats, making them the first STABs. The hulls were armored to withstand .30 caliber fire. Ten weapons stations were built into the hull, allowing the boat to mount .50 caliber machine guns, M60s, 40mm Honeywells, and later Stoners. The only limiting factor would be room for the ammunition. Twin hundred-horsepower Mercury outboards would push the fiberglass hull at thirty knots even carrying a six-man fire team and a load of ammo.

As it turned out, it was too difficult to rappel down onto that small STAB quickly. It was found to be much faster just to jump into the water and climb aboard the boat. It took a lot of practice to establish which was the better system, rappelling or jumping. I had helped pound the hell out of those speedboats while we were testing them, and I was looking forward to using them in Vietnam. Carrying a STAB underneath an HC-46 didn't seem to be a problem, except for once.

It was never determined how it happened, but a helicopter was carrying one of our boats down near Pelican Cove when the hook let go and dropped it. The boat was brand-new and mounted twin Mercuries that had not even had the ignition turned on yet. Falling from several hundred feet, the STAB hit a parked car standing in a lot, totaling the car and the boat.

The accident report must have made some real interesting reading for the insurance company. "My car was hit by a boat that fell out of the sky." That was the laugh of the Team for some time after the incident.

There was real camaraderie in the platoon then. We worked together, played together, and now would go to war together. Mutual respect gave us a real edge over most of the troops already in Vietnam. And that respect stemmed from us all having proved ourselves during training and Hell Week. It was the men in the Teams who got the job done, especially those men led by officers who respected their men and led by example. When a Team, platoon, squad, or fire team had that going for them, they operated like a single, coordinated organism. An organism that could wreak havoc on anything that got between it and its objective.

In October we showed what a tight team could do when we took training with the Marines at Camp Lejeune. The Marines had a counterguerrilla course that both platoons were going to take. An entire Vietnamese village had been constructed out of native materials with a training cadre who had all been in Vietnam. The Marines were constantly changing instructors to keep up with the latest developments in Vietnam. As Marines would return from Vietnam and new cadre members came to the school, the instructors who had been at the school the longest would leave. That would constantly bring in fresh blood to the course.

The training was in a variety of skills—how to search villages, where to look for hidden caches, where common booby-trap areas were, what booby traps looked like, how to approach a village or a hooch, how to handle a bunker. While we were there we lived in the field alongside Force Recon Marines who were also taking training. The platoons learned a lot while we were at the course. And the Marines learned a bit from us.

At the end of the course was one of the times I was very proud to be a SEAL. There is a long-standing, but good-natured, animosity between the Marines and the Navy. On our last day at the center, an old-time Marine gunny sergeant stood up and gave the Force Recon Marines a professional chewing out. At the end, the gunny turned to us and probably gave us the longest speech of his career:

"I wish to hell that the Marine Corps had a unit such as you in the way of devotion and teamwork. In all my years in the Corps, I have never seen a group of men who can act as one man like you can. A group that can pull together like you can. There are no individualists in your group. The common effort is to function as a team and get the mission done. You are constantly looking after each other and always trying to cover each other's ass."

That meant a great deal to all of us, and made part of the school really worth it. It was during this training that I had the idea to become the point man for my squad. The Marines were teaching us to just put Joe Shit the ragman on point. The most important thing was to protect your radioman and your corpsman. A point man is too exposed to be able to be covered. There has to be a better way, I thought.

It was now that I put forward my suggestion that the squad have the man with the most experience on point. Not only would this give the point man the best chance of survival, it would give the squad an edge in spotting the enemy before they saw us.

After we got back from Camp Lejeune, there was another formal school we were all going to attend. The Air Spotting/Gunfire Support Course (G-2G-6438) was taught at the Creek as part of the Amphibious School. It trained us in using the big guns—calling in artillery support or naval gunfire from offshore ships—and in calling in air strikes on ground targets and applying air support from helicopter gunships, aircraft, jets, even bombers. This was where we learned to use the radio as our biggest gun.

The course was great; it showed us the power of artillery and exactly how to apply it. After we learned the procedures for using the radio and ranging in rounds, we put the lessons into practice. One room of the school held a huge three-dimensional map board laid out on the ground. All kinds of targets were set out on the map, scale-sized to represent exact distances.

Overlooking the map room were galleries. We would sit in a gallery and, using binoculars, determine where we wanted fire. On our individual maps that matched the big 3-D map we would figure the grid coordinates of our targets and then call them in over a radio.

An instructor would point to a section on the map and announce, "Here is your target, troops in the open. Call in your fire mission."

For troops in the open you wanted either HE (high explosive) or Willy Peter (WP, white phosphorus), fuzed for an airburst. Using the radio, you would call in the fire mission. "I have a fire mission. I have troops in the open. I would like two guns and two salvos, HE airburst at grid coordinate such-and-such." As you would be calling in the mission, the people at the other end of the line would be giving you answers just as a real fire control would.

Even if you called the target in right on the money, the fire control people wouldn't let you hit the target on the first shot. The 3-D map had a mechanism underneath it that would indicate where your shot had landed. When you called in "Shoot," the answer would come back "Shot." On the map, a puff of smoke would rise showing where the rounds had landed. They wanted us to learn to bracket our shots. If the first round went over the target, you would call the next round in short of the target. Splitting the difference between the two impacts, the next call would be right on the money. "Fire for effect," and the entire battery would open up, obliterating the target.

The air part of the course would be much the same, but there were different procedures for talking to aircraft. "Angel Six Two, this is Whiskey Sour. What ordnance do you have on board? I have a target such-and-such." After he told you what he had on board, you would tell the pilot where you wanted him to place what.

One thing that was drilled into us was always to have the aircraft make its firing run from left to right or right to left in front of you. Never have the craft make a run directly over your head if you could possibly avoid it. In a sideways run, a short or long round wouldn't make much difference. If the run was right over your head, you'd best hope that pilot was having a good day.

One trick the Gunfire Support people taught us was the "center of sector" method of finding your own location. If you were confused as to where you were on the map—and there were not a lot of big landmarks in the jungle—you could call in fire and orient your map. Using either ground artillery or naval gunfire, you would call for "one round Willy Peter, center of sector." Naval gunfire was usually preferred, because it was a lot more accurate than ground artillery.

When the WP went off, you had both noise and smoke. You'd have your squad watching in all directions for the round to go off. Seeing the round detonate would give you your position relative to the center of the sector. Finding your way after that was usually easy. The only drawback to the system was that you might be at the center of the sector. That drawback kept the method from being very popular.

After gunnery training it was back to field training with the platoon. Team Two had a facility at Camp Pickett in Virginia where we were able to fire weapons and conduct field maneuvers. Camp Pickett was only a few hours' drive from Little Creek. We could fire any of our weapons there and set up our own specialized ranges. The area at Pickett was satisfactory for general training and weapons practice, but we needed something more to get us ready for the jungles and swamps of Vietnam.

Bob Gallagher had studied the maps and photos of where we were going in Vietnam. After getting a good idea of the terrain we would be facing, Bob started searching the areas surrounding Little Creek. He found what he was looking for in North Carolina. After locating the area, Bob took me down with him to examine the place. It was on the Black River—hundreds and hundreds of acres of woods, with small streams, marsh, swamp, and heavy areas of underbrush. The land belonged to the Union Camp Corporation, so our next step was to get permission to use the area.

The folks at Union Camp were sympathetic to our needs and agreed to let us use the area, provided we caused as little damage to the trees as possible and cleaned up after ourselves. We were even able to bring down small boats and keep them at the local marina. The boats let us run practice ambushes of all kinds. The information we had from Team One was that the ambush would be our primary method of operation.

Before we could make full use of the Union Camp facility we had to be more competent with our weapons. So it was off to Camp Pickett and live weapons firing. Even though he was in our platoon and undergoing training himself, Bob Gallagher, as the most experienced weapons man in the Team, ran the training at Camp Pickett.

The setup at Pickett was simple. The men would sleep in their car or whatever camping gear they had brought with them. The camping area was between the access road to the area and the weapons tent. In the sixteen-by-thirty-six foot weapons tent was stored every kind of ammunition we could have wanted. Along with the ammo were our weapons, securely locked in steel cruise boxes. On the far side of the weapons tent was where we had set up the firing range. Our range was considerably less strictly run than other military ranges. If you wished you could take an entire seventy-two-round case of 40mm ammunition over to the range and fire it all. The idea was for the men to get comfortable with their weapons. Stakes were set out on the range to indicate the firing line. Downrange were silhouettes, old truck bodies, sandbag emplacements, all kinds of targets. You would practice with your chosen weapon until you became proficient with it.

Instinctive fire, point-and-shoot style, was what took the most practice.

There were a few organized training evolutions, but they were spread pretty thin. You spent your time learning about your weapons on the range. Taking an M60 machine gun, you would experiment with different ways of firing it. Feeding it with the belt over your arm, your shoulder, from a bag. Holding the weapon with the sling around your neck, your neck and shoulder, just your shoulder; with no sling; from the hip, the shoulder.

With the M16, we practiced our marksmanship on a measured thousand-inch range with standard targets. For instinctive fire, we had pop-up courses—the targets would suddenly pop up anywhere from right in front of you to thirty-five yards away. Striking a target with a bullet would make it fall down, showing you a hit.

Gallagher's ingenuity showed up on some of the training ranges he designed for us. For our submachine-gun pop-up course Bob set it up so that you not only learned the proper way of shooting a submachine gun, but also became very familiar with handling a variety of weapons. On the range were a Schmeisser MP-40, a MAT-49, a Sten Mark II, and a greasegun. To run the course, you were given a single magazine for each weapon. Starting the course with, say, a Sten gun, you would walk along a trail, shooting at targets as they popped up. When the order was shouted to change weapons, there would be a different weapon somewhere at your feet. You would have to load the weapon quickly with the proper magazine. And Lord help you if you tried to use the wrong magazine—that sharp-eyed Eagle was just waiting to catch you doing something like that.

Very quickly, the whole squad became proficient at using different submachine guns and loading them by feel alone. We had no idea what it would be like for us in combat—none of us were combat veterans—so Bob would try everything he could think of to give us an extra edge. Anything our people could think of, from any of the military schools they had attended, was grist for our training program. Moving silhouettes would be used on night ambush ranges. Hanging from strings, the silhouettes would be pulled across the killing zone. You waited in your concealed position, and it might be one minute or three hours before that target moved. And you had better hit it as soon as you saw it.

We were all hotshot SEALs after weeks of this kind of practice. We knew our weapons and teammates. All of us were expert rifle and pistol shots. With an automatic weapon in our hands, nobody was able to stand in our way. We were the best there was. Then came our first squad night ambush.

Bravo Squad was all concentrated on a small line of dunes. The targets would be pulled across a clearing directly in front of us. After getting down into our positions, we were to wait for the targets to move into the killing zone. The clearing would simulate a canal in Vietnam, with our ambush coming down from the banks onto the "sampan" target. With two men in each position, we were able to cover each other easily.

Lying there in full combat gear waiting for the target was anything but a comfortable way to spend the night. But the lack of comfort helps keep you awake and alert. The weather was cool, but sweat would still trickle down your face, tickling the camo-painted skin. You could hear your own heart beating loudly in your ears. The sound of the breath going in and out of your lungs seemed loud enough to be heard some distance away, but you could barely hear the quiet breathing of the man right next to you. With me that night was the Eagle. I couldn't have asked for a better partner.

As the time slipped past, your eyes became adjusted to the amount of light available. You could see things in shades of black and gray. If you looked at one point too long, your mind would start playing tricks on you. Things that weren't quite there would seem to move. To combat that, you kept your eyes moving, always scanning the area in front of you. Peripheral vision is better at night, and you seemed to have a wider field of view. Things could be seen more sharply by looking next to rather than right at them.

The dusty smell of the cold sand would fill your nose, overriding the musty, earthy smell of the nearby woods. Most of all, you would be alone with your thoughts. You'd be watching carefully, but all sorts of thoughts would go through your head. When we get back in, I'm going to grab a beer to have while I clean my weapon. . . . I wonder if deer use this trail . . . When do deer sleep?. . . Do porcupines wander around here at night? . . . I still haven't seen one. . . . I've got to get off my dead ass and finish that letter home. Even professional warriors think of things other than war.

Suddenly, Rick's hand signal is passed down the line. "Enemy coming. Get ready." The sound of a jeep engine starting shatters the stillness. The roar of Rick's weapon firing is the signal to initiate the ambush. We all open fire. SOP is to fire two magazines and then cease firing. The target is a group of four standard cardboard silhouettes attached to a sled the jeep is pulling with a rope. The range to the target is maybe fifteen yards.

My night vision is gone from the brilliant flash of my weapon firing at eight hundred rounds per minute. When my first magazine is empty, I quickly eject it and seat a full one in the magazine well. Hitting the bolt release chambers a fresh round.

Noise and confusion fill the small clearing as the M16s empty their magazines. A shotgun is booming out spaced shots while the M60 thunders through a belt.

Rearing up from the prone position, I can get a better firing angle to sweep the target area. With my night vision gone, I can only fire where I think the target is going to be. I'm ripping off bursts, then suddenly my magazine is empty and the ambush is over. The sudden silence is deafening.

Rick was acting unhappy about our performance, but that was nothing compared to what he said when he examined the targets. The entire squad had fired hundreds of rounds, but you couldn't tell by looking at the targets. There were maybe half a dozen holes in an otherwise clean set of silhouettes. This was not a good thing.

Rick came absolutely unglued. "You highly trained, motivated bunch of fucking killers couldn't hit the broad side of a goddam barn if you were standing inside of it. What did you do with all that ammo you've been firing for the last week? Shoot it off into the goddam air? This is not fucking good enough, you pus-nuts, shitbag bunch of motherfucking assholes! We are going to do this all night until we get it right. *Do I make myself clear?"*

It wasn't much use arguing—we had done a piss-poor job of the ambush. If this had been a real shooting war, some of us would probably be dead. We had all been just too cocky. Instead of cutting the targets in half like the professionals we were supposed to be, we had just waved at the targets with most of our ammo.

In a real ambush, the only way out of it is to assault the firers. That was something I had learned back in the Army jungle course. You charge right into the ambushers' positions and kill them before they kill you. Any other actions just get you shot in the back.

I had explained this to everyone on the squad. It was anything but a cocky bunch of SEALs who got back into their positions on the dunes. If we had been in Vietnam ambushing a bunch of VC who knew how to counter ambushes, Team Two would be short one full squad.

Over and over and over again that night, the sound of gunfire would suddenly erupt. By the time the sun was coloring the horizon with the dawn, we were tearing the target area up.

Each SEAL had a specific field of fire. You did not shoot outside of the arc your field of fire covered. Each man would shoot exactly where he was supposed to and the squad would fully cover the killing zone. It didn't matter if you could see the target—you covered your area. If the target wasn't in front of you, it would be in front of your teammates. Our killing zone had earned its name.

Discipline was something the SEALs understand very well. Our training instilled it in us, and it proved its value in Vietnam. No matter what the situation, none of us would ever forget that night at Pickett and our first ambush.

Another point we picked up very quickly was initiating an ambush. Once you have placed your unit and the fields of fire have been determined, it is the person with the best view of the killing zone who starts the ambush. Once it has been decided, at the site, who will initiate the ambush, you hold your fire until the signal is given.

After ambush practice, it was more time on the firing range. By now we were able to reload any of our weapons in the dark. Malfunctions were taken care of instantly. A jam was usually because of the ammunition. When you take as much care of your weapons as we did, malfunctions just didn't happen very often.

We played with tracers a bit at Pickett, loading one tracer for each second or third ball round. The idea was to fool Charlie into thinking more weapons were being fired at him than he could see. The VC knew we ordinarily loaded one tracer for every four rounds. More tracers would suggest more rounds. But we found the idea wasn't worth the trouble. In a properly executed ambush, the target would be too busy dying to notice the number of tracers coming at him.

As hard as we worked, there was time for a little clowning and comradeship at both camps. And there was always time for beer.

Never would we mix beer and weapons, or beer and explosives. But the occasional blowout would take place. There was a little country store near Pickett where we would buy our beer. This place was lost in time. There was a potbellied stove in the middle of the room with old guys sitting around it smoking their pipes and talking about crops. Those farmers thought we were a little crazy, but they treated us like visiting kings.

We had developed our SOPs. Established hand signals so we could silently communicate with each other. Done just about everything we could think of to prepare for Vietnam. Now it was time to go.

Christmas was a little tight with the family. Some of the kids already knew that Daddy was going to war, but really didn't understand what it meant. Marlene knew what she had been getting into when she married me, but it still wasn't easy for her. Uncle Buck was there for Christmas with my family in Jersey. While we were visiting, Uncle Buck took me aside for a quiet talk. This was as close as Uncle Buck ever came to telling me about his time in World War II and the Rangers.

"When you get over there, Jimmy, it's not going to be anything like what you expect. When the time comes that you have to kill a man close up, don't hesitate. Shoot! Once you have made the decision, it's too late to back down. It'll be either you or him. Make sure it's him." And then Uncle Buck gave me his knife. It was a Fairbairn/Sykes commando knife he had been given by a British commando while sharing a foxhole in Italy. That knife had been with Uncle Buck through the battles he fought in Italy. Now I was going to carry it in the jungles of Vietnam. That knife hangs above my desk today. Uncle Buck, I listened.

It was on January 11 that we left for the West Coast. We were going to spend some time with Team One before going on to Vietnam. While we were being seen off at the airport, the Commander of PHIBLANT, a full admiral, came out to see us. We were waiting around the C-130 cargo plane that would take us to California. The admiral told us again that we were the first SEALs from Team Two to go into combat. The Navy had invested a lot of money in our training, and now it was time to see if the investment was going to pay off.

The admiral was sure that we would uphold the tradition established by our forefathers, the UDT, in World War II. If there was anything that we needed or wanted, the admiral invited us to write him personally and ask for it. Any one of us. He would see to it that if it was at all possible, we would get what we asked for. There was a short silence after the admiral had finished his speech.

Then Bill Brumuller shouted from the back of our formation, "We'll be all right, Admiral. Just keep the three B's coming."

Looking up with a smile on his face, the admiral asked, "And what might those be, son?"

"Beer, bullets, and broads!"

The frozen chosen. UDT 21 detachment on its way to an Arctic operation along the DEW line. On my first job as a UDT man, I'm standing on the far left. U.S. NAVY

Freddy the Frog, official symbol of the Underwater Demolition Teams

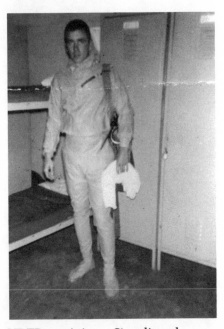

UDTR training. Standing by my bunk and locker as soon-to-be frogman. Today, the Little Creek chiefs' club stands at the same spot.

JAMES WATSON

One very young sailor,
Bainbridge, Maryland, 1955

The cover shot of *All Hands* magazine, January
1962. That's me jumping from a helicopter
while north of the Arctic Circle at Kulusuk,
Greenland.

St. Thomas with UDT
21. Testing the Fulton
sled pickup method.
That's me on the deck;
to my right rear is
Nichols; to my left, John
Tegg; behind Tegg is
Lowell Gosser.

St. Thomas with UDT 21. I'm just going over the side, practicing standard cast and recoveries.

Second Platoon first arriving in Vietnam at Binh Thuy air base. I'm facing sideways on the left, and the mustachioed individual on the right is a young Rick Marcinko.

Can Tho, first tour. Myself and the "family" dog, Prince.

R. A. Tolison (*kneeling*) and myself prepping the
STAB early during my first tour

R. A. Tolison and myself
an op. I'm the clean one
on the left.

The point man covering Rick Marcinko's rear
coming back to the boat. First tour, 1967.

Second Platoon arriving back incountry from our first tour in Vietnam. Bob Gallagher is just coming out of the plane, with Fred Kochey in front of him. I'm the "tourist" with the guitar.

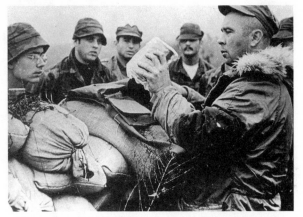

Here I'm giving Claymore mine instruction to Boat Support people as well as Greek students in the fall of 1968.

Vice Admiral L. C. Heinz pinning on my Navy Commendation Medal, November 6, 1968

Spider hole capture op, December 1968. I'm in the center, speaking into the radio. Joe Silva is to my left, with his Stoner. U.S. NAVY, SEAL TEAM TWO

Spider hole capture op, December 1968. I'm on the left, where the wounded NVA officer is hiding.

U.S. NAVY SEAL TEAM TWO

Two of the trucks that were illuminating the mine with their headlights. I was standing just to the left of the truck on the left when the mine went off.

U.S. NAVY

The dirty dozen, plus three. Union Camp prede-ployment training, Sixth Platoon, 1970.

Reenlistment, third tour, 1970. I'm not looking at the paper—I'm so drunk I can't keep my eyes open. But I'm doing better than Chuck Fellers; he's lying passed out on the floor between us.

JAMES WATSON

Front view of my helicopter, shot down during my
POW (Bright Light) operation

JAMES WATSON

My wedding, April 1993, with my
new wife, Linda, A SEAL always
knows how to make an entrance.

TOM BAUMKER

CHAPTER 8

Vietnam: First Tour, 1967

The C-130 was anything but a comfortable aircraft, especially when the plane was crammed with equipment, weapons, personal gear, and twenty-four SEALs. It was when we arrived in Coronado that the games really started. Our two platoons were assigned TAD to Team One. Since it was Team One that had the Vietnam commitment, we would be operating under its orders.

The West Coast people immediately told us that they had to train us before they could let us operate under their name. Give me a break! There wasn't a single man in the two platoons who was less than a second class. Each enlisted man had at least six years in the Teams, either UDT or SEALs. And now we had a bunch of people telling us we had to prove ourselves to them!

Jake Rhinebolt got a little hot under the collar about Team One's treatment of us. Fred Kochey and Rick kept their cool. Our fourth officer wasn't about to rock the boat, so he played the game. He wasn't the kind of guy to ruffle anybody's feathers, except those of people lower down. So we all had to go along with the schedule.

There were several small operations Team One wanted us to do, things like an overland compass course. We did the compass course they had laid on for us easily. When they gave us a problem that

151

was expected to take hours, we would complete it in minutes. Finally, they had enough.

"You know, there's no problem here. It's obvious you guys know what you're doing. All this is a waste of time. Let's go to the club." And all of the Mickey Mouse crap was over.

The differences between Team One and Team Two were due to more than just being on the West or East Coast. Team One was more traditional Navy than Team Two. Team One's officers were more aloof from the enlisted men and didn't fraternize as our officers did. The partying we did in Team Two brought the men closer together than if we just did our jobs and went our separate ways.

The geography of the area made a lot of difference in social habits too. Little Creek is part of Norfolk, and it was not difficult getting a home near the base for you and your family. There were whole subdivisions where 90 percent of the homes held people from the base. Not only were we Teammates, most of us were also neighbors. But Coronado is an expensive resort town. The cost of living prevented any but the highest-ranking officers from living near the base. Even San Diego, across the bay from the base, is a very expensive place to live for someone trying to make it on an enlisted man's pay. That fact alone tended to keep the Team One men from living near each other when they had a family. Bachelor enlisted men would often live right on the base, where the facilities were less than ideal.

And there were a lot of bachelor enlisted men in Team One. Team Two had more older, married men with established families. The average age of a SEAL in Team Two was twenty-eight, while the average age in Team One was only twenty. With the difference in age came a corresponding difference in rank. An officer in Team One felt lucky if he had a second class as his platoon's leading petty officer. Team Two was very rate-heavy. In most of the platoons, half the men were second class or higher.

The large number of petty officers gave Team Two an advantage in leadership in more ways than one. Besides the greater level of experience, the different styles of leadership also worked in our favor. When you have a large number of leaders, their different styles stand out. Given the range of styles in Team Two, from simple order-givers to hands-on, let's-all-do-it types, men would gradually move among the platoons to follow the kind of leaders they preferred.

When a man is following a leader whom he respects and enjoys working with, the overall efficiency of the Team improves dramatically. The retention rate of Team Two was higher than that of Team One, and this also helped to give us more senior petty officers. The first two platoons from Team Two going to Vietnam had greater levels of experience, excepting that of direct combat, than some Team One platoons that had already been in Southeast Asia.

Now it was Team Two platoons who were going into harm's way in Southeast Asia. Jake Rhinebolt, Jess Tolison, and Lenny Waugh went over to Vietnam ahead of the rest of the platoons, leaving us in Coronado. Jake Rhinebolt was going to be Det (Detachment) Alfa, in charge of the Team Two units in Vietnam. Jess and Lenny were both chiefs and went ahead of the rest of us to be sure everything was ready for our arrival.

Back in Coronado, the rest of us had our hands full finishing our preparations and packing our gear. The two STABs, complete with their trailers, had arrived in Coronado by truck. Along with the STABs, we had every piece of equipment we thought there might be a need for—enough materials to keep two platoons supplied and operating for eight months.

After being with Team One for over two weeks, we were all ready to go to Vietnam. At the North Island Naval Air Station a C-130 stood by ready to pick up our gear and us for the trip across the Pacific. There was some argument from the plane's pilot about the volume of gear we wanted to bring aboard. "There's no way you can get that much stuff aboard the plane, let alone yourselves."

As the loadmaster for the detachment, I had spent a great deal of time planning how to get all of our equipment aboard a C-130. With Bob Gallagher and Bill Brumuller helping, we had determined the center of gravity for every pallet, locker, and trailer. Exactly where each piece of equipment would go and how it would be secured had been decided back at Little Creek weeks earlier.

When I turned to Bob Gallagher, he just looked at me and said, "Handle it, Jim." That put the ball squarely in my court.

The pile of gear we had was huge, everything from seabags to two boats on trailers complete with big twin outboard motors hanging off the transoms. To the outsider, it did look as if we were trying to squeeze ten pounds into an eight-pound bag. But I knew everything would fit. Going up to the pilot, I asked to speak to the plane's loadmaster.

"We've got it all figured out, sir," I said. "It will all fit properly. I am a qualified aircraft loadmaster."

The pilot just looked at me, and then to our small mountain of gear. "Go to it," he said. "Call us when you're ready."

And with that, all the officers took off. Explaining to the loadmaster, I showed the man my figures and diagrams. Space in the cargo area was going to be so tight that the last STAB trailer would be on the rear ramp of the aircraft. The trailer would rise into the body of the plane when the ramp was raised for flight.

"Looks good to me," said the loadmaster. "Let's try it."

When the officers returned, we had the plane packed and ready for Nam. The pilot took a long look at how his plane was packed. Turning to the loadmaster, the pilot said, "Sergeant, you've known your business a long time. I'm going to take your word on this one. But I still don't believe it."

While we were taxiing out to takeoff, the loadmaster handed me an intercom headset. I could listen in to what the pilot was saying to the tower and the crew. After we had gotten into the air, the pilot called back, "Goddam, Sarge, good load. You got it." The sergeant just looked at me and gave a thumbs-up.

Now we were on our way to Vietnam. In our planeful of gear we had weapons, boats, field equipment, ammunition, clothes, personal gear, miscellaneous gear for trading such as a couple of cases of Navy MK 2 K-bar knives no one else could get, and even several sets of aqualungs and diving gear. We were on our way to a country at war. Team Two was going to be ready to come out fighting the moment the wheels of the plane set down.

The plane stopped off at Hawaii, Midway, Saipan, Guam, and more, most of them islands that the UDT had helped take back from the Japanese during World War II. It seemed that just about every rock that stuck up out of the Pacific had a landing strip on it where we set down and refueled. The long flight gave each man a lot of time to think. And I wondered about the future along with the others.

As professional military men, we were superbly fit, trained, and equipped, modern gladiators able to take on all comers. But how many of us would be on the return flight in six months? Who'd get hit? Me? Bob? Rick? Somebody I hadn't even met yet? Every warrior has to have his first taste of combat. But who would pay a warrior's fee? Sailors, soldiers, and fighting men throughout the ages have asked these same questions.

There wasn't any question about what we were going to do. But how we were going to do it was still up for debate. To combat guerrillas effectively you have to think, act, and fight like one. This was Marcinko's attitude, and I agreed with it. We would take the VC on in the rice paddies, jungles, and swamps of Vietnam. Taking the war to Charlie's doorstep rather than waiting for him to come to ours was going to be our trademark.

We were good, and I was able to stand up with some of the best men we had. But that one night in Virginia, and a bunch of untouched cardboard silhouettes during a practice ambush, kept me from being too cocky.

Rick Marcinko was a bold-ass hard charger. My job was to be part of the weapon that was the Navy SEALs. But it was Rick who was going to aim our part of that weapon. Very soon, a number of us were going to become "hunters."

There are SEALs who just get the job done. They are given their assignments and they do their jobs, but little more. Other SEALs are operators. You give them a target, and the job gets done no matter what obstacles might be in the way. If an operator cannot complete his job by conventional means, he will use any means available. A hunter doesn't have to be given a target, he will go out and find one. No matter what the cost to himself, a hunter will put the mission before any other considerations. The traditional "black-shoe" Navy has a hard enough time trying to figure out regular SEALs. Hunter SEALs are a complete mystery to the tradition-bound, by-the-book regular Navy.

But the time for thinking was over. Binh Thuy air base near Can Tho was where we would be landing in Vietnam. In our minds, the war was going to be on the moment the C-130's rear ramp hit the ground. Rick came back to us from up forward, where he had been talking to Lieutenant Kochey. "This is it," Rick said. "Get ready."

Lockers were opened and gear was passed out. We loaded our .38s and strapped them on. Out came the AR-15s and into them went full magazines. When the crewmembers of the C-130 were looking the other way, we chambered rounds into our weapons and put the safeties on. When that ramp went down, we were going to be ready. If the VC had planned an ambush, these SEALs were going to kick ass and take names.

My heart was thundering in my ears as we landed. The plastic grip of the AR-15 felt slick as my palms sweated. No matter how much you train, there is still a strong anticipation when the real thing comes along. We landed—*womp!* There was a heavy roar as the pilot reversed the engines to help the massive plane come to a stop. As the rear ramp whined down, we stood up, ready to go.

Can Tho was just a short distance inland from the South China Sea. Almost as soon as we were over Vietnam, we were in a landing pattern for the airfield. There hadn't been time to see Vietnam from the windows of the plane before we were getting ready for our arrival. When the ramp went down, that was my first glimpse of Vietnam.

People were driving around in jeeps. Planes and helicopters were taxiing on the ground or moving through the air. The heavy odor of rotting vegetation from the jungle was overlain with the civilized stink of kerosene and jet fuel. While we were standing there on the runway, weapons in our hands, Jess and Lenny came up.

"Relax, guys," they said. "Cool it. Take it easy. The war doesn't start until after sundown. It's that way every day." And then they handed out some cold beers.

The hot, humid air of the tropics struck me like a warm, wet towel. A cold beer sounded real good. But what was this shit about the war starting after sundown? Were Jess and Lenny putting us on? Truth was, they weren't.

This was a scary place to be. All of this war machinery was moving around us. Gunships, fighter jets, bombers, jeeps with machine guns mounted on them. I had never been in a place like this. This ain't no drill, I thought. What the hell have I gotten myself into? The hot, muggy air combined with the incredible noise made the airfield almost unbearable.

"Where do we go from here?" we asked. Lenny and Jess pointed out the trucks they had brought with them. We all got busy moving our gear from the plane to the trucks. Hitching up the boat trailers, we asked, "Where the hell are we going? We sure can't stay here.

Where's the river? Where's the base?" The direction was pointed out to us and we were on our way.

We made quite a little convoy driving down the road, the trucks hauling along our little speedboats from hell. We were gawking tourists looking around at the areas we were here to decimate. The truck drivers knew where we were going, and that gave the rest of us time to look around. Leaving the air base, we went north along a little dirt road. I had never been in this section of the world before, and I was taking it all in. There was just one big eyeball in the center of my forehead.

There were cyclos—pedal cabs—going by. Young and old men walking along with laden baskets on their backs or hanging down from shoulder yokes. Beautiful young china dolls in exotic flowing white gowns, just schoolgirls going to some destination. Old mamasans, wrinkled with the weight of years, stooped over from working in the rice paddies. In the air was the smell of the Orient, partly the fragrance of flowers and spice, partly the stench of too much humanity and a rotting jungle. Over all of this hung the pall of war.

Everybody and his brother was walking around with a weapon slung across his back. There were AK-47s, M14s, M1s, and carbines. "How the fuck do you tell the good guys from the bad guys?" I asked Jess.

"That's easy," he answered. "The guys shooting at you are bad guys. The guys shooting with you are the good guys."

"Oh," I said. "Okay." By this time I was starting to get a little hyper. Was this real?

Now we had arrived at our new base at Tre Noc, only a few klicks from the air base. There were PBRs (patrol boat, river) in the river and there was an APL (a barracks barge) that had been converted into a machine shop to support the boats. A line of little concrete buildings held what looked like small motel rooms. The river was the Bassac, one of the major waterways of the Mekong Delta, a flowing stream of brown water that looked like thin mud. Our reservoir of fresh water looked as brown as the river, only it wasn't moving water and there were ducks swimming in it. Unhitching the boats, we put them up for the time being. The first order of business was to get our room assignments, put up our personal gear, and settle down a little bit. Men were assigned six to a room. Now it was time to get something to eat.

Just walking around the base, inside of the wire, was an education. Now I knew what was meant by "the wire." The fence surrounding the camp was made up of rolls of concertina, big coils of barbed wire. Three coils would be stacked in a pyramid. After the first concertina stack, there would be an open space. Then there were more rolls of concertina along with claymore mines and tripwires. The tripwires wove through the fences, thin green lines connected to simple noisemakers, metal cans filled with pebbles, or tripflares, which would burn with a brilliant light, or even pop-up mines, ready to explode at a touch. Overlooking this whole mess were individual guard towers, sandbagged for protection and bristling with searchlights and machine guns. Every so often along the wire were sandbag bunkers. One of the first things we were told was which bunkers would be ours in case of an attack. SEALs were to be the base's defenders.

That's when the shit started to come out. The SEALs were to be the primary base defense if the VC attacked. Great, nice job, we thought, considering it some kind of joke. Only it wasn't a joke.

It was getting later in the afternoon and we continued to get settled in. The base bar opened up, and it wasn't going to be very long before we took advantage of that. All of our money had to be changed over to Military Pay Certificates (MPC). The MPC, more commonly called scrip, was supposed to keep money out of the black market but never really did. The scrip they gave us was entirely in small printed certificates. The little five- and one-dollar bills were easy to get used to. But the paper bills for nickels and dimes were odd. Again, this made the whole situation seem a little unreal. Paper bills for change? At least they wouldn't rattle in your pocket. Only we weren't supposed to pay the VNs with MPC. They lectured us on the importance of paying the locals only in piasters. Then they said you could only exchange so much MPS for piasters. All of this song and dance never did keep MPC or even U.S. greenbacks out of the local economy.

The lecture went on. The official exchange rates for MPC and piaster. Where could we go and when. All the rules of the base were laid out for us. The big rule was that you didn't leave the base at night. After sundown, the local land belonged to Charlie.

The first night at the base, we spent time getting caught up with the guys from Team Two who had already been in Vietnam for a couple of weeks. All of the gossip from back at the Creek was brought out and passed around. Then all of a sudden there was a new sound in our lives.

Whirrrrr . . . *kaboom!* Whirrrrr whirrrrr . . . *kaboom, kaboom!* "This is it, guys," said Jess. "It's dark-30. Time for the fucking war."

But Jess was talking to the empty air. The rest of us were diving under bunks, tables, whatever would give us a little cover. There wasn't anything out there for us to shoot at—the base was getting mortared. Right after the attack, sort of a VC evening wakeup call, we wanted to be out there to give Charlie back a little. Truth was, most of were a little embarrassed about our reactions. Jess just sat there and watched us dive for cover.

This was not the way SEAL Team Two was going to act our first day incountry! We had Prince, our scout dog, with us. Bill Brumuller had trained with Prince for weeks. That big German shepherd could track people down where the rest of us couldn't see any trail to follow. Taking Prince, we all went outside to try to track down our attackers.

Somebody said he thought he'd seen a guy crawling through the wire on the south end of the camp. Our rooms were on the outer perimeter of the camp. If someone came through the wire, we would be the first people, or targets, they would find. This was not something we'd accept easily. There was a bad guy in the wire and his ass was ours.

Bill got Prince ready to go scouting. Bob Gallagher and I were going with Bill to provide some cover. Then Prince picked up a scent. Bill had him on a leash; we didn't want to let the dog go. We weren't completely sure what was going on. Outside of the wire, Prince suddenly took a left turn and was heading for the road. Here was this VC walking down the road. The man didn't have a weapon, but Prince wanted a piece of his ass in the worst way. Trusting the dog, we snatched the guy up.

We brought our prisoner in and turned him over to security. After a few minutes, security turned the guy loose! Our dog had picked this guy out from everybody else as owning the scent that he followed from the wire. But security didn't believe Prince. The man had the proper ID and couldn't have been the guy in the wire. When they released our prisoner, there were some half-whispered comments about "cherries" and "new guys," but right then a fight with the base people was not what we wanted.

While we had been settling in, the officers had been checking in with the base headquarters. The unit we had been assigned to was Task Force 116, better known by the code name Game Warden. When we arrived, we had been expecting little more than tents and slit latrines. What we had found was a complete base with concrete buildings and support facilities. It was into one of the larger concrete buildings that Marcinko and the other officers had disappeared when we arrived. Marcinko came back later and gave us the dope on what was going on.

Rhinebolt, Gormly, Kochey, and another lieutenant were taking the majority of both platoons and going up to the Rung Sat Special Zone to operate with the Team One detachment. We were to wait until they had returned before we started operating. Wasn't this just a kick in the ass. On top of that, one of our officers insisted we do PT to "stay in shape." Hey, back off. This is the jungle here.

Rhinebolt backed the orders, so PT started the next day. We did our PT out behind a group of three buildings so that the natives couldn't see us. The PBR sailors didn't do PT, and the surest way to bring attention on yourself is to not act like the locals. You bring a new group into an area and start doing something like PT, and you are going to bring attention to yourself. But doing our exercise out of the public view helped. Having to do PT in the first place didn't help our attitudes at all. One day Bob Gallagher, a few other SEALs, and I showed up for morning PT wearing flak jackets. If we had to make targets out of ourselves to please this officer, we were going to wear body armor while we did it. The heavy armored flaks were not the most comfortable things to wear in that hot environment, and they made the exercises more difficult, but we did the whole PT wearing them. The lieutenant in charge never did seem to catch on to what we thought, or he just didn't care.

Some officers seem to think that since they have the rank, they are automatically better than you, no matter what your experience is. This one lieutenant just wasn't very well liked, and he brought it all on himself. He was superior to all the enlisted men, period. He had no interest in being part of the camaraderie normally present in the Team. He had to be addressed by his rank at all times. He never even noticed the respect we held for our officers, whether we called them by name or title. But titles are very important to some people. It would have served him right for us to have saluted him, out in the open, with VC snipers in the area. But we were professionals, and that is not how a professional plays the game.

Marcinko's Marauders were left behind when the rest of the detachment went up to the Rung Sat Special Zone. The Rung Sat was a large area of swamps, rivers, and canals just southeast of Saigon, and Team One had been doing most of its operations there. To keep our gear and the base secure was the official reason for our remaining behind. But we all figured that the higher-ups thought we would have caused trouble with the West Coast guys if we were allowed to rampage through the Rung Sat. Bravo Squad was a bunch of misfits, and we knew it. But we also knew how well we worked together. "Arrogant" and "headstrong" were two of the milder terms used to describe us. If we thought we were right, we would argue with anyone to defend our position.

With the rest of the platoons gone, we just hung around the base. The two STABs were tied up to the dock, and Bob was just champing at the bit to put them into action. Gallagher had been the primary push behind those two STABs. They were his babies and he wanted to see them do their job. "Why can't we go on an operation?" we asked. Marcinko wasn't any happier with the situation than we were. But orders were orders, weren't they?

Rick and Gallagher talked their way aboard a PBR patrol one morning, supposedly to get a feel for the area. The PBR was carefully chosen because of the chief who ran it. The story was that Chief Ganby had lost his entire family in a car crash several years earlier. Since there wasn't much back home for him, Ganby just kept extending his time incountry. By the time we talked to him, Chief Ganby had been in Vietnam almost three years and had more experience in the Delta than any two SEAL platoons.

The PBRs were a real piece of work in themselves. Thirty-one feet long with a water-jet propulsion system, the PBRs could operate in water too shallow for us to swim in. There wasn't any shortage of weapons aboard the PBRs. The bow held a sunken gun tub with two .50 caliber machine guns along with a whole bunch of bullets. On the stern deck was another .50 on a pedestal mount. In the center of the boat were more mounts that could hold M60 machine guns or 40mm Honeywells, hand-cranked machine guns. On top of all this were the personal weapons of the four- or five-man crews.

All of those weapons packed on a boat with a half-pirate crew made us SEALs feel right at home. And Ganby knew the river like nobody else. This was the man to buddy up with and learn the river. One thing we picked up early was that a cautious, slow-moving man would get hit much easier than an aggressive fast-mover. Ganby was a hard charger and willing to talk to us. That gave us an edge.

But before we could operate, we needed permission. Lieutenant Commander Hank Mustin was the operations commander of the base. He wouldn't let us operate because we didn't have "rules of engagement" yet. This was not a war and we had to follow rules. Rules of engagement told us when and how we could fire our weapons against the enemy. Rick's opinion, one that we all shared, was that when they shot at us, they were the enemy. If they didn't shoot at us but had weapons and were in the wrong place, they were still the enemy and we would shoot first.

The more rules that were handed to us, the more pissed off we got. Finally Rick said, "That's enough." He was going to get Ganby to lead us out on an op. If anyone asked, we were just taking the STABs out to shake them down and make sure everything was operating okay. Including the weapons.

All morning we loaded the STABs with ammo. Walking by a PBR, we would grab a can of ammo when nobody was looking. Going past the boat, we would drop the can inside the hull. By the early afternoon, both boats were so loaded with ammo we could've attacked North Vietnam.

It was well before dark when we set out. One moment we had just been messing about with the boats next to the dock. The next moment, we were gone. Those twin hundred-horsepower Mercuries could really push the STABs when we opened up the throttles. Radios kept the boats in contact with each other. Gallagher was running one STAB with a couple of guys, and I was the coxswain of the other. In my STAB were Rick and Chief Ganby, who had come along to show us the way. All of us were pretty stupid for doing what we were doing. No one in headquarters knew our location. If we got into trouble, help would take a long time finding us.

But with the wind flying in our faces, it was easy to ignore the danger. Heading south, we poured on the fuel. Gallagher had designed bulletproof covers for the Mercs and the inside of the crew area. Even the gun mounts could take any weapon we had brought with us. Each STAB was carrying a .50 caliber machine gun on a central pedestal mount and an M60 machine gun on the gunwale mount. A lot of thought went into the STABs, and now was the time to see if they worked. In my seat up front there was even a fiberglass hood I could pull up to protect my neck and head from hot brass.

While we cruised along, Chief Ganby pointed out areas of interest. All of a sudden, somebody commented, "Look at the fish jumping."

Behind us and to the side you could see the water popping as the fish jumped around. Then somebody shouted, probably Ganby, "Fish my ass! That's automatic weapons fire. They're shooting at us from the beach!" There was a small island to the east of us that was in a free-fire zone. There was not supposed to be anyone on the island. Anyone who was on the island could be assumed to be the enemy. And besides, these pricks were shooting at us.

Oh, so that's what it looks like, I thought as I spun the boat around. We had been traveling south, and the fire was coming from the east bank. "Okay," shouted Rick, "saddle up. Get behind the guns and let's have some fun." With plenty of ammo available, Rick didn't have to give that order twice.

Back at the Creek, we had practiced working with the boats in pairs. Now that practice was paying off. The loud outboards had kept us from hearing the enemy's weapons. But Charlie could sure hear the firing coming from us. Coming in at the beach on an angle, we gave a small target to the enemy. Turning away hard put all the guns on the target in a broadside, and we opened up.

The M60s were roaring, the heavy thunder of the .50s drowning out the sound of the motors. Every weapon we had was unloading on the riverbank. "Get the Japs!" was the order of the day, and every one of us was working hard to obey that order. As the coxswain, I had an M79 grenade launcher I could fire with one hand. While steering the boat I would clamp the M79 between my legs to pull out the fired case and reload. I wasn't sure if I was hitting much, but at least I was getting in on the fight.

We made pass after pass on the bank, strafing the area with our weapons. An incoming bullet ricocheted off the water and nailed Harry Mattingly right between the eyes. The bullet went in just above the nose, skidded along the skull, and exited out the top of his head. "I've been hit!" Harry shouted.

We quickly checked him out and told him, "Yeah, you're hit, but you're all right. Get behind the 60—we're fighting a fucking war!" The SEALs are not known for their delicate compassion. Besides, Harry was just a bloody mess, he wasn't really hurt.

Rick was on the radio calling back to the base for support. Nobody else was with us, and the rest of the detachment was up at the RSSZ—the Rung Sat Special Zone—doing ambushes with Team One. Good things were happening—we had found the enemy and were engaging him. But some supporting fire would be a nice thing right about now.

The time was just zipping past. We must have been out there firing for hours. Ammo was being burned, and Rick was trying to call in anything that was available. With my own headset, I could hear everything that was going on between Rick and the people back at the base. "Return to Home Plate, repeat, return to Home Plate," the radio ordered. Rick reached past me and fiddled with the radio controls. "You're weak and unreadable," he said, and then he turned the radio off. On a separate set, Rick called over to Gallagher in the other boat.

"Is everybody all right over there?" Rick asked. "Have you got plenty of ammo?"

"Everything's fine," was the answer.

"Well, since we don't have anybody hit and there's plenty of ammo," Rick said, "let's stay here and fuck with them."

So we just kept making passes at the beach. None of us had any idea of what we were doing. But finally, we were in a war. All those years of training, and now we got to shoot off the guns. There were people shooting at us and we could shoot back. Mattingly was all right. He had a headache, but even he was having fun. If we had actually lost somebody, things would have been a lot different. But for right now it was a big laugh. We had become combat veterans.

Finally, we had fired just about every round in the two boats.

Rick had called in air support and the fire from the bank had stopped a long time ago. The amount of fire we had been taking didn't seem like much, perhaps only a few VC. But the size didn't matter. We had our first taste of combat and had come out okay.

When we pulled in to the dock at the base, there was Mustin, jumping up and down and screaming at us. Mustin was shouting how we would all be court-martialed for direct disobedience of orders, engaging the enemy without authorization, calling in air support under false identification, and pissing in the Bassac. The list of our "crimes" covered two pages. It must have taken Mustin longer to write out the list than it had for us to do the action.

Jake was Detachment Alfa and our direct superior. When he came back from the Rung Sat there was going to be hell to pay. But for right now we all felt pretty good. A whole bunch of ammo had been fired and we had had our first taste of combat. There was even going to be a decoration for Mattingly. The first Purple Heart awarded to Team Two.

The next morning, Bravo Squad was in a world of shit. We were restricted to our rooms, and could just go to the mess hall or head. Then intelligence started to come in about our operation. Reports from agents in the field stated that we had stopped a large number of VC from crossing the Bassac. The largest crossing of VC to date in the area, and we had prevented it from happening.

But Rick was still in trouble. The rest of the detachment was still up in Nha Be playing in the Rung Sat—that is, "becoming familiar in SEAL combat operations"—with Team One. Since Rick had been our leader and responsible for us, he would get in the most trouble. Shit normally goes downhill, but Rick doesn't let his mistakes get paid for by his men.

It was a week before we finally received some information to go and pull an op on our own. The other squads had been back and operating for a few days. But we had been assigned as backup for the other squads. That first tour, we always had a backup squad ready to support one that was in the field. We looked out for ourselves, and it paid off in the long run. But now Marcinko's Misfits were going to be allowed out of the barn to go run and play.

The squad was ready for some action. Finley didn't care if the sun came up tomorrow—you just couldn't get him excited. He did what he had to do when it had to be done. When Finley was alongside of you, you knew your flank was covered. Gallagher was a hard charger. If things didn't go Bob's way, he could just explode. Ronnie Rodger was as strong as a bull and packed his M60 like it was a .22 rifle. The squad didn't have a corpsman, but that was okay. Rick said we didn't need a corpsman; we were so aggressive we weren't going to get shot. Joe Camp was one of the guys who would always give 120 percent when the rest of us were putting out only 110 percent.

When the squad was on patrol, I would be on point, out a few meters in front of the rest. Behind me would come Ronnie and his M60. If I spotted an ambush, Ronnie was going to chop it into hamburger. Joe Camp was the radioman and would sometimes alternate positions with Ronnie. Finley would sometimes alternate with Joe as the radioman. Otherwise Finley acted as a rifleman. Gallagher brought up the rear as our rear security, and Rick would move around in the squad as he saw fit.

The idea was to put our squad's most experienced men at the front and rear. Joe Camp would change places with me as point man when the strain got to me and my attention suffered. When Joe had point, Finley usually carried the radio.

The intelligence we had picked up for the operation reported an increase in VC activity near Juliet Crossing, very close to the island we had shot up the week before. The plan was for us to insert on the southwest tip of Dung island and move across to where we could set up an ambush overlooking Juliet Crossing. When a VC courier came across the area, we would ambush him and recover any intelligence he was carrying. Since the area was a free-fire zone, the only people moving in it at night would be VC.

Juliet Crossing was where a canal emptied into the Bassac. The point of the island, where we would be hidden, was downstream from Juliet Crossing and directly across from another canal. Intel reported that Charlie was using Dung island for cover from the patrolling PBRs, since they couldn't go up the smaller canals. Couriers would come out one canal, use the island for cover, and duck into the next canal down near Juliet Crossing.

Now we had our rules of engagement. Anything that moved after dark in a free-fire zone was a target. With our planning ahead, we could use one of the SEAL/BSU (Boat Support Unit) boats for fire support. The SEAL Mike boat was a modified LCM (Landing

Craft, Medium) Mark 6. It had the sides of the troop well cut down and armored. Weapon stations along the sides gave the craft several .50 calibers, at least one M60, and a 40mm Honeywell on each side of the boat. The troop well was practically covered with armor plate. In the front of the troop well was an 81mm mortar. All in all, a very heavy piece of firepower.

The Mike boat could also carry a full SEAL platoon. Team One used the Mike boat a great deal during its operations in the Rung Sat. But my thought was that the boat was too distinctive a craft. The only people who used it were SEALs, and it wouldn't take the VC long to figure that out. But on this, our first land operation, the weapons on board that big boat were a comforting addition to our firepower. Our PT-loving lieutenant was going to be commanding the Mike boat. Along for their additional skills were Bill Brumuller, Pierre Birtz, and a number of guys from the other squad to support us by manning the boat's weapons.

Tying our STAB to the side of the Mike boat, we moved out to our ambush. Since the STAB didn't have radar and the target was so far down the river, we would use the Mike boat as a mother ship with its radar guiding the smaller craft in to the target. Getting within range of the island, we moved out. The STAB took us in to the shore, and then we left it and inserted. We had an IBS with us, inflated and tied up next to the STAB. The IBS was in case we got into trouble and had to leave the island before the boats could come in and get us. This was going to be our first on-land op. We looked at anything that could help cover our asses if things went sour.

After we inserted, Bob and Joe Camp moved out to hide the IBS. The rubber boat was to be hidden on our right flank as we went in, putting it close to the tip of the island. Since the IBS was inflated, Bob and Joe just pulled it along the water until they dragged it into the jungle and hid it. After making all the noise we were going to, we went inland about ten yards and lay down.

The idea was to listen to the area and give things a chance to settle down from the insertion. Just sitting still and listening can sometimes give you all the warning you need that things aren't the way they should be. Lying there, you can hear all the sounds of the jungle around you becoming active again. Insects buzz and whir, birds start to move about and call to each other. The jungle sometimes seems almost peaceful. But somewhere out there is a man who will gladly kill you if he can. Is he also waiting and listening? Has the round with your name on it already been chambered into a weapon? Thoughts like that can drive you crazy. You have to break off that kind of thinking and get on with the job at hand. Too much imagination can be a very bad thing.

Lying there in the mud and humus of the jungle floor, you pay attention to the area around you in a different way. Any small warnings of an enemy presence have to be filtered out from the sensory assault of the jungle. There's the earthy rotting smell of the ground less than a foot below your nose. Or is that the body odor of a Vietnamese, a man who habitually flavors his food with nuoc mam, that fermented fish sauce that's so common in this part of the world? If it is a Vietnamese, is he VC or a friendly?

Is that a normal vine near the trail? Or could it be a tripwire for a booby trap? Is that patch of dead leaves where some animal foraged for food, or is it the covering of a punji pit? The bottom of such a pit is covered with glass-sharp bamboo stakes, dipped in rotted excrement. One slight cut with a stake will cause festering and possible blood poisoning in an unbelievably short time in this heavy jungle environment.

The quiet drip-swish of the riverbank just behind us adds its share to the sensory stew around us. And the constant heat and humidity do their part to keep that stew cooking.

Moisture dripping from the leaves. The feel of oily sweat trickling down camouflage-coated skin. It itches, but you don't move to scratch it. You notice the feel of the webbing harness around you, comfortable with the weight of war tools. Sudden violence waiting for you to release it. The rough, slick feel of the plastic gunstock is reassuring, a close friend in this hostile environment.

But with all of this, you have to choose what doesn't fit. Incidents you can't even describe will help alert you to what could be there. Help you keep yourself and your squad alive. I was the point man, and the lives of my teammates could depend on my next judgment.

As we lay there, I started to hear a sound that was out of place. An intermittent tapping, rustling sound was coming from ahead of us. Was it a VC on guard and moving around? The squad was waiting for me to move out. It seemed like we stayed that way for hours, but it was really about forty-five minutes. All that time Rick was right behind me. But he never said a word to hurry me on my way. I was the point man, and the squad was going to follow my lead.

Finally, in my own mind I said, This is bullshit. We're wasting time. If we stay here, we'll miss the courier when he goes by. The squad should be on the canal by now. I've got to find out what that noise is.

Crawling back to where Rick was, I put my mouth up close to his ear. "There's a noise up ahead. I can't distinguish what it is."

Rick whispered, "I know what you mean. I can't figure it out either. I've never heard anything like it."

"Well," I answered, "we can't stay here any longer. Cover me. I'm going to move up and find out what it is."

I hadn't moved forward ten yards when I found the source of the noise. A palm tree had dropped a dry frond that hadn't completely broken off. As the light breeze blew through the jungle, the frond would tap against the palm's trunk and rustle against other plants. We chuckled about that for a second, but everybody was tense. You couldn't have driven a ten-penny nail up any one of our asses that night, the pucker factor was so high. We were all scared, and anybody in a situation like that who tells you different is either a damn liar or a fool.

Now it was time to move out to the ambush site. Rather than go around the tip of the island, we crossed overland through the jungle. The distance we traveled wasn't far, only a few hundred yards. But when you're moving in enemy territory, every step has to be thought out. The rest of the squad was depending on me to warn them about any enemies ahead or booby traps along the way. As the point man, you try to see everything at once and hear everything there is.

The weather in Vietnam is normally hot and humid, and you sweat all day long. But when the strain of being on your first combat patrol and being point man is added to the situation, sweat runs off you in streams. You have to be careful not to let yourself get dehydrated, you lose that much moisture.

The underbrush is nasty. Thorns constantly grab at your clothes and exposed skin. The ground squelches as your boots sink into the marshy soil with each step. Insects are everywhere. The rumors about Vietnamese insects actually being attracted to U.S.-issue bug repellent sound more truthful with each stinging bite. But none of this can distract you from the primary job at hand. Every sound, bent leaf, broken twig, and scuffed piece of earth could be the clue that will warn you about enemy activity.

We finally reached the bank overlooking the canal on the far shore. Being near the point of the island allowed us to cover the water from three different directions. Settling in silently, our squad moved into place for the ambush.

For this operation I was armed with a CAR-15 fitted with an AN/PVS-1 starlight scope. The CAR is a shortened version of the M16 rifle. The one I had was the early 07 type with a solid, sliding stock. The CAR is supposed to be a lightweight weapon, but I had sure changed that. The AN/PVS-1 starlight scope is a large chunk of glass, metal, and electronics that lets you see in the dark, magnifying available light 35,000 times. Everything takes on a greenish hue when you look through the scope. The scope is a heavy bastard, weighing almost as much as the CAR-15 it was mounted on.

Using the scope lets you see things more clearly, but when you take it away from your eye, all your normal night vision is gone. On top of depriving you of your night vision for up to thirty minutes, the starlight left a green ring around your eye the other guys could see. If the other members of my squad could see a glowing green ring on my face, Charlie could see it too.

The starlight worked well and seemed like a really neat piece of gear when it had been shipped to us incountry. But I was never going to carry that heavy sonofabitch again.

The night was clear and cool. It's amazing how chilly the jungle gets at night. Here we were in the tropics, and I was colder than hell. After the adrenaline from the patrol had worn off, I could feel the chill in the air. Time went by. Time to think, time to wish for a cigarette, time to curse at this goddam heavy starlight scope. It was around 2300 hours and we had been in position about an hour and a half when the sound came out of the darkness.

It was a quick, muffled thump-creak-thump, thump-creak-thump, repeating with a regular rhythm. My skin tightened up and all my senses went into overdrive. Time seemed to suddenly slow down, and I could see everything more clearly than just a moment before. The sound was a sampan being sculled with an oar. The Vietnamese row using a single oar between two wooden pins at the rear of their boats. This was a free-fire zone. At night nobody was supposed to be on the water. Our courier had arrived.

The sampan was moving from south to north. He couldn't have come from the main river or a PBR would have picked him up. He had to have come from the canal. Intelligence had been right. There were three men in the sampan, one sculling the oar and two others just riding along.

As the sampan moved into the killing zone, I turned the safety of my CAR to the full-auto position. It was too dark for me to see the sampan, and I was not about to risk the glow from the starlight. Besides, I hadn't zeroed the scope to my weapon. Moving my finger from alongside the receiver, I gently touched the trigger. When Rick opened fire, the ambush was initiated and I pulled the trigger. The sampan wasn't more than ten meters away.

The night lit up with the flashes from our muzzles. Every man stuck to his sector of fire, and we completely covered the kill zone. When my first magazine was empty, I quickly reloaded and continued to fire. We each had about a twenty-degree sector of fire to cover with two magazines. As suddenly as it had started, the ambush was over. Only this time the silhouettes hadn't been missed.

Rick hollered, "Cease fire," and we quickly reloaded our weapons. The sampan had drifted close to me during the ambush. Rick quickly jumped into the water to grab the boat before it could drift away. The current was too strong for Rick to control the sampan by himself, so I jumped into the water to give him a hand. Finley remained on the bank to cover our flank.

By this time Bob, on the other flank, was shouting, "What's going on?" After all the firing, noise discipline wasn't as important as staying in contact. Rick and I were too busy stripping out the now sinking sampan to answer him.

The inside of the wooden boat was covered with blood and bits of tissue. Two of the VC that had been in the boat were obviously dead. The glow of our dim flashlights also pointed out a small pouch of documents along with some gear. One body had been blown out of the sampan by the murderous fire, but there were still plenty of things to pick up and take back to intelligence. I spotted a small plastic cigarette package and stuck it into my pocket along with some other items.

Sloshing back to the shore, we let the sampan go with the current. It was done, a successful op. Now it was time to go home and have a beer. Or at least I hoped Rick felt that way. Camp was on the radio calling out to the Mike boat to tell it we were ready for extraction and to meet us on the south end of the island. Only there wasn't any radio contact. The high I had felt just a moment before evaporated like a puff of smoke in a whirlwind.

Now on top of not being in radio contact with the Mike boat, we started taking fire from the far bank. It wasn't very heavy fire, perhaps only one man firing sporadically, but how big does the bullet that kills you have to be? And in our frame of mind at the time, it seemed like the entire NVA were out there shooting at us.

Now things were getting tight. Calls were still going out on the radio for the STAB to come in and pick us up. Where the hell was the STAB? For that matter, where was the Mike boat? It was supposed to be supporting us. The incoming fire was starting to get worse. The SOP for this operation called for us to light up our flanks with WP grenades if anything was happening. The STAB coming in would then be able to suppress any enemy fire on either side of us and know exactly where we were.

Rick called out to Bob and me to throw our WP grenades. Bob threw his to the east and I threw mine to the west of our position. The M15 white phosphorus grenade explodes like a deadly flower blooming, white streamers of dense smoke trailing from brilliant yellow/white fragments of burning phosphorus. At night, the smoke can't be seen, but the blossoming explosion has a dazzling center of light.

The fragments of phosphorus burn at over eighteen hundred degrees, setting fire to almost anything they touch. But the soggy jungle had too much moisture to burn well, and the phosphorus burned out after a minute. Only there was more to burn than just the jungle.

There was still no supporting fire and no pickup boat. The SOP was that when we marked our flanks with the Willy Peter, the boats were supposed to put down covering fire everywhere but

between the two grenades. Since the boats didn't come in, it wasn't that the radio didn't work. They just weren't out there.

The sporadic fire we had been receiving was probably lighter than we thought at the time. When you're on your first op, things get magnified. But we had been waiting long enough. Rick and Bob both decided it was time to leave. We could use the IBS to take us over to the main stream of the Bassac, where we would eventually contact a PBR.

"Jim, go get the IBS. It's time for us to get the hell out of here."

"Where is it?" I asked.

"Over on your side in the bushes," answered Bob. "Just go over there and you'll find it."

In the bushes? I thought. But that's where I threw the grenade.

I found the IBS, all right, and so had my WP grenade. The grenade had landed right inside the boat and completely destroyed it. The stink of the burning phosphorus had covered the smell of the burning rubber.

"Back to the drawing board, Boss," I said when I had gotten back to Rick. "It's time to go to Plan B. We don't have an IBS."

Right then, I think the VC would have given me a friendlier reception than Bob Gallagher did. Bob was seriously pissed and called me everything but intelligent. Rick just laughed it off with a quick "You dumb shit!"

Later on, thinking about the IBS, I realized I had not known where that boat was. Bob should have told me and the rest of the squad right after they had hidden it. But that didn't help the situation at the time. I had destroyed the insurance we had brought with us. If the squad had been really deep into it, it would have all been over. I should have known where the boat was before I threw the grenade. At least we learned that lesson without anybody getting hurt or killed.

Now the STAB finally showed up. As the boat got in close to shore to pick us up, neither of the M60s opened fire to cover us. Besides Bill Brumuller and Pierre Birtz, there were some extra sailors from the Mike boat's crew aboard the STAB. What was going on?

We piled into the STAB, and it was a tight fit with the extra men. The hull grounded briefly, but we got it loose without any trouble.

Fire was still coming at us from across the river channel, near the canal. With the STAB we could now get out of here. But where the hell was the Mike boat with all the heavy firepower?

"What in the hell are all these extra people doing here?" I asked. "Where's the Mike boat?"

Somebody answered, "The lieutenant has the Mike boat chasing sampans."

"You have got to be shitting me! He's supposed to be here with us. And who are these other guys?"

"They came along to help if you were in trouble."

No disrespect to the Boat Support people who were manning the Mike boat, but we could have used another SEAL on that STAB. SEALs would have had a much better chance of handling the kind of situation we might have fallen into. I was pretty pissed off, but Rick was coming absolutely unglued and Gallagher was going ballistic.

The STAB took us upriver to find the Mike boat. As we got closer we suddenly had great radio reception. The sonofabitch had been out of range! As we tied up to the Mike boat, we started feeling a little better. Our first land op was over and we had come out of it okay. The anticipation about what could happen is worse than the action itself. It's like a football team before the big game—once you've started playing, training takes over.

As we tied up alongside of the Mike boat for the trip back to Can Tho, out of the darkness came another ship. It looked about as big as the *New Jersey*, with much bigger guns than we had. But it turned out to be an RVN (Republic of Vietnam) ship patrolling the deeper part of the river. After we made contact with the RVN ship and told it about the situation, it turned toward the area we had just left. Since it was a free-fire zone, the RVN ship peppered the area of shore that the fire had been coming from earlier.

Rick had calmed down by the time we had gotten aboard the Mike boat, but he was still pretty sore. The Mike was heading north, up the Bassac, and our STAB was tied up to the starboard side. We were all leaning back in the troop well feeling good. "Oh, shit, we made it. First op and we made it." Rick had headed up to the conning cabin to talk with the lieutenant about what had happened.

When Rick came back he was breathing hard and was seriously

pissed off again. Off in the distance we could see flares going off and hear the sound of gunfire. "The outpost up ahead is under siege," the lieutenant shouted down. "We're going to support them. Everybody grab a weapon."

There were four .50s, a bunch of M60s, and other weapons all over the boat, so arming ourselves wasn't a problem. The outpost was on Cu Lao May island and had been under attack by an unknown number of enemy forces. We could see the outpost on the far left side of the river. Then the Mike boat went past the outpost!

Turning around upstream, our boat was going to make a gun run past the island while moving downstream. The Mike might have been heavily armed and armored, but she moved about as fast as a sunken rock. Going downstream would put us past the island faster, but now our STAB was on the side that would face the incoming fire. When we passed the riverbank the enemy was on, they would be able to look down into the Mike boat.

Gallagher hollered out, "Everybody into the STAB! Jim, take the wheel!"

Ya-hoo, two firefights in one night. Over the side I went, quickly followed by Finley, Gallagher, Rick, and the rest of the squad. "Charge the weapons," shouted Gallagher. "Everybody get ready to shoot." We had taken the .50 off the STAB earlier because the ammo just took up too much room for the amount of fire it gave us. Now we had the M60s in place and a whole bunch of linked 7.62mm. We pulled off the port M60 and put it on the starboard side, giving us two guns on that side. After checking the engines and the fuel lines, I climbed into my seat at the front of the STAB and made sure my M79 was loaded.

The lines tying us to the Mike boat were still in place, and we were waiting for somebody to cut us loose. But on board the Mike boat, things were about as organized as a bucket of worms. Everyone was shouting orders at everyone else and no one had enough leadership, the senior man included, to get the boat squared away before we had committed to supporting the outpost. The BSU people crewing the Mike boat didn't know who to follow. The BSU lieutenant was supposed to follow the direction of the senior SEAL lieutenant. Only trouble was, our lieutenant was tripping over his own feet.

By now, the Mike boat had turned around and was starting to

pass close by the enemy riverbank. The bank wasn't more than twenty meters away when the firing started. The starboard side was facing the enemy, and no one had cut us loose yet. The STAB was acting as a buffer for the Mike boat! Brumuller was manning a .50 right above us just smokin' the Japs. You could see the enemy on the riverbank, silhouetted against the light of the parachute flares. Bru told me later that he had felt sorry for us because he could see the hot brass from his .50 pouring down into the STAB.

The STAB was full of gasoline tanks and ammo. If a piece of hot brass melted through a rubber fuel line, it would be all over. But Brumuller was doing what he had to do, firing his weapon and keeping the enemy's heads down. Looking up, you could see the barrels of the .50s starting to glow from the heat of the firing. I had an M79 and a full box of 40mm ammo right next to me. Charlie didn't like 40 mike-mike, and I was putting out rounds as fast as I could. Gallagher was shouting at me, "Get up on the bow and cut us loose."

"Hang it," was my reply. I was crouching down behind my quarter inch of fiberglass and glad I had it. But we had to get out of there. I had fired the engines up, but there was no place for us to go. Somebody finally cut us loose, and I pushed the throttle full open. Moving away from between the Mike boat and the shore, we spun out to the open, and turned back to make some firing runs of our own. The STAB could spin rings around that wallowing Mike boat but didn't have the range or firepower of the much slower craft.

Again and again we rushed past the shore, pouring fire onto the enemy positions. Being busy with the wheel, I didn't get much shooting in, but I did manage to fire my M79 now and then. Finally, over the radio came the call that the enemy attack had been broken. Coming back over to the Mike boat, we climbed aboard again. The STAB sucked up a lot of gas, and we might not have had enough to get back to the base. Otherwise there was no way you could have gotten us back aboard that boat. Twice in one night, poor judgment on the part of our support had put the squad in a bad situation. If we weren't a little more careful, our luck was going to run out.

Later on, back at the Creek, I would receive my first Bronze Star for the action off Cu Lao May island. Part of the citation reads that

I saved "the valuable craft [STAB] from destruction." Truth is that the "valuable craft" happened to be wrapped around my ass at the time I was "saving" it. Other guys did as much as or more than I during the operation. Personally, I think a medal should go to whoever finally cut us loose from the Mike boat.

But the next day at the base I had another little discovery to make. That plastic cigarette case I had taken off the dead VC was still in my pocket. When I finally got around to looking inside it, there was a watch ticking away. If I had heard that watch ticking when I first found the case, I sure as hell wouldn't have put it in my pocket.

Things were getting a little rough around the base. I don't know what Marcinko told Rhinebolt and Kochey about the snafu with the Mike boat the night before. But the general attitude of the squad toward a certain lieutenant was not friendly. Just what the hell did he think constituted "supporting" us? Being in the same general neighborhood? Somehow, Bravo Squad was in the shit again, and all we had done was our mission. It quickly became evident that getting Bravo Squad off somewhere operating by it-self would prevent any embarrassment to Det Alfa and a certain lieutenant.

Rick had gotten the word that a commander up in My Tho wanted a team of SEALs. My Tho, pronounced "Me Toe," had a big PBR base and was soon going to be reinforced by units from the U.S. 9th Division. To check out the area, Bravo Squad was going to go up to My Tho and pull some ops. If the situation warranted, more SEALs could be called up to operate in the area.

We left with not much more than the clothes on our backs but every piece of firepower we could carry. There was a general feel-ing of relief on both sides. The Can Tho group could breathe easier now that Marcinko's Mob was gone. And we could operate the best way we knew how without somebody trying to hold a leash on us. On March 30, a Caribou transport plane landed at Binh Thuy and Bravo Squad loaded aboard.

The flight to My Tho became interesting very quickly. I was over the feeling of unreality by now, but it was obvious some people still didn't realize where they were. After we were airborne, an Air Force colonel came walking back to where we sat toward the rear of the plane. Since the flight was over enemy-held territory, we had every round of ammunition we could carry strapped on. If we were forced down, the VC would find they had a fight on their hands.

But this colonel didn't seem to know where he was. "Excuse me," he said, "but are those live hand grenades?"

"Sure hope so."

"They're against regulations. You can't fly in an Air Force aircraft with live explosives aboard. Those are going to have to be properly packed away."

"Well sir, we don't know where you're going. But where they're letting us off, there's a war going on."

There are some real good men in the Air Force, and some of them are my friends. But some dingbats show up in the higher echelons. Maybe they've flown too long without oxygen. "Are those live grenades?" What did that jerk think? That we'd carry practice grenades in a combat zone?

We arrived at My Tho without further trouble. The plane landed on a dirt runway where there was supposedly a jeep and driver waiting for us. Somehow we had the impression that this was a less than friendly area. The pilot had said before landing that as soon as the plane came to a stop, he was dropping the ramp and we were to get out fast. He wasn't going to shut down at all, just put the brakes on long enough for us to deplane. I think if there had been chutes available, the pilot wouldn't have even landed, just asked us to leave while he flew by.

"There's supposed to be a three-quarter-ton or jeep to pick us up," Rick said. "Let's hike over to the road and wait for them." No problem, the map and aerial photo Rick had showed a road nearby, so we started walking in that direction. As we stepped away from where the plane had landed, we all slipped a magazine into our weapons. This was strange territory to us—no sense taking chances.

As we approached the road, here came a three-quarter-ton weapons carrier to pick us up. The man riding shotgun with the driver had a loaded M60 with him. They ain't shitting, I thought. This is not a friendly neighborhood.

Rick climbed into the front seat with the driver and M60 man while the rest of us climbed into the back. Bob moved up toward the cab, where he could hear the conversation between Rick and the sergeant driving the vehicle.

As we drove down the road, traffic started getting congested. Pedestrians and cyclos were all around us. The driver had to slow way down to avoid hitting anybody. We noticed that the M60 gunner was starting to get nervous. His eyes were trying to look everywhere at once.

Looking at him, somebody asked, "What's going on?"

"They've had a couple of ambushes here in the past week."

There was no answer, just the clack of bolts being pulled back and rounds being chambered. Now we all were nervous. Everybody tried to look everywhere at once.

But the trip went along without incident, and we finally got to My Tho. We pulled up to this little villa, like an old-fashioned hotel with courtyards, slow-moving ceiling fans, and shuttered windows. If there hadn't been a war going on, you could've filmed a Humphrey Bogart movie there. We had assigned rooms and lived pretty well. The villa was a few blocks from the My Tho River, another silt-laden flow of yellow-brown water.

Four men were assigned to a room, with a bunk and footlocker for each man. After we had dropped off our stuff, they took us up to the roof. On the roof were sandbagged positions where we could place our weapons and fire from cover. Most of My Tho was spread out in front of us. They called it a city, but I've been in bigger villages. Everything outside of the city, especially at night, was owned by Charlie.

As good as our quarters were, the base was something else again. The dock was wooden planks laid out over floating oil drums. Buildings were either half-round Quonset huts or flat-sided aluminum Butler buildings. Not as built-up as Can Tho had been, but plenty good enough for us to operate from.

At the PBR base, we had a ready room assigned to us. In the ready room we could keep whatever ammunition we wanted strictly for ourselves. No more scrounging bullets from PBRs for us. They even gave us an allowance of ammunition to draw from the ammo bunkers. Right away, we started setting up our ready room. At the moment, setting up consisted mostly of unpacking the few boxes we had brought with us, mostly cleaning gear and some supplies.

Rick and Bob had separated from us early on. They both went into town to the safe house, intelligence headquarters, to find out what was going on in the area. The higher-ups in My Tho had heard about SEALs and were glad to see us. Many people were glad to see SEALs, but once we had arrived, they didn't know what to do with us. My Tho was not that situation. These guys wanted us to go into action, the sooner the better.

The PBR commander had been getting his boats sniped at all over the place. Sometimes they took fire very close to the base itself. All he wanted to know was if we could do anything about the situation. Could we run some night patrols and find out what was going on?

What? A free hand to operate and support without an argument? Ya-hoo—Marcinko's Marauders were back in business.

Before we had left Can Tho, a bunch of new and deadly toys had come in from the States. Our first Stoner machine gun had arrived, along with the instructions and a supply of ammunition and extra links. Since there was only one Stoner for Second Platoon at the time, we had left it back with the other squad. But other items had come in that we took with us. Bob Gallagher now had a Remington 7188, a selective-fire 12-gauge shotgun. With the selector switch set to full automatic, the 7188 would empty its eight-round magazine in about one second. Quite a handful of firepower.

For myself, I had found a weapon I particularly liked, the XM-148 grenade launcher. Looking like quite a complicated piece of hardware, the XM-148 was designed to be fitted underneath the barrel of an M16 rifle. The XM-148 fired the same round of 40mm ammunition as the M79 grenade launcher. Only once you had fired the XM-148, you still had the M16 in your hands, ready to go. This was a lot better than the single-shot M79, and I could hardly wait to use the weapon.

Bob Gallagher set up a target range for us to try out all the new weapons. To be sure that none of the VC could see our new hardware, we only used the range at night. Bob liked the shotgun, even though it was a bitch to hang on to during full automatic fire. The trigger of the XM-148 stuck out a bit and could hang up on brush, and the weapon was a little more fragile than I cared for. But outside of that, I liked the additional firepower it gave me.

Now it was time to start operating. Information was available to us about a small group of VCI (Viet Cong infrastructure, officers and leaders of the VC) who were living in a small village only a short distance from the water. This was going to be our first operation in the area, and we had some special help for the occasion.

Special Navy helicopter gunships were now available, committed to supporting the SEALs and Brown Water (Riverine) forces in Vietnam. The gunships, called Seawolves, operated most often in detachments of two aircraft. Each chopper in a detachment was armed with two seven-round rocket pods, four fixed, forward-firing M60C machine guns, and two flexible M60 door guns, one on each side. These Navy birds were quickly going to become a close friend to the SEALs operating on the ground.

So with Seawolf support on call, we went out on our operation, inserting from a PBR and following a fairly well defined path to the village. The path ran along a line of paddy dikes, and we stayed close to it without exposing ourselves above the dike. It was first light when we reached the village, only a few klicks from the river.

We observed the village for a while and saw no movement out of the ordinary. Setting up a perimeter for security, we busted into the village and charged into the hooches, weapons at the ready. We had been all set to catch us some high-ranking Viet Cong. Trouble was, the only people in the village were women and children.

The village was in a free-fire zone, and there were not supposed to be any civilians in the area. The women and children were at least VC sympathizers and family, and some of them were probably active VC. We would have been within our rights and orders to level the whole place. But you have to show some humanity and compassion, even in a war. Searching the village, we found a lot of food and gear—much more than should have been in a village of that size with the people who were in it.

We knew that the men were out in the jungle somewhere doing what the VC do. But no weapons or military equipment turned up in our search. The squad fell back from the village and left. Gallagher was covering our rear, and Rick had me up on point. This time I was armed with my XM-148 grenade launcher. I had mounted the weapon underneath the barrel of my CAR-15. This was a nice piece of firepower without too much weight. The 40mm grenades weighed about half a pound apiece, so I was carrying only one bandolier of six HE rounds.

As the squad moved out of the village, we suddenly found the men who had been missing. The VC had been waiting in the jungle around the village while we had been searching the hooches. As soon as we left the village, the VC sprang an ambush on us. This was not fun.

It was only because the VC had not been able to organize a proper ambush that we were able to get away from them so cleanly. That and the fact that the Seawolves showed up almost immediately and started firing the area up. Concealment didn't make much sense now, so the squad got up on the paddy dike and started moving out in no small hurry.

This was one of the Seawolves' first operations with SEALs, and the crews were making the best of it. As the choppers made their gun runs, flying low along the paddies, we could see crewmembers leaning out the doors to get a clearer shot. These guys had M16s along with their M60s and M79 grenade launchers and were pouring fire down on the VC.

"Don't worry about it," they radioed. "We've got the guys spotted. Head toward the river and we'll cover you for extraction."

You didn't have to tell me twice. I was moving along in front of the squad as quickly as I could while still keeping an eye out for enemy activity. There was a tree limb hanging low over the trail in front of me. I ducked down under it while pushing the branch out of my way. This was a mistake.

When I ducked under the branch, I knocked down a whole bunch of red ants that had a nest under the leaves. Those little suckers fell right down the back of my neck, stinging and biting all the way. I clenched my hands in reaction to the sudden pain. That was my second mistake.

While charging along, I had my fingers on both triggers of my weapon. When I clenched my hands, both weapons went off. I had been carrying the attached weapons at a forty-five degree downslant while running. The roar of the CAR-15 didn't quite drown out the *thoop . . . smack* of the 40mm going off. As my hands clenched, all that went through my mind was "That 40mm has a ten-meter killing radius!" The round impacted into the mud not six feet from where I was standing.

Those 40mm HE rounds have to spin over 150 times before the impact fuze will arm. The grenade travels at least fourteen meters in that time. This safety is designed into the weapon so that operators will have a harder time killing themselves when they make a mistake like the one I had just made. I watched the grenade smack into the mud right in front of me and not go off. Now I only had the VC and a bunch of red ants to worry about.

The rest of the squad didn't see the ants and wondered why I had suddenly gone apeshit right in front of them. "It's goddam ants or something. They've gone down my back!" I said.

"Shit," Bob said. "Jump in the canal and drown them."

Sounded like a great idea to me, so I did. The VC were still trying to find us, so the entire squad jumped into the canal with me. Seawolf was right down on the deck, covering us all the way out. Later, Seawolf told us that the VC were chasing us all the way back to the river. As the point man, I watched out for any VC in front of us. I hadn't seen any on our way out, but nobody had told me I had to look out for ants.

Up till then I usually wore a regular Marine cap or sometimes a black beret when in the field. After my little adventure with Vietnam's insect population, I started wearing a wide-brimmed floppy bush hat on operations.

Getting back to My Tho after the operation, we cleaned up and talked about what had happened. Maybe we should have greased that village—it was a free-fire zone and VC were obviously using the place. But our decision to leave the people alone still seemed like the right one. There had been women and children killed by both sides during the war. Friendly fire isn't always as accurate as we would like it to be. Women and young children had been used by the VC as soldiers, and had been treated as the enemy when they came at us armed. But that was the kind of war Vietnam was. War is hell, and Vietnam proved that better than most.

Rick contacted Jake Rhinebolt down at Can Tho and told him what was going on in My Tho. There was plenty of intelligence about VC activities. A full SEAL platoon would have more than enough operations to keep busy for a while. Jake agreed and sent the rest of Second Platoon up to My Tho to hook up with us. Alfa Squad showed up with Lieutenant Kochey, Bill Brumuller, Leg Martin, RA Tolison, Ronnie Fox, and Kenny Robinson adding to our merry band.

Once the rest of the platoon arrived, we spent a short time getting everyone organized. Intelligence had come in on a big target—a VCI finance chief, a security chief, and some other targets, five in all. The intel was pretty good, we had locations, the men we were looking for, the equipment we should look for and where it was hidden, even names of some of the targets. This was going to be a big operation, and we were not going to let the opportunity slip away. To keep any warning from going out, all five targets were going to be hit in a single night.

Rick gave us a full briefing on when, where, and how we were going out. Alfa Squad was going to be our backup on the op, and we would be using the Mike boat and PBRs. The Mike boat would act as the mother boat and give us fire support. The PBRs would insert us at the target and take us away after the mission. Since the PBRs were seen on the river every day, they wouldn't attract attention. The idea was to avoid using the STAB too much. Intelligence was already coming in that the unique-looking STAB was drawing attention to our activities.

The 9th Division had moved into nearby Dong Tam along with units of the Riverine Force. With the Riverine Force in the area, Mike boats and monitors were common on the river around My Tho and no longer drew attention. The heavily armored monitors with their 20 and 40mm cannon and 81mm mortars would back up the lighter PBRs giving the Riverine Force a heavy punch to conduct their Brown Water operations. And we would be an integral part of those operations.

After the briefing up in our quarters, it was time to prepare for the mission that evening. My job was to break out the ammunition we would need and make sure all the equipment was laid out and ready. It was right after lunch when I finished and went up to the chow hall to tell Rick and Bob everything was squared away. After I'd spoken to Bob in the hall, Rick called to me to come outside. Rick was standing just outside of the doorway with a message board in his hands. Flipping open the board, Rick handed it to me and said, "Here, read this, Jim."

Right in the middle of the page, surrounded by all the other message traffic, it said: "Watson, James D. Advanced to QMC (Quartermaster, Chief)." The effective date on the message was two months earlier. I had been a chief for two months and hadn't known it.

"Holy shit! Wahoo! Mr. Rick, I ain't going on that op tonight."

That set Rick back a few steps. "What do you mean, you ain't going on that op tonight?"

"You've got to be shitting me," I answered. "One of the biggest operations we're going to pull, five targets, and I'm the point man. My ID card says I'm a first class petty officer. If I'm going to get killed, I'm a chief and I'm going to get killed as a chief."

"You made CPO, not CNO.* Get your shit together—we're going."

Then we both walked around the back toward where the TOC (Tactical Operations Center) and sick bay were. There was a little beer hall there, and we went in. Vietnamese beer wasn't much, but right then it was available. Rick bought two beers and gave me one. "Congratulations, Chief," he said, and we drank our beers.

The operation that night was going to be a long one. After getting what rest we could in the afternoon, we loaded aboard the Mike boat and left My Tho. Since the op was going to run all night, we took some chow from the mess hall with us—ham sandwiches, salami, cheese, bread, practically a picnic lunch. The Mike boat usually had come C rations aboard, but the mess hall had made up these box lunches for us. Hell of a way to fight a war—take a box lunch into combat—but that's the way Vietnam was sometimes.

At the first target, we came up empty. Nothing but women and kids were in the area. There was a bunker in the village—most villages had them for protection. Cans of fuel were around, but it was hard to tell if the fuel was for sampans or just the village's lanterns. If we had found twenty gallons or more, that would have been unusual and gotten our attention. But the amount wasn't that great and we just passed on the target.

Pulling out, we went back to the Mike boat and grabbed a sandwich while we chugged on to the next target. By the time we reached the target area, a couple of the guys said they weren't feeling very good. Not thinking anything of it, we left them on the boat. Picking up a couple guys from Alfa Squad, we climbed aboard a PBR for insertion.

---

* CPO Chief Petty Officer, CNO Chief of Naval Operations, the highest ranking officer in the Navy.

Going in, we found an unoccupied sampan. This was another free-fire zone and there was supposed to be absolutely no people around. While we were lying in the area of the sampan, a single VC walked up and we took him under fire. Though we hit the man, incoming fire from the flank forced us away before we could recover the body. That caused the kill to be listed as a **VC KIA PROB** (Viet Cong killed in action, probable). Pulling back slightly, we called in fire from the Mike boat's 81mm mortar, and that silenced the enemy guns.

Moving in closer to the target hut, we followed our guide in. We had a VC woman who was acting as a guide and identifying the targets for us. She had been captured and turned over to work for us and the RVN forces. The same thing happened as on the first target. Women and children only, and the village had a small bunker. Another dry hole. Women and children were not the targets we wanted. Again we pulled out. Back to the Mike boat.

The men we had left on the boat earlier were now really getting sick. I was starting to get pretty squeezy myself. But the Mike boat was moving up the river for the next target, and I wasn't about to let my squad go on without me. Pride kept me from speaking up; I didn't want to be listed among the complainers, or, as we called them, the sick, lame, and lazy. That was pretty much macho stupidity on my part as it turned out.

Inserting on the third target, we came up with a capture. The man we had been looking for wasn't in the village. We spotted one man walking along the dike path we were covering. The squad was inland from the river about three klicks. When we called out for the man to stop, he suddenly took off running. A short burst of fire caused the guy to come to a stop. Now we had brought attention on ourselves. Suddenly the VC we had been looking for showed themselves. Fire started coming in from the jungle. Mattingly took a round in the hand, losing his M16. Time to go home, bye now. While withdrawing along the paddy dikes to the river, it suddenly hit me.

Food poisoning. I was retching and vomiting all over the place. Diarrhea hit me so bad it felt like my whole insides were turning inside out. God, it was awful—getting hit in an ambush couldn't be much worse.

Rick came running up to me all concerned. Grabbing me by the back of my neck, Rick showed his sympathy as only a SEAL could.

"You dumb sonofabitch," Rick growled into my ear. "If you ever go on an operation sick again, I'll kill you! Get outa here."

Now the squad had to move. Lights were coming on in the area surrounding us. The cat was out of the bag, and the dumb point man had almost walked us into it. The squad broke out into a run, and we headed for the river. Extraction went off without a problem, and we got out of there with our prisoner and guide intact. Now on board the Mike boat, even the Vietnamese woman who worked at the TOC at My Tho and had come along as an interpreter was getting ill. A total of six people came down sick. It was so serious that a medevac chopper was called in to evacuate us to a hospital.

When we arrived in My Tho, all of us were immediately taken to an Army hospital near Dong Tam. At the hospital, they gave us shots that were damn near as bad as the illness. Whatever it was we had, it was nasty. I felt so horrible I wanted to die. Anything to stop the pain. You couldn't tell how long the agony was going to go on, and there was nothing the hospital people could do to relieve it. This was the most painful episode of my life. It felt like something was inside of me trying to claw its way out. I wouldn't wish something like this on Ho Chi Minh.

Mattingly wasn't hurt too bad, but losing that M16 was a problem. The platoon went back to the area where the weapon had been dropped to look for it. The canal where Mattingly had been standing and the surrounding area were closely searched. The rifle never turned up. Normally losing any ordnance is just short of a disaster. But the location of Mattingly's wound, combined with the way he held his weapon, kept us from worrying about that particular M16 coming back to haunt us. The round that hit Mattingly had probably destroyed his piece by going through the breech section. Some things even a VC jungle workshop can't repair.

The food poisoning op took us several days to recover from, especially those of us who were ill. Slack time gave us all a break from the war and patrols. Somewhere, the platoon had acquired a monkey as a pet. Jocko was the critter's name, and we kept him with us most of the time. Weird things seem very funny in a war zone, and one day that kind of slopped over on the monkey. Did you ever see a drunken monkey? None of us had when the question was raised one day. Out comes Jocko along with a bottle of scotch. A monkey with the staggers is funny to a bunch of guys in the middle of a war. But a monkey with a hangover . . . brrrr. I'd rather meet the VC than deal with a hungover monkey. The VC just have guns. That little ape would try to bite you all over.

One of the places we hung out was the gun shed, a secure location where we kept our exotic weapons. Now that the rest of the platoon was with us, we had a Stoner to go along with our other deadly toys. Alfa Squad had been operating with the Stoner and thought the world of the weapon. The Stoner fired the same round as the M16 but fed from a disintegrating-link belt at over 850 rounds per minute. The high rate of fire and 150-round ammunition capacity made the Stoner a real popular weapon with some SEALs. The weapon had to be kept very clean and was difficult to maintain, which is what kept it from being as popular as it could have been.

The limited number of Stoners in use gave us another headache when it came time to load ammo. The special linked ammo for the Stoners was in very limited supply. The Stonerman carried a empty sandbag to recover the links whenever he could. After a mission, a bunch of us would be sitting around the ready room, swapping stories and relinking ammunition by hand.

Other weapons were in the gun shed, including the Remington 7188 full-auto shotgun. When the weapon had first arrived, Bob had grabbed on to it as the best thing since sliced bread. Since the episode with the ants, I had started carrying a shotgun, a five-shot Ithaca Model 37. Bob tried to convince me that the Remington 7188 was the weapon for a point man to carry. But I considered it just too heavy. Besides, my pump-action repeater was much more reliable than that complicated full-auto weapon.

Bob carried the 7188 on about six patrols and finally gave up on it as just being too sensitive to dirt. The fact that I could take my Ithaca and just rinse it off in a muddy stream was one of the reasons I liked it. During one ambush, Bob used the 7188 on full auto, and the results were devastating. But the reliability problem finally caused Bob to switch to either another Ithaca like mine or the CAR-15 and M16 rifle.

My favorite shotgun ammunition was the XM-257 round with the hardened-lead #4 buckshot. The twenty-seven pellets in the shell would knock down any VC I aimed at, which was exactly what I wanted. The flechette shells that were sent to us later would certainly kill a man, at even longer ranges than the XM-257. But the sharp-pointed little flechettes—they looked like finishing nails with fins—wouldn't stop a man as quickly as a load of #4 buckshot.

As the point man, I wanted to walk as light as I could while still carrying a decent weapon. That's why I stopped taking the starlight scope—it just wasn't worth the weight. My job was to be the forward eyes and ears of the squad. If you get tired from carrying too much weight, you start thinking about being tired rather than what you are doing. When on point, I tried to be as comfortable as I could to keep anything from bothering me.

Within reason, each man could choose what kind of uniform he wore and what weapon he carried. Most of the time, I wore the canvas coral shoes we had instead of boots. The coral shoes had a rubber sole and canvas upper, much like a light tennis shoe. I liked the way it gave my feet some sensitivity while still protecting me from thorns and such. Other guys would wear boots, jungle boots, or even bare feet on occasion.

Regular Levi jeans tended to be the most popular pants for operations. Team One had told us jeans wore better in the brush and thorns than the issue fatigues. Issue uniforms in mangrove swamps wouldn't last for six hundred yards before they were torn to rags. For our time in Vietnam, we had each brought four sets of fatigues. Since we didn't expect to be in any parades, no one brought any dress uniforms. The lack of dress uniforms did cause some trouble if you had to go home early for some reason. For the most part, we wore jeans and fatigues during our first tour.

Operationally we had been improving considerably as our experience grew. The PBRs were quickly becoming our favorite insertion boat. The Brown Water sailors who operated with us knew their jobs and the waters they operated in. Depending on the area, we had different ways to insert. If we had the boat nose in to the bank, we would climb out over the bow and remain still longer than usual to see if the noise had attracted attention.

Another technique for inserting, and one we liked better than nosing into the bank, was the simplest for a SEAL. With the PBR moving at a moderate speed, the inserting squad would just roll off the back of the boat into the water. That brown water tasted like dirt and wasn't the most pleasant swim I ever had. But when we inserted off a moving boat, there wasn't any noise to alert Charlie that we were coming to visit. A drawback to that insertion was the lack of flotation for our equipment. All we had at the time was the small inflatable UDT lifejackets. Those jackets just weren't enough when a man had a machine gun and several hundred rounds of ammunition. The lack of buoyancy was a question that was going to be addressed once we got back to Little Creek.

When we rode the PBRs we tried to stay out of the way of the crew. Those sailors knew what they were doing, and they didn't need us to get in the way. We especially stayed out of the bow and the twin-.50 gun tub. Those .50s were the biggest weapons on board, and you did not want to limit their field of fire. A squad was about the biggest unit that could ride a PBR at all comfortably. In the case of a firefight, we would add our weapons to those of the crew. But for the most part, we just rode quietly along and let the PBR crew do their job, get us to and from the target.

Alfa Squad had an operation. Kochey, Ron Fox, and two other SEALs had some good intelligence about a reported sapper living on the south side of Thoi Son island. The reported location was only about six klicks from My Tho—you could see the north side of Thoi Son from the PBR dock. Using a STAB, a four-man combat patrol would insert a few hundred meters from the suspect's house just before dawn. The local VC were doing their operations at night and returning to their hooches just after dawn. After they had hidden their weapons, the same VC who would snipe at us at night would wave to us from the rice paddies during the day.

The suspected VCI member was supposed to be the equivalent of us in the NVA (North Vietnamese Army). I didn't understand what that was supposed to mean, but he was a bad guy and that was all that mattered. Early in the morning, Gallagher, Finley, and I went along on the op to run the STAB and man the guns. The suspect was supposed to have from three to five bodyguards returning with him at first light.

This was a bad dude, and we wanted his ass. The STAB was

taken in about a klick upriver from the water taxi landing where the suspect was supposed to land. When we got to the insertion point, around 0515 hours, two of the other SEALs said they weren't feeling well. Deciding not to press the issue, Gallagher and I switched equipment with the two ill SEALs and went in on the op. Both Kochey and Fox were good operators, and neither Bob nor I had any reservations about operating with them.

Kochey knew I was the point man for Bravo Squad, so he turned to me and said, "Okay, Jim, you go ahead and take point." We had inserted west of the target after having come around the island the long way. Working our way along the riverbank, we soon came to where the water taxi landing was. Aerial photos of the area had showed several native huts in the target area. In fact, the building that the main action took place near was even printed as a black square on the topographical map we had.

The terrain was mostly just brush and palms. By taking care, we were able to move silently through the underbrush without anyone noticing our passing. Not a word was spoken—all messages were passed with the hand signals we all knew well. Coming close to the water taxi landing, we moved in toward the center of the island. We hadn't gone very far, only about thirty yards, when we came across a small drainage canal. The drainage canal, really an open sewer, was close to the target hooches. Moving along the canal, I found an opening with a small trail leading to three huts. The lair had been found. Now we just had to wait for Charlie.

To the east, my right, more native huts could be seen in the gathering light. Those other hooches were where the water taxi would be landing. Signaling Kochey to come up, I whispered into his ear what I had found. "That's what the intel told us," Kochey whispered. "This is where that fellow's coming to. You stay right here."

With that, we settled down to wait. Kochey put Ronnie to the east of me, Gallagher to the west, and he set down near Bob. I was the only one who had a clear view of the trail. The rest of the patrol was going to act on my go signal. The darkness gradually gave way to the dawn. We didn't have long to wait before company arrived.

Off in the direction of the river, we heard a chugga-chugga-chugga sound approaching. The water taxi had arrived. Then there was the confusing babble of a group of Vietnamese. In the rosy light of the tropical dawn, I could see a group of VC walking home from their evening's work, AK-47s slung across their backs.

Immediately, I gave the bad-guy signal, hand in front of the face, palm in, fingers spread. If there had been any question about the quality of our intelligence, it had been answered now. Those were some important VC, and they were not getting away. The AK-47 was in very short supply among the VC in 1967. Only the highest-ranking VCI, number one ichi ban, and their number one body-guards were seen with the weapon. The only greater giveaway was if the man had a sidearm. And now I could see four men in front of me, all of them carrying AK-47s!

Not twenty meters in front of me, they all went into a hut to-gether. But I was the only member of the team who saw them. I motioned to Ronnie and gave him the bad-guy signal and held up four fingers. Signaling to Kochey, I gave him the same message. There were four men who had gone into that hooch. Who was the number one dude and who were the bodyguards, I didn't know. Maybe they were all bodyguards. It didn't matter—it was time to go hunting.

This wasn't like earlier operations. It wasn't 0-dark-30 and we weren't shooting at muzzle flashes. I had four assholes directly in front of me with absolutely no question as to which side of the fence they were on. This was paydirt. For me, this was exactly the kind of thing we had been training for all these years. What should I do now?

They had gone into the hooch; I had to go and get them out. Capturing these guys was the preferred thing to do. It was so hard to get information from a corpse. If this VC was who they said he was, he could be a gold mine of information for intelligence. But I had to get him first.

Motioning to Ronnie to cover me, I signaled that I was going to move up. Placing my 12-gauge in the crook of my arm, I signaled for Gallagher to move up the far side of the hooch. There was now nothing else to do, and I moved out from the cover of the canal. My shotgun had five rounds in it, and I had an additional fifty rounds loose in my pockets. I went scooting up the trail toward the target, my heart hammering in my chest. I actually wasn't scared. This was why I had trained so long; my training just took over.

When I wasn't more than twelve meters away, the front door opened!

There was one of the VC. His hands were empty, but he had an AK slung across his back. We were eyeball to eyeball, and he froze in position.

I remembered Uncle Buck's advice, back when I was preparing to leave for Vietnam. "The first time you have to take a man out one-on-one, don't hesitate. It's not going to be easy. But after that first one, it's easy and just becomes part of your job. But I hope you don't hesitate."

Holding my shotgun on the man with one hand, I used my other hand to give him the signal to "lai dai"—"come here," in Vietnamese. Putting my hand out flat, I waved down toward the ground. The Vietnamese wave at each other differently than we do, but this was a signal he would understand. I didn't want to use my voice and alert the other guys in the hut. If this man cooperated, perhaps we could complete the mission without firing a shot.

The business end of a 12-gauge must look like a five-inch cannon when you're looking at it from the wrong side. I thought for sure that I had my man under control and he would do what I wanted. I was wrong.

Moving so fast that I couldn't really tell how he did it, the man in front of me bent forward, hunched his shoulders, and now had an AK-47 in his hands. As he swung the gun up toward me and fired his first shot, I let go with my shotgun. That's it, this prick isn't going to give up, I thought.

My first load of #4 buckshot smashed into the man's chest and flipped him over backward. *Clack-chunk*—I racked another round into the shotgun and moved forward. He was still moving! *Blam! Clack-chunk . . . blam! Clack-chunk . . . blam!* I was running toward the hut, shooting as I went.

As I fired my fourth round, my left hand went into my pocket and I started feeding rounds into my weapon. Men started pouring from all sides of the hut. Working the action without conscious thought, I ripped off another five rounds from my shotgun.

In the meantime, the first man I had fired on started crawling away. He still had his weapon in his hands and could open fire on me at any time. "Bob, they're headed your way!" I shouted as I turned my attention on that first man. It was obvious that he was terribly messed up, but he was still a danger. I didn't care what happened with the other three men. The rest of the squad would deal with them.

Time seemed to slow down to a crawl. All the time I was next to the hooch, I had been firing and reloading. Now the first man I had ever killed, which was how I saw it, was still moving. The situation had to be dealt with, and I was the only one there.

This was not an ambush. I had been the only one shooting except for that one round fired from the AK. It was one-on-one, a regular shoot-out. And I had come out on top.

I must have appeared like some demon from hell to those men, green-faced with camouflage makeup and armed with a weapon that roared horribly. The natives had taken to calling us "the men with green faces" and had given us almost unearthly powers. But that had not impressed that first man. He had tried to take out a "green face" and lost.

He was still moving, still crawling away with his weapon in his hands, when I came up to him. It was obvious that he was dying. I just kept pumping rounds into him. Shit was happening all around me. The hooch was being almost blown apart, and firing was going on where the other men had disappeared. But my whole concentration had centered on the man in front of me and what I had to do.

I still couldn't catch him. He was crawling, but I was also moving very slow. I had already seen one punji pit, and there had to be more. It had rained the night before, and the covers over the stake-lined pits had settled slightly. But where there are some booby traps, there can be others. There was no way I was going to run through this guy's backyard.

Then I found him. He had crawled behind a punji pit and was trying to get his weapon out. He must have known he was going, but he still wanted to take me with him. There was more buckshot than bone inside of his body and his arms wouldn't work anymore. Every shot I fired hadn't hit him, but those that had had done a terrible amount of damage. When I came up to him, I did what I had to do. There was no way he was going to surrender, even now. With a final blast, the fight was over.

Bending over the body, I started stripping his gear off. Fire was now coming at us from the other flank. Reaching into my pockets for more ammo, I found them empty. Without realizing it, I had fired all fifty rounds during the fight. With my shotgun empty, I needed another weapon. And there was one right close at hand. Bob Gallagher's training proved itself once again as I took the dead man's AK-47. The magazine in the weapon was dented from the buckshot, so I reached into the three-pocket ammunition vest on the man's chest and pulled out two loaded magazines. Shoving the magazines into my pockets, I moved out after the other hooch.

Everything was pretty much suppressed, and the fight was just about over. One of the men had a radio, I think it was Kochey, and he called in the STAB. It was now full daylight and we could see all around us.

As the STAB came in, Ronnie called up, "What do you want? The STAB's here."

"Bring me a can of gas," I hollered back. The name of the game was, if we found anything, burn the hooches. Let them know that the men with green faces had been there. And there wasn't much question that we had found something.

Up from the river came Finley carrying a can of gasoline. About the time he got up to me, Finely realized that he didn't have a weapon with him. He was not a happy camper. My 12-gauge was still slung across my back. "Here, use this," I said, and I thrust the shotgun out toward Finley. He didn't know it was empty, so he felt good—now he had a gun.

Moving up to the two hooches, I started spreading gasoline all over them. "All right," I hollered, "let's pull back." While I was talking, I was also pulling a Mark 13 day/night flare off of my rig.

When I thought I had moved a safe distance away, and all the other men were clear, I would use the Mark 13 to start the hooches burning. That was one of the real dumb things I have done. Thinking that I would toss the flare at the hooches, I pulled the firing ring igniting the night end of the Mark 13. I forgot that the wind was blowing in my direction.

Surrounded by fumes, I popped the flare.

Woommpp! My eyebrows were gone, my eyelashes were gone. I didn't have to shave for three days after that. All that shooting and I damn near set fire to myself. Now some of the other guys were starting to laugh.

The hooches were starting to burn, and I was going back to the

STAB. Picking up the man I had shot by his web gear, I started dragging the body back to the river. He was getting too heavy, so I just said fuck it. I already had his gear, so I just went through his pockets stuffing their contents into my pocket.

When I got back to the STAB, the adrenaline was starting to wear off. Reaction was setting in a little bit over what had just happened. But when I got to the boat, no Gallagher. Nobody had seen him for a few minutes. That man is like a brother to me. Boom, the adrenaline was back!

Running back to the hooches, I started screaming, "Bob! Bob!"

"I'm over here," came out of the jungle.

"Over where?" I shouted as relief started rushing through me.

"I'm playing pop goes the weasel with some asshole."

Bob was behind one dike and there was a VC across from him behind another dike. The two of them were playing World War I games peeking to see where the other one was.

"Goddammit," I shouted as relief started being replaced with anger, "throw a grenade at him!"

"Good idea!"

The next thing I heard was *kaboomf* as a grenade went off in the mud. The fight was now over. "I'm on my way!" shouted Bob.

Here came Gallagher trotting along. Bob had not seen anything that had gone on. He said later, "They were just pouring out of that hooch like ants, trying to get away from Jim and his damned shotgun."

Filling Bob in on what happened, I said excitedly, "The guy had an AK! Here it is."

"Where is he?" asked Bob.

"Back there," I answered, indicating where I had left the body.

"Let's go get him," said Bob. "He's got to be big-time." And he walked over to where the dead man was. We dragged the man down to the STAB. The AK I was holding was dented all over from my buckshot, but the weapon still worked. On the way back in the STAB, I took some time to look at the weapon and noticed something strange.

The safety/selector switch on an AK-47 goes into the full automatic position first and then all the way down for semiautomatic —the opposite of most Western weapons, which go into semiautomatic first. In his excitement to open fire on me, that VC had

pushed the selector all the way down into semiautomatic. That was why he had only got off a single shot at me. If the weapon had fired on full auto, he would have cut me in half, he was moving so quickly. Lives turn on such small mistakes.

We took the body back to the base, letting the villagers see what had happened. The VC would quickly learn. The easy times were over. The men with green faces were taking back the Delta. And now the villagers could plainly see that we could protect them. Even the most powerful VC in the area, as our target had been, couldn't hide from the green faces. The villages in our areas would not be terrorized by the VC or NVA.

Getting back to the base, we put the body up on the pier. The man was a mess. His arm and leg were obviously broken. The buckshot had torn terrible wounds in his body. But he had still tried to get me, even while I was killing him. Bob and Kochey immediately went over to intelligence to turn in the documents we had taken from the bodies and the hooches. Figuring that we had a good one that would lead us to something else, Kochey had looked into the hooches before we burned them. He had found a pouch of documents he had brought out with us.

Coming back to me, Kochey and Bob had these big grins on their faces. "Jim," they asked, "do you know who you got out there?"

"No," I answered. The guy had had an AK and that indicated he was important. But beyond that I had no idea.

"You took out an NVA Medal of Honor winner, buddy. His medal was in his pocket. And that package of documents you took out of his pocket—they identified him as the man who took out the *Jamaica Bay* last year. You took out a big one, bud. You took out one of us on their side."

"You have got to be shitting me," I said, stunned. The *Jamaica Bay* had been the third-largest dredge in the world. It had been sunk by NVA swimmers the year before. The event had made headlines around the world. This man actually had been the closest equivalent that the North Vietnamese had to the SEALs.

The guys were just bouncing around. "That's our Jimmy! That's Patches for you!" It was celebration time.

Later on, when I was going through the man's papers, I found a picture of a woman and a couple of kids. It hit me that the situation could very easily have gone the other way. A VC could be sitting

somewhere right now going through my things. Only I didn't carry a picture of my wife and kids when I went out on an op. The things that happened didn't really bother me. Uncle Buck was right—it just becomes part of the job. But it was then that I realized just what kind of hell war was. I really believe that if we had the chance to meet before the fight, if that man and I had just sat down over a beer, we might never shot at each other.

Other times, the war wasn't so bad. Things could be fun working with the Brown Water Navy people. Their layout at Dong Tam was interesting. There was a small inlet leading into the basin that sheltered the RAG—River Assault Group—force and the Brown Water Navy boats. Our docks were further down the river in a slightly more exposed location. That basin might have been secure, but it could sure be a bitch to find at night.

One night when we were coming back from an op with the Mike boat, nothing was going on and we were basically fucking off. A lot of jabbering suddenly started coming over the radio. About eight or ten RAG boats were lost in the river. They weren't in trouble, they just couldn't find the entrance to the Dong Tam basin.

The RAGs were calling the base asking for illumination rounds. Something was wrong at the artillery battery and it couldn't support the RAGs just then. Bob looked around and said, "Hell, we can illuminate them. Guys, break out a case of parachute flares."

The radar on the Mike boat had no problem showing us the mouth of the inlet. Opening a case of twenty-five hand-held rocket flares, we prepared to act as Bob's artillery battery. Getting on the radio, Bob started talking to the RAG boats. After identifying ourselves and giving them our call sign, Bob said, "Call your fire. We'll illuminate." There we were for a good twenty minutes popping off these rocket flares. The damned things would go up several hundred feet and eject a magnesium flare on the end of a parachute. Pop . . . woooosssssshhhh . . . *poof*, and in the wavering light of the flare we could see all these RAG boats running for home. They had been out there for hours looking for the inlet. We had a blast that night, firing cases of flares. That was the only time a SEAL squad acted as artillery support for an Army unit.

The intelligence we were given didn't always work out as well as it had at Toy Son. Sometimes we seemed to operate more on

hunches than on hard data. Rick came up with an op like that. To this day, Marcinko will not say exactly why we patrolled Ilo Ilo island when we did. He says there was intelligence on VC activities that guided our op. I still think Rick was running on a hunch.

The word we had was that the ARVNs (Army of the Republic of Vietnam troops) had swept Ilo Ilo some time before and hadn't found anything. We had a fairly low opinion of the competence of ARVN operations. Our intelligence was reporting a possible NVA field hospital on the island. The office after-action report on our operation lists intelligence reports of a medical training center on Ilo Ilo island. We expected to find something roughly in the middle of all the above reports.

Located at the mouth of the My Tho River, the island is not very big, maybe half a mile by a quarter mile at low tide. If there was something there, even the ARVNs should have found it. But Rick had this gut feeling. The place was so uninhabitable and unapproachable at low tide that putting a medical facility there made perfect tactical sense. Rick would listen to our advice and opinions. But when it came right down to it, he was the officer. Ilo Ilo, here we come.

From the aerial photos and maps of the island's layout, the easy way in was obvious. There was a canal running from the west end, the upriver side, almost to the center of the island. Working our way down the sides, or even the center of the canal, would put us through the hardest part of the island without any strain. But the longer we looked at the path, the easier it appeared. It finally just looked too easy.

The decision was to come in from the east, the hard way. We would have to cross five or six hundred yards of mud just to reach solid ground. Once we finally reached the land, we would cut across the island in a crisscross pattern, covering every foot of the place. The plan was to insert early in the morning, just before sunup. The highest point of land wouldn't be more than eighteen inches above water. This was going to be a soggy op.

Problems began almost as soon as we left the base. The Mike boat developed problems, and we didn't get to Ilo Ilo until after sunrise. We inserted from a STAB at 0600 hours on May 18, and the smaller boat grounded on the mud flats while it was still low tide.

Something had gone very wrong. Instead of high tide and dark, it was low tide and sunrise. We hadn't made it three quarters of the way to the beach when it was full daylight.

The mud flat was hundreds of yards wide, and it was a thin, gooey, grasping type of mud made up of silt from the river. You couldn't stand or swim in the stuff. The only way to cross the flat was to crawl slowly through it. With the sun up, there we were, crawling along like bugs in tar. We couldn't have been more exposed.

Back in training, during Hell Week, they had made us go through mud flats like this. We had learned that the best way through the mud was to lie on your back and push with your feet. That was how we crossed these flats. I wouldn't have believed that years later I would use that Hell Week training in a combat zone. Not like this.

Finally we reached the solid ground of the island. It wasn't much drier than the mud, but at least we could stand up. On a normal operation we lie still for half an hour to listen. This time we sat there and tried to clean ourselves and our weapons. I was carrying a CAR-15, because there was supposed to be open terrain on the island. In thick vegetation, I carried the shotgun for close-range work. But in the open, I wanted the extra range of the CAR.

Moving inland a short way, we found a canal where we could wash ourselves and our weapons off a little. We stripped down the guns and even the magazines. Finally everything was finally squared away enough for us to start the operation. Now it was time to move inland.

Now was also the time to start paying the price of being a point man. Stress! The word is used so much today that it almost loses its meaning. But for the man on point, stress keeps you sharp, and that helps keep you alive. The sense of danger throws all of the body's systems into high gear. Adrenaline pours into the bloodstream, the heart rate goes up, muscles tense for fast action. The animal that you live in screams *do something!*

But the brain says no! Instead of running or fighting, the things your body wants to do, you concentrate on the job at hand. The steel-hard discipline and will that is forged into SEALs during training comes out. You will concentrate on what you have to do. The lives of your teammates could depend on it.

Slowly, deliberately, you go forward. Every movement is a

trained response, thought out well beforehand. The body is still running at top speed. Calories disappear as stored fat and even tissue is ripped apart for energy. Sweat runs off you as if you were in a shower, literally pouring off you as the body tries to cool itself down. More water is consumed inside of you as the body's functions stay in high gear. Damn but you can get tired and thirsty on point!

It was one of those hot, muggy days that the tropics are famous for. Just crisscrossing over the island, we covered every type of terrain Vietnam had to offer except mountains. There were canals, streams, banks, swamps, and flats. But mostly mangrove thickets where you couldn't see two feet in front of you. Joe Camp and I had been trading off point all morning long. The heat and strain of running point would drain each of us in just a short time. When the mangrove was at its thickest, we thought we were in the center of the island. It was time for a break.

I had been up front, and Joe reached up and tapped me on the shoulder to signal take he would take point. We had been on Rick's ass all day about the op. After long hours of searching, we all were tired and nasty. There wasn't any talking in the squad. But during a break, we would whisper to each other mouth to ear. There were no footprints on the trail, not a sign of life. This island, and the op, sucked. "Do you have any intel that there's something here?" we would ask Rick. "Just call the fucking Mike boat and let's get the hell out of here."

"Don't worry about it, just do your job," he would answer.

The last break was taken about two o'clock in the afternoon. I was tired, and so were the rest of the squad. Finally, I'd just had enough and voiced the opinion we all had. "This is a typical Lieutenant PT goatfuck! Somebody's got his head up his ass. There is no intel. This is just a hit-or-miss operation, and it sucks. I am fucking wrung out and ragged."

"That's the way you feel about it, Jim?" Rick asked.

"Yeah, that's the way I feel about it," I answered.

After resting a moment, Joe moved out on point. He hadn't moved four steps when he turned around with the danger sign, a spread hand across the face. Right out loud I said, "You have got to be shitting me!"

Joe was frantically signaling silence and danger. It was then that I realized what I had done. Boy! I must have been tired. I've done a lot of stupid things, but talking out loud on a patrol was one of the dumbest things I have ever done.

I moved up alongside of Joe, and he pointed out to me what he saw. In front of us was a small canal. Across from it was a little boheo, maybe four or five feet square and elevated two feet into the air. Since the VC used them to sleep under and to store supplies, there was no question now that the area was in active use by the Viet Cong. Packages of supplies could be plainly seen piled on the boheo's platform.

All kinds of goodies were in that boheo, and we wanted to know where the owners were. Motioning to each other to scan one direction and then the other, we visually searched the area. Joe and I stayed there fifteen or twenty minutes, just quietly watching the area. Motioning up Rick, we pointed out what we had found. The rest of the squad didn't have the vaguest idea what was going on. All they had seen was the bad-guy signal that was relayed back.

Bringing the squad up, we formed a skirmish line. Crossing the canal, we reached the boheo and set up a perimeter. Searching the boheo was not my job. I took up a position near the canal on the west side to see if anything came in that way. Gallagher did the same thing on the other side. Fred Kochey, who had come with us, and Marcinko both had empty rucksacks with them. Kneeling down at the boheo, Kochey and Rick started stuffing the materials into their rucks.

All the gear was medical supplies. There was even a logbook. Later on we found out that the book listed what a man had taken, when, and who he was. Talk about an intelligence find. That book listed known VC and even gave us an idea how effective actions had been against them. The majority of the supplies were either French or had the crossed helping hands of U.S. aid.

Calling out on the radio, Rick said we had hit pay dirt. The Mike boat was to stand by on the west end of the island. We would take the canal route out, the route we would have used for the easy way into the island. Taking point, I led the way down the canal.

We hadn't moved fifty meters before I heard noises and smelled smoke. Turning around, I pointed to my ear—"I hear something"—and to my nose—"I smell something." Then I gave them the danger

sign. All simple signals worked out long ago at Pickett. Joe came up and whispered that he smelled smoke too. Telling Joe what I was going to do, I moved out to check on what I had heard.

Signaling Gallagher to join him, Joe explained what was going on. Since Rick and Kochey were loaded down with stuff, Gallagher was moving around the squad. Going down the canal, I saw a clearing off to the side. Looking over the bank, I could see two good-sized boheos that men could sleep in. Sitting around a fire were six men eating rice and talking. Weapons were stacked against one of the boheos nearby. We've got a turkey shoot, I thought.

I had been crouching low in the murky water of the canal, barely looking over the top of the eighteen-inch mud bank. Thirty meters away, the VC ate their rice, not one of them suspecting I was there. Silent as death, I slipped away through the dark waters, back to my squad.

We considered our next step. Bob would move us up in a skirmish line, just below the rim of the bank. Kochey and Rick would keep rear security, since they had all the confiscated material. Bob was calling the shots, and we moved on his order. I was on one flank and Bob was on the other. Bob would count to three, and on three, we'd fire. Each man would empty two magazines. Bob and I would go through one magazine, then throw a grenade. One . . . two . . . three, Happy New Year.

I ripped off a long burst through my CAR, covering my field of fire. Then I hit the magazine release and grabbed a frag grenade. Taking an instant to look at Bob, I could see he was ready with his grenade. I shouted "Grenade!" and threw mine to the left. Bob threw his to the right.

Nobody was sure whose grenade hit the tree. Some say it was Bob's; I think it could have been mine. In any event, one of our frags hit a tree and bounced right back at us, landing in the canal. These weren't old-fashioned Mark II pineapples. They were modern M26A1s lined with notched wire. All of our eyes were huge, watching that grenade bounce back at us. We smacked our faces down and ate mud. The frag detonated harmlessly in the canal. Feeling the thud of the explosion, we all jumped up out of the canal and charged the boheo.

Five dead VC were lying around, and one was breaking the land speed record running away. No matter how carefully you planned an ambush, one person always seemed to get away. We shot at him, but missed. Running up to the bodies, I saw one of them moving toward a weapon. Having reloaded my CAR, I used it to finish the job. One of the squad grabbed me when he saw me fire. "Is he dead, Jim?"

"He is now," I answered.

Policing up all the weapons and equipment, we quickly searched the area. The weapons consisted of AK-47s and bolt-action Mausers, a good haul. Ronnie Rodger found some odd "snowshoes," bamboo frames holding woven strips of inner tubes. They were mud shoes, and that was how the VC crossed the mud flats surrounding Ilo Ilo. Before leaving the site, we did a little stunt the VC had shown us. We pulled the pins on some grenades and slipped them under the dead bodies. The weight of the body held down the spoon of the grenade. As soon as someone tried to move the body . . . boom!

A couple of sampans were in the canal, and we threw the gear into one. Now it was definitely time to get out of Dodge. "Okay," Rick said, "let's get back in the canal and move out as quick as we can. Jim and Bob, stay back and cover the rear."

Joe Camp was on point, and the squad pulled out. Kochey and Rick were pushing the gear-laden sampan. At least, they pushed it until Kochey decided he was going to ride in it. He settled his big American ass in the VC sampan and promptly sank it. Raising the sampan from the bottom of the canal, we poured the water from it and continued on our way.

Following the canal out, we passed under overhanging trees. A deadly fruit was in those particular trees. While moving along, we could see grenades hanging from limbs. Lines ran from the grenades to the shore. Lines were attached to the grenades' pull rings with the ends leading back to the boheos. If we had followed the easy way in, all that Charlie would have had to do was pull the lines and they would have probably gotten us all. Those grenades weren't six feet over our heads, a perfect height for an airburst.

Now we started to hear gunfire behind us. Nothing was whistling past, but we had overstayed our welcome. The one guy who had gotten away must have found some friends. Gallagher took a moment and took down one of the grenades. Since Bob was qual-

ified in EOD (Explosive Ordnance Disposal), he wanted one to examine.

The Mike boat was on the radio, asking if we wanted covering mortar fire. We did, but since we weren't sure of our location, we told the Mike boat to hold her fire. Then we came out of the canal into the open water. The goddam tide was out again. We had been on the island all day. The Mike boat was way out in the water, and the STAB couldn't get closer than about three hundred yards. Fire started coming at us from the island. Only now we were out in the open!

We called out to the Mike boat and had her put fire onto the island. Now it was time to play mud flats again. While the Mike boat put out 81mm mortar fire, we crawled out through the mud. The 81mm Mark 2 mortar on the Mike boat is a direct-fire weapon. The mortar can be lowered and fired like a cannon. Apparently, the Mike's crew could see the VC on the island, because they were direct-firing the 81. We were sure of that because of our visitor.

As we crawled along the mud as fast as we could, suddenly an 81mm HE round came skipping along the mud right past us. Like a flat rock over water, that mortar round skipped off the mud every few yards. The pucker factor went up real high. Somebody must have been on our side that day, because that round didn't detonate until it hit the island.

When we finally reached the STAB, we looked like a bunch of Hell Week rejects. But we had hung on to our captured material, even the sampan. It had been a successful op.

Now we had some free time on our hands, and there was a party overdue. "Bring all the money you've got and borrow what you can. Jim's made chief and it's time to party." That was a general order the squad had no problem obeying.

I had not only made chief petty officer in the Navy, but I had done it in one of the finest units in the world. The fact that I wasn't sure that I would be going home to buy the uniform tempered things a bit, but not much. Gallagher had gotten me a set of collar devices that I could wear on my fatigues. Then it was off to Dong Tam, where they had a bar that served whiskey. Some of the Boat Support people were with us, and we were having a great time.

Then someone leaned into the bar and shouted "Hey! The last bus is leaving." It was about four miles to the first checkpoint to get into My Tho. One of the Boat Support guys and I said, "The hell with the bus—we're partying." He thought it was all right and wanted to keep drinking with us. As long as you're buying, everybody's your friend. But the Boat Support people were a great bunch of guys themselves.

It was getting to be around ten o'clock, and they were closing the bar. There wasn't any place to stay in Dong Tam, so we walked back to My Tho. It was only four miles. When we went drinking in what was considered a secure area, we didn't carry weapons. So we were unarmed.

On the walk back to My Tho, our situation started to set in. The farther we walked, the more sober we became. The more sober we became, the more we realized just what we had done and the more scared we became. "Chief," the young BSU guy said, "I'm not in as good shape as you're in. But if you'd like to jog, I can stay with you. If you want to run, I'll bet I can stay with you."

"Doesn't sound like a bad idea," I said. Now we were in Charlie's backyard. We also knew where our security forces normally set up the roadblock. It was across a little bridge near town. Getting to that bridge soon seemed like a great idea. So we started jogging, and the more we jogged, the more sober we became. The more sober we became, the more we thought about our situation and the faster we jogged. By this time I was thinking, Holy shit! You dumb asshole. I was calling myself everything but smart.

Now we could see the roadblock up ahead. The guard was made up of White Mice, the Vietnamese police. Sprinting was now the order of the day. As we came close to the roadblock, both of us were at a dead run. Those Vietnamese police had never seen Olympic runners do the high hurdle before. They had now. But we cleared that roadblock and kept going all the way to the villa.

That wasn't the only time we had a little problem while in town. But it was the last time we were caught out without a weapon. Downtown My Tho was fairly secure, but we carried weapons there when we went into town. Buckling on a Smith & Wesson in a hip holster didn't take any time, and the weight of that revolver felt good on the street.

There was a little joint down near the river where we could sit out and watch the people. While we were doing that one day, VNs looking at us and smiling, Bob Gallagher made an observation that summed up the difficulties of the Vietnam War. While drinking our Bammebah beer over ice, Bob leaned over and said to me, "Jimmy, you know these guys are the ones we're shooting at when we go out on an op." Some of these guys we would sit and drink beer with. They'd look at us and we'd look at them, and we both knew the situation. Certain nights when we would be outside the city limits, we'd be shooting at each other. They were the bad guys, come into town for some relaxation at the saloon.

Not all of our operations were run out of My Tho. The word came down from Jake for the entire platoon to go to Long An for some operations. The platoon from Can Tho was going to be there, as well as a West Coast platoon from Team One.

Along with other operations, we ran one three-man op out of Long An with Rodger, Finley, and me as the team. They put us on the point of a small island where intelligence had said we would pick up data on VC crossings. What was going to happen was that a VC would come out of his hooch and wave his lantern. The way he moved the lantern would signal the local VC if the way was clear or not. If the way was clear, the VC would make a river crossing.

Snatching this guy would tell us a lot, and we wanted him. We settled in at the water's edge, between two paths leading down to the water. To cover all the area, we sat in a triangle back to back. I was facing west, Rodger southeast, and Finley north. Sunken down in the mud, our bodies were exposed only from the chest up.

We crouched like that for hours, and the night dragged on. Then I felt a nudge from Finley. "What's the matter?" I asked. "Did you see something?"

"Naw. But if that guy comes out and waves that lantern again, what am I supposed to do?"

"*You have got to be shitting me!*" I said a little more loudly than a whisper. "What?"

"Yeah—the guy came out and waved the lantern, then went back in his hooch."

"Goddammit. That's what we're here for. If we had snatched the guy or blown his legs out from under him, we could've called in a PBR. We could've been home by now."

Instead, we sat there all night. Just before dawn, a PBR came in to get us. The trip back was so long, we ended up transferring PBRs three times.

By now the platoon was getting a little "short"—coming close to the time when we would be heading back to the States. One SEAL platoon was going to go home a little early and the other was going to head back a little late. The reason was that Team Two had only one relief platoon available to come over to Vietnam right away. Second Platoon won the draw, and we were heading home.

A C-130 was taking us across the big pond. This was going to be a more comfortable trip, since we were leaving the STABs behind for the other platoons. It was just us and our personal gear—plus about every kind of souvenir that hadn't been nailed down. No one was going to check our gear, and customs wouldn't look in our bags much. Besides, the worst thing we might bring in would be too much booze. Nobody, and I mean *nobody*, in the Teams would even consider bringing back some of the stuff that SEALs have been accused of carrying. Besides, everything we brought back was Team equipment, confiscated or otherwise. Even my AK-47 was the property of the Team, but they presented it to me later in Little Creek.

When the plane arrived in Japan, we had a little while to move around. Gallagher took me down to the Navy Exchange and bought me my first regulation Navy chief's hat. Now I had the right hat to go home in.

On the main flight home, somewhere over the Pacific, the C-130 lost one of her engines. It wasn't that the engine fell off, it just stopped working. After a safe landing on Guam, the pilot managed to convince us that he could get the plane home the way it was. We made the flight back without being too nervous, thanks to a little help from our medic, Leg Martin.

Pilots are a funny lot. Some of them drink like fishes but won't allow alcohol on their planes. But Leg Martin had a way of supplying us with what we wanted. On the landings, we'd pick up grapefruit and oranges from the local vendors or even the mess hall. Leg would use his syringe and pump the fruit full of vodka. No problem with open booze now, and besides, it prevented scurvy.

When we finally reached the North Island Naval Air Station near Coronado, the whole platoon was tired. The civilian plane that would take us back to Little Creek was going to show up in a few days, so there was time to kill with Team One. The war stories were flying thick and fast at the chief's club. We were regular heroes—we'd been to war and seen the elephant.

Climbing aboard a National flight, we flew to Little Creek, more than a little hungover. When we arrived at the Creek we looked like anything but returning warriors. Bob, Finley, and I were just walking down the ladder in civilian clothes. I had a guitar in my hands. With our deep tans, we looked like a bunch of guys just coming in from California. Which we were, but we had sure taken the long way around between flights.

It wasn't long before our new combat experience was put to practical use. Rick and I worked on an R&D program for new materials. We now knew what some of the problems were with SEAL operations in Vietnam. And we had some ideas for solving them.

The inflatable UDT lifejacket had proved just too small to support a fully equipped SEAL. With the help of the Switlik Parachute Company, we developed a vest that would keep a man afloat and carry a load of ammunition as well. I tested the first vest myself in a swimming pool, and it worked well. After the first thirty prototypes were made and went to Vietnam, the Navy modified the design and it was produced for the SEALs. The buoyant ammunition-carrying coat was made for riflemen, grenadiers armed with a 40mm weapon, and radiomen. It was well received by the SEALs and was one of our first big R&D successes.

At China Lake, California, the engineers asked me about my thoughts on the M79 grenade launcher. "A nice weapon," I said, "but it would be better if it held more shells. Couldn't there be some way you could make it a repeater?" As I said that, I was making a pumping action with my two hands.

Only a few weeks later, when I was back at China Lake, the engineers handed me an answer. It was a five-round pump-action 40mm grenade launcher. Only a handful of the weapons were produced for the SEALs in Vietnam.

Other weapons were investigated. While at China Lake I fired the first .50 caliber sniper rifles developed for the SEALs. Today, these weapons give the SEAL snipers the ability to take out targets at up to two thousand meters. Colt made the CMG-1 machine gun for us to test. Frankfort Arsenal gave Rick and me the opportunity to fire the first small Ingram submachine gun. "Nice weapon," we said, "but it needs a front strap to give you something to hold on to."

New silencers for the M16 rifle. Special adaptors for our shotguns to give them a wider shot spread and larger magazine capacity. Liquid explosives, subsonic M16 ammunition, improvements on the Stoner, miniature blasting caps and primacord—all were supplied to us, used by us, or tested by us. Aberdeen Proving Grounds, Frankfort Arsenal, China Lake, Colt, Smith & Wesson, Dupont Powder Company, and other manufacturers were contacted by the SEALs for new ideas and equipment.

Training was constantly improved on. Now there was a definite purpose to much of our training and material development. Vietnam was taking up more and more of the SEALs' concentration.

CHAPTER 9

Welcome Back to Vietnam

Refresher training was the order of the day in November. I was going to be the platoon chief for Sixth Platoon and we were going to Nam in December. In early November it was Course G-2G-64, Introduction to Supporting Arms, at the Naval Amphibious School. Welcome back to Gunfire Support. The entire platoon attended the course. For the new guys, it was their introduction to calling in artillery, naval gunfire, and air support. For the old guys, like me, it was refresher training to make sure we hadn't forgotten anything and learned the new wrinkles that had been developed in the last year.

It quickly became a game with us. Bets were made as to who could get on target fastest, call in the support best, problems like that. Time on the big target board was limited, so preference was given to the new guys in the class. After an older man had shown he remembered how to do everything, his place was turned over to one of the new guys.

There was a Marine major who taught the air support end of the course. The man had a very practical way of ending the training. "All right, gentlemen," he would say, "you have now learned all the proper procedures, nomenclature, targeting, and effects. All that is well and good, but remember, if you get in trouble out there, we speak English. So do you. Just tell us what you see and where it is. We'll take it from there. You don't have to ask for 'one round white phosphorus' or 'fuze super-quick.' We know what we have and what it does better than you do. Just tell us what the target is and where you see it. We'll take care of it."

Predeployment training was following a regular outline now. After the Gunfire Support course, the platoon went down to Camp Pickett for weapons training. At Pickett the platoon worked on ambushes, popup target courses, weapons familiarization, and zeroing in weapons. Each man would take his own M16 and zero the sights on the thousand-inch range.

Carefully sandbagging his weapon, the firer would adjust his sights until he held a good three-shot group exactly an inch below his point of aim at one thousand inches. For an M16, that would put the bullet's point of impact on the point of aim at 250 yards. After a man had zeroed his weapon's sights, that weapon would be assigned to him by serial number for his tour incountry.

For myself, I was going to carry an early-model CAR-15 this tour as one of my primary weapons. The firing procedures were the same, and I lay down with my platoon to zero my CAR on the thousand-inch range.

The early-model CAR-15, the Colt Model 07, had a hard sliding stock rather than the tubular stock on the later XM-177 model. With the stock slid in, the weapon was only 26 inches long, as compared to 38.6 inches for the M16. During my three tours of duty in Vietnam, I don't think I extended the stock and fired the CAR from my shoulder once. Instinctive firing from the hip or under the arm tended to be the rule for a point man. But I still zeroed my weapon right along with the other members of my platoon.

Things at Pickett went very smoothly during training. Now I had experience in Vietnam and had some idea of what to expect. Instead of going in cold, as we did that first tour, Team Two now had a solid cadre of combat veterans who were constantly improving the training. My mistakes and experiences were being taught to the new guys to give them an edge.

When the platoon had been forming up in late October, I had a lot of input as to who would make up the platoons when it deployed. As the platoon chief, I had very close to the final word on who would go with us. Out of the fourteen men in Sixth Platoon, only about four of them had already been to Vietnam once. The two officers, Mr. Williamson and Mr. Thames, were brand-new to the Teams and had very little experience with how the SEALs did things.

Both the officers were good men. As officers, they had to take the brunt of the responsibility for the platoon. After we had arrived in Vietnam, they learned what was expected of them and how to operate. Both were young, but Thames really looked like a kid—he had one of those very youthful faces. And there I was, over thirty, a hardened chief raised under Gallagher.

We had a meeting with the skipper soon after the platoon was formed up. Since the two officers were new to the Team, Lieutenant Commander Lyon wanted to give them some special guidance. "Both of you are new to the Teams. This chief has been here since the day the Team started. He has one tour under his belt already as a leading petty officer, and he made chief while he was over there. He is seasoned. If you want to do a good job and come back alive, listen to him. If you want to be bullheaded, do it your own way. I would listen to what he has to say."

The new officers hadn't spent any time in the fleet, so they didn't know the byword of the Navy: When you have a problem, ask the chief. After getting the backing of the skipper, we went outside for a break. Now looked like a good time to have a little fun at Thames's expense.

Lieutenant Pat Patterson, Louie, and a couple of others were standing outside when I started in on Thames. Turning to Thames, I said, "Mr. Thames, you're my ticket to the one they hang around your neck"—meaning the Medal of Honor.

"What do you mean, Chief?" asked Thames, puzzled.

"When you get shot," I said, "I'll carry you out. They'll give a chief the Medal of Honor in a minute for carrying out a wounded officer."

Thames was just staring at me by now with a real serious look coming over his face. "Well, Chief, what if we get to the end of the tour and I haven't been shot yet? Are you going to shoot me?"

Pat had been leaning against the building with a cigarette in his hand, just listening in. Now he spoke up. "Tell you what, son," Pat said. "If you screw up he will."

Thames never did go into the field with me. He was a little guy—I wouldn't have had much trouble carrying him. Williamson would have been a bit too big. But I had just been joking. A few years later, Mike Thornton actually did carry out his wounded officer and they gave him the Medal of Honor for it.

After finishing training at Pickett, the platoon moved on to the Black River and the Union Camp site. Among all the work at Union Camp, we found some time for fun. Bob Gallagher was back from Nam and took over as training platoon chief. Bob never passed up a chance to stick it to me. "Come on, Watson," Bob would say, "you're the big seasoned chief now. This training can't be that hard for you. After all, you're going back for your second tour now." But Bob meant the best for me, as he did for all the men he trained.

On December 9, Sixth Platoon left Little Creek for Coronado. After a few days on the West Coast, it was off for Vietnam. The platoon was made up as follows:

Alfa Squad

LT Bruce S. Williamson
BM2 Michael W. McQuillis
SFNP2 Joseph M. Silva
RM2 John W. Rowell
AE2 Charles W. Fellers
SN David E. Rutherford

Bravo Squad

LTJG James F. Thames
QMC James D. Watson
HM1 Larry S. Johnston
SN Slaytor C. Blackiston
FN Ronnie E. Rodger
ED2 Clayton Sweesy
EM3 David Hyde

The platoon was given eleven enlisted men instead of the normal ten so that without shorting one of the squads we could supply an adviser to the South Vietnamese PRUs (Provincial Reconnaissance Units) or LDNNs (SEAL-like troops).

The platoon was going in to Tan Son Nhut to relieve Rick Woolard's platoon in Nha Be. Things had changed now in Coronado and
Team One. Our training had been completely accepted, and most
of the platoon's time in Coronado was spent processing paperwork.

This time the flight over wasn't going to be on a C-130—we
would be on a Super Constellation. The big, broad-tailed Constellation would be a more comfortable ride than a C-130. The pilot
came down and met us, laying down the rules first thing. "Chief,"
the pilot said, "since this is a Navy aircraft, the regulations will be
followed. There will be no alcohol aboard my aircraft. Do I make
myself clear, Chief?"

"Yes sir," I answered. After the pilot had left, I grabbed Doc
Johnson, my platoon's corpsman.

"Doc," I said, "get all the grapefruit and oranges you can. You
know what to do with them."

Doc pumped up the fruit and we were shit-faced after only a
couple of hours in the air. I don't think that pilot ever did figure out
how we did it. But this was our last fling.

We landed at Tan Son Nhut International Airport just northwest of Saigon at 1000 hours on December 17. Within three hours
we had arrived at Nha Be on the shores of the Soi Rap River. Nha
Be looks down at the Rung Sat Special Zone (RSSZ) roughly from
its northwest corner.

Soon after arriving at Nha Be, I met with the chief of the base.
After getting a briefing on the local situation, I got the platoon
together and laid out the information.

"Now look," I said. "This is the name of the game now. At 0-dark-
30, the gates close and the sandbags go up. We all have to be on the
base except for those men on a mission. This isn't back at the
Creek. Things are real here, and a serious fuckup will get you
killed. Here's the places you can go downtown."

Downtown Nha Be was not exactly like San Diego. Nha Be was
an average-sized village just on the edge of the Rung Sat. It was the
first major town you would pass after getting by the Rung Sat on
your way from the South China Sea to Saigon. The Rung Sat had
been a pirates' and smugglers' haven for centuries before the Viet
Cong came onto the scene. Bordered by the Soi Rap River to the
south and the Long Tau River to the north, the Rung Sat is thirty
by thirty-five kilometers in area—over a thousand square kilome-

ters. It includes mangrove swamp, nipa palm, and jungle. Among all those plants are scorpions, spiders, snakes, crocodiles, jungle cats, and VC.

We were on the outskirts of an unpleasant neighborhood. But our little portion of the world wasn't too bad. Just outside the base gate was the local PRU compound with a Marine Advisory building nearby. A small restaurant was outside the base, and I was soon taking most of my meals there. The dirt road leading toward Saigon was lined with little shacks and storefronts. Several small bars, a couple of whorehouses, and Nha's Laundry were all close to the base along that road.

After giving the men the layout of the area, I told them which were the best places for what. "But remember," I repeated, "you've got to be back at dark. Let your conscience be your guide." With that, liberty went down and we all headed into town.

The whole platoon, less the officers, ended up in the same bar just a short while later. Thames and Williamson just did not mingle with the troops, and they were off somewhere on adventures of their own.

Before we ended up at the bar, I met with the local PRU adviser. This guy wasn't SEALs, Marines, or Army. I didn't know what he was. He liked playing the Agency game. Some guys, no matter what they actually were, wouldn't admit their military connection when they were assigned to work with the Agency on the Phoenix program. "Oh, I work for the Agency. My name is Smith and I'm a plumber." Fuck you, Charlie.

Bob Gallagher, myself, and a few others had made a joke about these guys all being plumbers. A more phony bunch of bastards you couldn't find. And the more they played the Agency game, the less they accomplished.

The bar was a good break from this particular jerk. It looked like I was going to pick up the PRU slot, and that made me feel pretty good. So the time went by fast in the bar. Being from the old school, I knew the rule about being back on the base, but rules were meant to be broken. Just don't get caught. Most of the platoon and I spent all night at that little bar.

That was one of the dumber things I did that tour. None of us were armed. After that first night, whenever you thought you might spend some time out, you carried a sidearm. But that first night, we got away with it. Or at least most of us did.

The next day, the base chief brought me in two of my own men. These two kids, Blackiston and another man, had gotten caught outside the base after curfew. I was in my little office in our barracks, just across from our ready room. When the chief handed me these two guys, I just chewed their asses up one side and down the other. "Thank you very much, Chief, for bringing this matter to my attention," I said. "I'm glad you saw there was no need to bother the base commander. We handle our own problems. Right, Chief?"

"Right," he answered. And with that, the chief left. Now I really set into my two lost children. I gave them some half-assed extra duty, cleaning weapons, stuff like that, and I restricted them to the base for a few days. "But, Chief," they complained, "you were out along with us."

"Yes," I answered, "but you got caught. Now, I don't want to hear any more shit. What you do is one thing. What you get caught at is another. You two fucked up—you got caught."

The kids respected me for that, because I used the same rule on myself. I call them kids, but as soon as the shooting started, they grew up in a big hurry.

After those two left, into my office came a guy who was working for the Agency. I knew the man was a Marine. He wanted to know if I would be interested in taking over the local PRU adviser slot. Just outside of the gate were 150 PRUs without active leadership. I had already received training in the administrative end in dealing with PRUs, so I jumped at the chance.

The Provincial Reconnaissance Units were groups of Vietnamese, Humong (montagnards) from the mountains, Chinese, even Viet Cong and NVA deserters. The units would act as native troops under Agency-controlled guidance. PRU targets were high-ranking VC, members of the infrastructure or leadership of the Viet Cong. The VCI were captured whenever possible to give us more information for further missions. As the PRU operations became more successful, rumors started to surface back in the States about "assassination squads."

The problem was that the Agency paid the PRU men more for a corpse than for a prisoner. That was a mistake held over from the early days of the war. No matter how hard Bob Gallagher and I tried, we just couldn't change the Agency's attitude.

What I liked about the PRUs was the action they saw and the results they came up with. Now my Agency friend took me to meet the PRU chief and a couple of the squad leaders. Along with the leaders, I met my interpreters. One of the interpreters, George, was a real piece of work. To hear this man talk, you'd swear he was from Brooklyn. Apparently, George had been taught English by a native of that well-known borough of New York.

The situation was laid out for me, and I accepted. But there was something else I wanted. The Agency issued 9mm Browning High-Power automatics to their men, and I wanted one. In the Team, you couldn't get a Browning unless you bought your own, and now this man was willing to issue me one. A nice pistol, it holds thirteen shots, letting you be obnoxious longer between reloadings.

The average guy would only count up to eight shots from a pistol. Then he would think you had to reload. Surprise—with a Browning, you had five more shots ready, something I like in a pistol.

Rick Woolard had stayed behind when his platoon returned to the States. Rick would remain to break in the new platoon to the area, introducing them to the people around the TOC (Tactical Operations Center) and the district advisers, making sure the new people had the lay of the land before he left. Since we were the new people, I thought this policy of Rick's was just fine, and he did it every tour he had.

Before we arrived at Nha Be, the base officers' club had been closed for renovation. The chiefs had told the officers that they could use the chiefs' club until their own was completed. This was a courtesy that isn't always seen in the Navy.

Within a week of Sixth Platoon's arrival at Nha Be, the new officers' club was finished. The skipper of the base told all his officers to invite their chiefs to the new club. And while the chiefs were in the club, they couldn't spend any money. It was payback time, and they did it in a nice way.

Woolard invited me. Thames and Williamson were there, a couple of PBR officers, a Seawolf pilot, and a couple of Seawolf chiefs. All of us were sitting around a single table passing around a Mateuse wine bottle. This was a nice relaxed evening with no rank getting in the way.

While we were sitting there, this big bosun's mate master chief came over. This guy was the master chief of the base and was known for being a pushy loudmouth. Poking Rick Woolard in the shoulder, he growled, "You one of those loudmouth SEALs, aren't you, Lieutenant?"

Rick isn't a tall man, only about five-eight or so, but he's a tiger in a fight. But this was the officers' club and Rick shouldn't make any trouble in it. Standing up from where I had been sitting next to Rick, I moved between Rick and this big master chief.

"Chief," I said, "You're a little out of line. Number one, we're guests in this club and you're making the chiefs look bad. Number two, I'm certain that if you stepped outside and took your anchors off, Mr. Woolard would be glad to accommodate you and take his bars off. But I'll tell you right now. That would be the second mistake you've made this evening. That lieutenant will turn you every way but loose. The first mistake was when you came over to this table and started shooting off your mouth."

"Oh, you're one of those loudmouthed SEALs too, aren't you?" And the guy came up to me.

Now the master chief was on my left side, and Mr. Woolard was sitting down on my right side. Looking up at this big chief, I just knew he wasn't going to back down. "Excuse me," I said and I turned away and bent over to talk to Rick.

Rick could see that I had closed my fist and was reaching down to the floor with it. "Hey, Boss, this is the officers' club and I'm your guest. I request permission to—"

Woolard never even let me finish: "Permission granted, Chief."

The only way I was going to take this big guy out was to sucker-punch him one real good one. Swinging up from the floor with my fist, I nailed that loudmouthed chief right square in the teeth.

The chief flew backward over two tables and crashed down on the floor. While he was lying there groaning, the XO of the base came running over to me.

"I'm sorry, Chief, but I'm going to have to ask you to leave."

"I know, sir, and I understand. I apologize for causing trouble in your club. But no one bad-mouths one of my officers."

Woolard was starting to get up from his seat, but I stopped him. "No sir," I said. "You stay here and enjoy yourself."

That big chief was starting to sit up by now and was looking about groggily. "Hey, Chief," I called out. "When you sober up, I'll take you on one-on-one anyplace you choose." But I was sure hoping that big sonofabitch wouldn't take me up on my offer.

Once I was outside, the XO came out and put his hand out to me. "The Navy needs more chiefs like you. I hope you understand. I would love to have you come back inside, but I can't."

"I understand, sir, and thank you."

The next day, I was going into the chiefs' club when a Marine gunny sergeant I knew shouted out at me "Hey, Jimbo! It had to be you. I heard what happened last night. You're the only one who would have balls enough to hit that loudmouthed sonofabitch."

The whole base knew about the incident real fast. That chief walked around for a week with his face all screwed up. The punch must have just landed right—I've never done that much damage before. And it must have really impressed that master chief, because he never did take me up on my offer of a fair fight, thank God.

Now it was time to start running ops with the platoon and the PRUs. When I didn't have my PRU running ops, I would have my platoon in the field. With the quality intelligence that started to come in to us, we had Charlie running almost from the start.

Our Agency contact was giving us top-notch intelligence from his agent net. A report would come in from a native agent that a VC finance chief, along with two bodyguards, would be coming down a specific canal on such-and-such a day at such-and-such a time. Most VC travel was done at night, but some of the VC had the balls to travel during the day. Disguised as fishermen, the VCI members would be very hard to pick out from the general population. But there were times the intelligence would be detailed enough for us to pull a daylight op and nail some of these gutsy bastards.

Using the intel report, such as on the finance chief, the platoon would go out on an op. Setting up an ambush on the indicated canal, my men would turn up the proper target close to 75 percent of the time. Most of my operational intel came from my Agency man, and I quickly came to trust his information.

Keeping my men operating well was my primary concern. If

the men stayed on the base more than three or four days at a stretch, they started to get rusty. But putting them out on a number of back-to-back operations where they didn't hit anything was even worse. If they kept pulling dry ops, the men would get lax in their attention. And doing that is a quick way to end your tour in a body bag.

There was a fine line I had to follow as a leader—when to give the men a break and when to send them out. But Christmas soon answered my question about operations.

The Christmas Truce was in effect from the 23rd to the 27th of December 1968. It was time out. No offensive operations would be conducted by U.S. forces during the truce. Charlie now had time to reload. He could hit us, but we were under orders to follow the truce and couldn't go out after him. At least the U.S. forces couldn't go out after him. Charlie wasn't a Christian—he'd hit us anytime he wanted to.

The PRUs were not held to the same truce requirements as the U.S. forces. And I worked my PRUs right through the holidays. I had been working in the field with my PRUs since well before the Christmas truce. When I would go out with my PRUs, I would take along either Jack Rowell or Joe Silva as a Stonerman to back me up. They could tear down a Stoner, clean it, clear it, and reassemble it practically at a dead run.

A good Stonerman was of real value in a firefight. That weapon had the respect of both the enemy and the men who depended on it. The deadly spray of 5.56mm projectiles from a Stoner would make a believer out of anyone. It kept enemy heads down long enough for us to vacate the area.

The parakeet op became my favorite PRU operation. Eddie Leasure had developed and perfected the parakeet. What Eddie had noticed was that a single helicopter would be ignored by almost everyone on the ground. They were such a common sight in Vietnam, carrying mail and ferrying people, that even the VC gave a single chopper flying at altitude no notice. In a parakeet op, that single lone chopper would have an agent aboard who would point out the target, at least one SEAL adviser, and a squad of PRUs ready for action.

The agent was the most important point of a good parakeet.

Without good intelligence, the parakeet operation was just too risky. We wanted to be as sure as possible about an agent's sincerity before we committed to an op.

The intelligence had to be exact, that such-and-such a man would be in a particular hooch at a specific time of the day. The Vietnamese rested, had a siesta, from roughly eleven to one or two, to escape the hottest part of the day. So the time around noon was our daylight target time.

The story would be checked. The man would be given aerial photos of the area, layouts on a map. Maybe we'd even take him up in a chopper to recon the area by sight. But always, the guy would be checked. Photos of other similar areas would be slipped into the pile, different locations pointed out on a map. Anything to slip the guy up and make him change his story. Once you had the feel that the intel was straight, it was time to plan the op.

All of these precautions were due to the fact that during a parakeet op, your ass was hanging out big-time. The one guide chopper, flying at altitude, would have four or five VNs in it, usually PRUs. Along with the PRUs would be the Team leader and one other American, preferably a Stonerman. When I was the Team leader, I would be armed with either the Browning or my shotgun. On my back was my radio, the big gun of the operation. That radio could call in the evac bird, a dust-off if things got real bad, or the air support we brought with us.

We had two primary helicopters in Vietnam, the armed Huey gunship with its rocket pods and machine guns, and the slick. The slick would be a regular Huey UH-1B helicopter without any outside mounted weapons. Without the rocket pods and machine guns, the bird would have "slick" sides. Since the inside of a slick was not filled with ammunition boxes, it could carry ten or so fully armed troops. The two door gunners would still have a machine gun each, so even a slick had some claws.

Behind and below the guide bird, an unarmed slick, would be at least four gunships, either Army birds or Seawolves. The slick would be flying along at fifteen hundred feet, approaching the target village. The gunships would be right on the deck, just skimming the treetops. The noise of the slick would cover any noise made by the gunships until the last minute.

When the slick dropped down on the target fast, the four gunships would rise up and start circling the target area. Dropping as fast as he could, the pilot would put you as near the target as he possibly could. I always liked the pilot to put the left door of the bird toward the hooch. With the bird's door gunner and my own men in the door, we would have a pretty good base of fire facing the target if something went wrong on the insertion.

When the slick came close enough to the ground, the strike team would pile out. As soon as the team was out of the bird, she would lift off. That slick was our ticket out of there, and we didn't want it to be exposed any longer than necessary.

The VNs would quickly put out a close-in perimeter while I would usually take the Stonerman with me against the target. As soon as the target was identified, we would snatch him up, secure him, and call in the extraction bird. If the target man had bodyguards, they were fair game for the team. If there was time, Mark 13s would be tossed into the hooch. My rule of thumb was that if we found the enemy or contraband, then the area was dirty and we burned the hooches.

Willy Peter grenades were nice to burn the hooches with, but the smoke could block the incoming extraction bird. Thermite and incendiary grenades were just too heavy to bother with, so the Mark 13 became our primary fire starter.

The ops could go incredibly fast sometimes. On one parakeet, we had inserted almost against the target hooch's door. I ran toward the door, and the target's bodyguard opened it just as I came up to it. Snatching the man's AK-47 out of his hands, I cold-cocked him with my fist, laying him out like a sack of potatoes. It was hard to say who was more surprised, the bodyguard or me. My shotgun had been hanging around my neck on a string, but the action took place so fast I never had a chance to reach for it.

Now with the target secured in the extraction bird and my men accounted for, we pulled out, on our way home in only a few minutes. That was what I really liked about parakeets—you're not in the mud all night and no cold, wet boat rides back to the base afterward. But they were risky ops.

A man had come to Nha Be to sell us some information. The man knew where a wounded NVA officer was hiding in a spider hole near a small village. The agent told us the man had been left by the

NVA because he couldn't travel. Even better, the agent said he could point out the hole where the officer was hiding.

The NVA had been through Long An Province earlier, so the report made sense. With the agent to guide us in, the operation sounded like a good one, almost perfect for a parakeet.

There were no tunnel complexes in the Mekong Delta like those you could find all over the rest of Vietnam. The Delta was only about three feet above sea level at its highest point. The spider holes were dug into what little high ground was available and then lined to help keep the water out. A woven grass/bamboo cover would be over the hole, camouflaged to blend in with the ground. It was just like the lair of the trapdoor spider, which is where the spider hole got its name. But it would be a rough place to hide if you were wounded.

Silva, myself, an interpreter, one PRU man, and the agent went out on the op. The slick set us down in a rice paddy, and we quickly moved over to the cover of the dike. The agent said the man's hole was dug into one of the dikes near a group of huts. We could see the huts nearby. The agent just walked up over the dike and lifted a mud-covered straw mat. Underneath the mat, looking up at us, was the NVA officer.

The man wasn't armed. His arm was infected, and he had also taken a round through the leg. He had not received any medical attention. An easy op with a worthwhile prisoner. We had won the war that day.

The speed of a parakeet was what I really liked. You had to go out on a limb and expose yourself. But you either hit or you missed. And it didn't take all night to figure out if you had missed. In an hour or an hour and a half, it was over. Back to the base and party time.

The platoon pulled about three or four operations on which I led them in. I would lead both the platoon and the PRUs. Even though I was working the PRUs, I wouldn't go with them all the time. The PRUs would never know when I would go with them on an operation. Setting a pattern was a great way to let the enemy know that an American would be with the PRU at any specific time. The VC and the NVA had set a high price on the head of any American who could be taken while leading a PRU. A SEAL was worth ten thousand dollars' reward just as a "green face." That tended to make you a bit more careful.

The way to limit the problem was to never tell the PRUs when you would be going out with them. The PRU leader would give the patrol order to the men after I had briefed him. That was all they expected. If I showed up that morning in gear, then the PRUs would know I was going with them.

But keeping the PRUs' trust was important to me. The PRU men wouldn't know when I would go out with them, but they always knew I would back them up. I ate with the PRUs down in the little restaurant in Nha Be. A PRU adviser could write off the ten dollars a week his meals cost him. The men knew I would work with them, eat with them, and never abandon them. The ARVNs and other Vietnamese units would look down on the PRUs, ignoring them when they called for help. But my PRUs knew that I would always back them, and that trust helped make for a very effective unit.

I was having trouble getting AOs (areas of operations) from the senior district adviser for Long An Province, an Army colonel. My requests just weren't being cleared as my platoon was starting operations. When I would put in for an area, I would always ask for three. Besides asking for three AOs, I would ask for them to be active over a seventy-two-hour time period. Separating the requested areas all over the province would keep Charlie from knowing exactly which one you would be operating in and when. District headquarters wasn't exactly the most secure place in the world. Often enough, the VC would have your AOs and plans before the paperwork had filtered down to the operating unit.

Not announcing exactly where we would be operating or even what day we would be out there helped increase the security for my platoon. But my requests kept getting knocked down by the district adviser. Now it was time to go over to headquarters myself and see what the problem was.

Putting on my civilian clothes, I tucked my papers in my pocket and my Browning under my belt. My papers identified me as working with the PRUs and being an Agency man. I would not tell this guy my military affiliation or rank. When necessary, I could play the Agency man to the hilt. The only thing more that I could do would be to call in an Air America chopper to take me over to headquarters. If you stepped out of an Air America bird, it was like having a rubber stamp smacked onto your head—"He's a plumber."

Arriving at the adviser's office, I identified myself and asked him, "What's the problem?"

"Well, those damn SEALs down there in Nha Be, every time they go out, they get something. I'm operating people around here and can never get anything."

He went on like this for a while. Then he finally said what he wanted.

"In the Navy, lieutenant commanders and above, they all have their own swimming pools over here."

Oh, really, I thought. "Colonel," I said, "it sounds to me as though you would like a swimming pool."

He just looked at me.

"If you had a swimming pool, do you think those SEALs would have any trouble getting AOs?"

"I doubt it," he said.

Back to Nha Be I went.

"You three!" I shouted at several of my platoon who were standing nearby. "Get over here. Here's a three-quarter-ton truck. There's two things I want you to come back with. One's a jeep for the chief. Number two is a swimming pool, complete, in its crate. They bring them in at Saigon. You've got four days. I don't want to hear any reports about anything, clear? Saigon's that way. Why are you still standing there?" Off they went.

Later, my little gatherers came back with big grins on their faces. "Look what we've got for you, Chief." In the back of the three-quarter-ton was a big crate containing one each, swimming pool, complete w/equipment. Behind the truck was a brand-spanking-new, shiny green jeep. Now I chewed their asses out.

"What the hell are you doing bringing me a brand-new jeep?" I bellowed.

"What do you mean, Chief?" they asked, looking a little crest-fallen.

"There's not a new jeep anywhere around here."

"It was in Saigon."

"Yeah, in Saigon new jeeps are all over the joint. In case you haven't noticed, this isn't Saigon. All we have around here is

beat-up old jeeps. That bitch is going to stand out like a hooker in church. Take it down to the pier, beat the piss out of it, tear the roof off it, and make it look old."

That was an order they could follow without any problems. Using hammers, crowbars, and enthusiasm, my men soon had that jeep looking like an old wreck. But underneath all the damage was a brand-new engine and chassis.

I had a real good platoon. In fact, I never had a bad platoon, or knew a bad SEAL. There were some SEALs who weren't operators, but even they weren't really bad SEALs. But this bunch of thieves and maniacs I had now—they were going to make a name for themselves.

One day, I was in the little bar we had in our barracks. I don't know what it is about SEALs, maybe it's that we have so many different rates in one outfit. But we could always find what we needed. The rest of the men on the base were making do with open windows and fans, but we had air conditioners. We walled off and insulated our section of the barracks so we could keep cool in our off-duty time.

Our bar was a simple affair, two stacks of demolition crates with a sheet of plywood across the top. Sometimes the plywood was even missing. But the important thing was our refrigerator, found along with the air conditioners, full of beer. While I was relaxing one day in civilian clothes, in came this Army officer.

"Excuse me," he said, "I'm looking for Chief Watson."

Hmm, very interesting, I thought. "Yes sir," I said, "I'm Chief Watson. How can I help you?"

"Well, Chief, I understand you have a jeep."

Oh shit! We'd been caught. I could hear those brig doors closing now.

There was nothing for it but to brazen it out. "Yes sir," I answered. "What do you need?"

"Well, I've got to get up to Saigon. There aren't any vehicles available on the base. The chief over at the motor pool said that one outside belongs to you and suggested I talk to you. Do you think I might be able to get a ride?"

"No problem sir. Just let me put down this can of beer I've accidentally crushed and I'll even get you a driver."

Commander Strany, the OIC of the Tactical Operations Center

was tickled pink with the results my SEALs and PRUs were getting. We had gotten along just fine right from the start, which was more than I could say about the commander and my two officers. Williamson and Thames called me over to their room. I didn't know that Strany had chewed them both out thoroughly.

The gist of what Strany said was: What kind of officers were they? And what kind of leaders did they think they were? He had been looking at after-action reports, and apparently the two of them had not been out. And it didn't appear that they had any intention of going out.

When the two lieutenants pointed out that the holidays were here, Strany cut them off: "Your chief is in and out of the TOC constantly and pulling operations day in and day out."

The result of this was that Williamson and Thames read me the riot act. Apparently I was making them look bad. And that really pissed me off.

"Look," I said, "let's get something straight right now. This is my Team, fellas. You're only here for a short stay. A year and a half or two years at the most, and you're gone. We're over here to do a job. If you don't want to do it, if you'd rather sit in the o-club or here in your rooms, fine. Be my guest. That way, when I need paperwork signed, I know where you are."

Well, that got the two of them off their asses. We sat down like three grown men and talked about what had to be done. They had never realized quite what I had been doing. I had never cleared it with them. Which may have been wrong on my part. But it's very hard to argue with success.

Most officers then came into the Teams from the reserves, either OCS or NROTC graduates. After UDTR training and jump school, much of their military commitment was already gone. An officer's career track for Special Warfare was just getting started, and it would be several years before it would be fully instituted. Most officers did their time in the Teams and then rotated to other duty for a while. Williamson and Thames had just been part of the system for too long.

Neither one of the officers wanted to take me away from my PRU operations, which they could have done. But the better the platoon looked, the better they looked. The problems were soon ironed out, and both of the officers started operating in the field. While they actively led the men, I ran the PRUs. And we were both making things difficult for Charlie in Long An Province.

The platoon was working hard and I was rampaging all over the place. With the 112 PRUs outside the gate and the twelve SEALs inside the gate, I was operating all of the time. With the Agency feeding me intel for the PRUs, I had all the information I could handle. Mixing the units together, I could have them give each other mutual support. And support wasn't something the PRUs got all the time.

The ARVNs would almost never support the PRUs. If an American wasn't with them on an operation, calling in air or artillery support was real hard for them too. About the only people who would consistently support the PRUs were the PBRs and us.

Gallagher had taught me a long time ago that if you were going to get your men's respect, you had to live, eat, sleep, and fight right alongside them. Most of my meals were taken in the same Vietnamese shop where my PRUs ate. To be a good adviser, you had to become one of the men you were leading, at least in spirit. And Bob's teachings worked. Those PRUs would do things for us that other advisers just wouldn't believe.

After the holidays had passed, new intelligence started coming in. I started getting reports about big movements just northeast of our little base, in the narrow part of the channel leading up to Saigon. We had code-named the narrows Hanging Tree. The intel was that Charlie wanted to sink a ship in the channel, something he had tried in the past. A large boat could easily block the channel for some time if it was sunk in the right spot.

The Agency man, my boss with the PRUs, had me up to his superior's place over the holidays. And those people lived well. A real big villa, houseboys, and mamasans all over the place taking care of things. The best of booze and food. You name it and they had it. Watching their gates were hired killers, montagnards, the Mafia of Vietnam.

So I had been hitting it off pretty well with my Agency liaison man. When the reports started coming in, we both sat down to discuss what we could do about the situation. We had one hundred some PRUs, and what was the best way we could apply them to mess up Charlie's plans?

My thought was to put patrols out and man LPs and OPs (listening posts and observation posts) around the clock. Relieving the posts at different times, we could slip in a relief crew without Charlie knowing it. We'd let the initial group go in during the day, not being too obvious but letting Charlie see what was going on. The next day, we'd extract the people, also letting the operation be seen, but before we left the area, we'd secretly release a crew away from the extraction site. The new crew would slip into the post and man it while Charlie thought it had been abandoned.

The operation sounded good, and we initiated the program. The fake extraction system had been going on for three or four days and looked like it would yield results. Now it was the middle of January and I had been running operations with the PRUs. We had been hitting well and moving fast. The feeling was good and I was really enjoying myself. Between the platoon and the PRUs, I ran about twenty operations that month.

Out of the last eight days, Charlie had hit us five times at the Hanging Tree location. The LP/OP system we had set up had given us enough warning to prevent Charlie from mining a ship. One afternoon, I had come in after an eight-man fake extraction. It was about three-thirty in the afternoon and I was pretty beat.

Commander Strany and a couple of other guys commented on how I looked. I had been operating the last several nights and been up most of the days. The general opinion was that I looked like shit and should take it easy. This sounded good to me. Going back to my room, I scrubbed up, put on some clean fatigues, and headed for the chiefs' club.

It was about eight o'clock that evening when Commander Strany came into the chiefs' club. "Your boys have hit, Chief," Strany said. "They've got pay dirt and are in trouble. You'd better get over to the TOC."

The Vietnamese weren't going to support my PRU, so I had to move fast. Without an American with them, my men couldn't call in air support either. On my way to the TOC, I stopped to get my Browning. I also grabbed Jack Rowell.

"Get out to the camp and get George," I shouted. "Get him to the TOC now. And bring back some more PRUs too."

George was one of my interpreters with the PRU, and I was

going to need his help tonight. Inside the TOC, chaos ruled, but there was purpose in the confusion. Over the radio you could hear gunfire and the sounds of battle. There was so much cigarette smoke in the TOC it almost looked like the haze over a battlefield. Commander Strany filled me in on what had happened.

One of my PRU outposts was on the banks of a small canal near Hanging Tree. A sampan had come by with four armed men and a large box in it. The PRUs ambushed the boat and killed the four men after a short firefight. When they grabbed the sampan, the big box fell over the side and landed on the beach. The five PRUs who tried to lift the box couldn't budge it. While they were tying a line to the box to let the PBR tow it back to the base, all hell broke loose.

Fire started coming in on the PRUs and the PBR that was trying to get them out. The enemy was on the far bank, and the reports were that there was a bunch of them. When the one PBR pulled out because of the volume of incoming fire, the towline caught and snapped.

Commander Strany asked me what I wanted in the way of backup.

"Get me two PBRs," I said. "Loaded and ready to go right now."

While the commander went to tell the PBRs to get ready, George came in. With George's help, I talked to the PRUs on the scene. What they wanted to know, after I had told them that support was on its way, was what I wanted done with the big box. I told them to wait until I got there to see what it was. Into the TOC now came three EOD men.

Lieutenant Mac, in charge of the EOD unit, wanted to know what was going on with the big box. I told him that my men had the box in custody and that it was about a foot and a half square, maybe five feet long, and floated. "But five VNs can't pick it up," I finished.

"It sounds like they've found a water mine," Mac said, "I haven't heard of one quite that size. Chief, you've got to let me go with you. This sounds like something for us."

"Okay," I said, "you and your men can come." He had two more EOD men with him. "But be ready—we're pulling out of here right now."

The radioman said he had the Air Force on the horn. "They've got a Spooky in the area," he said. "Do you want it?"

"Hell yes," I answered. A Spooky was an AC-47 gunship. "And get me a Seawolf as soon as possible."

Strany asked me what I was going to do. I said, "I'm going out there to support them. Jack brought me four PRUs and I sent back for four more and my PRU chief. The EOD men are going in with me to check out that big box. I'll take two PBRs with all the ammunition they can carry. Now if you'll excuse me, sir, I've got to get out there and control the air support." With Commander Strany's nod, I was heading out the door.

There were already two PBRs on their way that Commander Strany had called up for me earlier. The boats were just pulling up to the pier when I arrived. Reloading quickly, we got ready to move them out. I now had eight PRU men, my PRU chief, and the three EOD men going along. All I had on me at the time was my Browning. There were guns on the PBR, and I didn't intend getting out of the boat anyway. What I wanted to do was just get into the area and control the air support for my men.

It was only about a fifteen-minute boat ride to the canal my PRUs were on. We stopped the boats at the mouth of the canal. Two other PBRs were on station, having supported my men from the start of the firefight. Seeing where my PRUs were, I called in Spooky to hose down the area. "This is Whiskey Sour. Light 'em up." This was the first time I had personally called in Spooky, what the Vietnamese called the Dragon.

When the gunship banked over the target on her left side, I could see why the VNs held the craft in almost superstitious awe. The three 7.62mm miniguns pointing out of the side of the plane poured out their fire with a thrumming roar. The miniguns fired so fast that the sound wasn't recognizable as a weapon. It sounded more like a long, deep note from a gigantic bass fiddle, or maybe the roar of a flying dragon.

Each of the miniguns would spin its six barrels, spewing out steel-jacketed death at a rate of six thousand rounds a minute. Eighteen thousand rounds a minute would pour from the side of the plane, every fifth round a tracer. The tracers would burn out before hitting the ground from Spooky's altitude of three thousand feet. Looking up from the ground, all you could see in the darkness was a moving black shape against the stars, licking down at the ground with three long fuzzy red tongues of flame.

For fifteen or twenty minutes, tracers rained on the target area. After her gun runs, Spooky dropped flares for us, lighting up the canal with a flickering, otherworldly glare. We moved in to pick up my PRUs.

While one person manned the rear .50 caliber on the PBR, I picked up an M60. With the .50 covering the left side, I covered the right side of the canal as we backed the PBR up it. The idea was that we could cover the canal enough with all of our weapons in the back of the PBR. The twin .50s in the bow of the boat would make sure that no one was able to block us in.

My PRUs had just about finished off the situation before we had arrived. When the Dragon showed up, that was the end of the show. With no trouble at all, we found the mine.

The mine was a long sheet-metal affair, about four and a half feet long and eighteen inches square. The box was made up of four separate compartments. They were numbered one through four and were held together with flanges. Mr. Mac, the EOD officer, called over to the lead boat, "Pass that line over here. We don't want you messing with that thing."

The lead boat had gone in ahead of us. Coming onto the mine, the boat's crew had picked up the line attached to the mine and were attempting to tow the box. We were only about twenty or thirty yards up the canal and had a straight run out of there. While I was on the radio, Mr. Mac came over to me.

"Can I go over and have a look at this thing?"

"Yeah," I answered, "but don't take long. I want to get my boys together and get out of here."

The PRUs wanted to go back into the jungle and look for the bodies of the VC they had greased. Putting my foot down, I said no, it was time to leave. The gunship had us spotted without any problem. The PBRs had an infrared beacon on top of the cabin that Spooky could see without any problem. She just kept circling above us, tossing out flares as needed.

Mac had gotten back in the boat. "That's definitely a water mine. I've never seen anything like it. There are devices sticking out of two of the compartments, and one of them looks like a timing device. Chief, I would definitely like to take this back to the base with us for study."

"You have got to be out of your mind," I said. "Okay, we'll do it. But at the end of a long rope."

As far as I knew from Bob Gallagher, who was EOD-qualified, the only way to learn about new devices was to take them apart. Dragging that bitch back wasn't exactly how I had planned to spend the evening, but EOD wanted it.

Making sure everyone was aboard the PBRs, we pulled out. We had attached the towing line to the mine and were pulling it along behind us. Just in case it broke loose, I made sure there wasn't anyone else behind us.

When we reached the main river, we let the line out until that mine was bobbing along about 150 feet behind us. Mr. Mac said, "I'm going back there to check it."

Stripping down to his shorts, Mr. Mac went over the side and swam back to the mine. Illuminating the mine with the PBR's searchlight, Mr. Mac gave the mine a close inspection. When he climbed back onto the boat, he said, "It's all right—it's not ticking."

Just to be a little more sure, I had all the extra people transfer off the PBR and onto the other boats that were with us. That left the boat captain, one member of his crew, the three EOD men, and myself aboard. Calling back to the TOC, I told Commander Strany what we were bringing back.

Requesting that the area be cleared where the old EOD shed had been standing, I also asked for at least three vehicles to be at the site. The headlights from the trucks would illuminate the concrete slab where the shed used to stand. We were moving very slowly back to the base, so there was plenty of time for them to set up before we arrived.

Mac then came up to me, "Chief," he asked, "have you ever seen one of these before?"

"No."

"Chief, there's something wrong with that sonofabitch, but it isn't ticking. I don't know what it is. None of us have ever seen a mine like it. But since it isn't ticking, I want to take the bastard in."

If that had been meant as a reassuring speech, this guy had to work on his public speaking. But I was going to try to bring the mine in as safely as I knew how. The beach we were going to land the mine on was just south of the piers that we tied the PBRs up to. We pulled even with it and got ready to cut the mine loose. The plan was to swing the boat past the beach, cut hard out toward mid-channel, and cut the towline. A couple of guys would jump into the water and swim the mine in to the beach.

Mr. Mac and his second class stripped down to their shorts again for the swim in. I stripped down as well. Mac said he thought it would take only two men. Handing my Browning to the boat captain, I said, "Here—somebody will pick this up at the pier when you tie up."

"What are you going to do?" asked the boat captain.

"I'm going to give these guys a hand swimming this mine in."

"I'm sorry, Chief," said Mac, "but I can't let you do that."

"Wait a minute, Lieutenant," I answered. "This isn't your operation. Your operation doesn't start until this thing's on the beach. Until then it's still my show. I'll give you a hand—we've gone this far together."

If we had had swim fins, two men wouldn't have had any trouble swimming the mine in. With just the few of us, it was going to be a real job keeping control of that unwieldly bastard in the river's current. After I pointed that out to Mr. Mac, he relented.

"I guess I shouldn't, Chief," he said, "but let's go."

Jumping over the side, I grabbed the towline to the mine. The second class hung on to the mine itself, and Mr. Mac swam alongside, helping guide the mine in. The water was illuminated from the lights of vehicles along the beach. As we swam the mine in, Mr. Mac gave me more instructions.

"As we get into shallow water," he said, "Don't let it bounce on the bottom."

Both ends of the mine were buoyant—you could hear they were hollow when you tapped them. The two middle compartments had the dull sound of a full box. With all of Mac's warning I was starting to get more than a little concerned about the whole thing. Was this really such a smart idea?

Mac checked the mine again when we could stand in the water. "When we get into shallow water, we want to get our hands under it," said Mac. "We'll lift it up and set it on the concrete slab where the shed used to stand. Don't drag it or knock it."

"Okay," I said. Bob had taught me a little bit about working with explosive ordnance. I had been a demolition man for about nine years now. But EOD is something very different. Most of what Bob taught me had consisted of "Don't fuck with this kind of shit." But I trusted the EOD men and they needed my help.

"Okay, Chief," Mac said. "Give me a hand and we'll get it on this concrete slab."

There was a handle on the mine, so we lifted it up and gently placed it on the slab. Sitting there, the mine just looked like a metal box, gleaming wetly where the river water was running off it. In the center part of the mine was a dial, much like the dial from a safe. To the left of the dial, two thin copper tubes were sticking up about an inch and a half, like the prongs of an electrical plug.

"Damn," said Mac. "I just can't figure this thing out. I've never seen anything like it in my life."

"Yeah," I said. "It looks weird to me."

"Well, screw it," said Mac. He called up to the men gathered by the trucks, "Get some sandbags down here. We'll sandbag the bitch in place and study it in the morning."

The three of us, Mac, his second class, and I, were standing over the mine looking at it. We were wearing nothing more than our shorts and practically dripping on the mine. There was a Base Support man standing nearby with a big power light in his hands, lighting up the mine. Noticing that the man was standing in a pool of water, I told him he had better move before he fried himself.

About that time, someone called to me from the trucks. "Chief Watson!"

Since the trucks had their headlights on and pointed at us, I couldn't see who was calling.

"Who wants me?" I shouted as I shaded my eyes from the glare.

"This is Commander Strany, Chief," he shouted. "Get up here."

I hadn't taken ten steps toward the voice when I heard a quiet *click* behind me.

With as much time as I had in demolitions, this was the first time I had heard the click of a detonator firing. Time seemed to slow down. A giant hand thudded into me, and I flew through the

air. All the lights around me had gone out. The blast was so strong that I couldn't hear it. Some explosions are so loud that the ears can't react to the sound—you feel it more than hear it. This time, there was just a weird kind of keening silence, like a dog whistle you can almost hear. I never even felt myself land.

As I struggled up off the ground, things were pitch-black. There weren't any lights. The trucks weren't working anymore, and we had been too far from the base for the base lights to reach us. I hadn't fully lost consciousness, but I was sort of numb all over. I hadn't lost my cool, and I was still thinking straight. Just then a thought hit me.

There had been three other people standing practically on top of that mine when I walked away from it!

When I tried to reach up to my head, I couldn't move my left arm. I still couldn't feel anything. What's wrong with my arm? I thought. Reaching down with my hand, I grabbed my left hand and pulled my arm up to the moonlight. I saw muscle and tissue hanging down from my arm and blood pouring out onto the mud.

Grabbing at the mess, I squeezed down with my hand to try to stop the bleeding. "Is everybody all right?" I shouted, my voice sounding hollow in my ears. There was no answer, just some moaning and groaning.

Nobody from the base knew what had happened. They all thought the base was under attack. As far as I knew, I was the only person moving at the blast site. And I wasn't going to be able to keep moving much longer.

Even in the dark, I knew the way to sick bay. Moving as fast as I could, kind of a lurching stagger, I headed toward it, about three hundred yards away. I kicked open the door, fell through it, and smacked into the floor.

They were in the middle of field day, scrubbing and painting the place! Looking up at a corpsman, I said, "Doc, would you please stop my bleeding. I don't want to die."

The second class I was looking at said, "What the hell happened? We heard the explosion."

"There's guys lying all over out there. And those EOD guys are gone."

They grabbed me and threw a tourniquet on my arm. I heard a corpsman bellow, "I told that silly son of a bitch that you don't tear down a whole sick bay just to hold field day, not in a combat zone!''

I didn't fully lose consciousness, but the whispered buzzing in my head got louder for a while. Putting me on a stretcher, they set me outside the sick bay while they brought in other wounded. Because of the field-day mess they didn't have enough room in the sick bay to handle more than one person at a time.

They brought in Commander Strany. He had also been wounded in the blast, along with a number of others. I met the corpsman who had been there almost two years later. He told me that out of all the wounded, I was the most severely injured. The blast had just obliterated the EOD men. Estimates later put the amount of explosive at four hundred pounds. There was a huge crater in the ground where the mine had gone off. Even the concrete slab the mine had been on was blown into powder. Sandbags had been tossed about. The trucks that had been facing the explosion were totaled. They looked like those shown in the films of atomic blast tests in the Nevada desert, just smashed and mauled by the shock wave.

Now the corpsmen were calling in the dust-off choppers. They placed my stretcher on the bird and started to strap me down. Now the pain was starting to hit me like a wash of flame. I must have stated making some noise, because one of the men came at me with a morphine syringe.

There were already three or four other people on the dust-off. As soon as I was aboard and secured, the bird lifted off, putting down later at a MASH unit in Ben Wha.

Just like in the TV show, a bunch of people came out and grabbed my stretcher. By now, I was starting to hurt again, but that wasn't the worst. I was terribly thirsty, willing to drink damn near anything. My mouth felt as if it had been stuffed with cotton rags. And I wanted a cigarette in the worst way.

A nurse came over to me and started wrapping my arm with pressure bandages. I don't know if she released the tourniquet or not. While she was working on the wounded arm, my attention was drawn to my good arm. A medic had grabbed it and tried to put an IV needle into it.

And tried is the right word. He didn't stab me once with that needle, it was more like half a dozen times. He was sticking that needle all over my arm. Then he asked the nurse to try. Now it was her turn to stick me a number of times. These people were going to stab me to death trying to save me.

Finally I heard the nurse say, "This man needs blood right now and I can't hit a vein."

Great! I thought.

Now a doctor came in. At least I think it was a doctor—he was wearing a lot of OR gear on him. Finally, he hit a vein in my ankle. Now with the bottles hanging and flowing into my leg, I started to calm down again. The nurse came over to me and talked.

"You're going to be all right now," she said.

"Can I have a drink, please?" I asked.

"No, you can't. You're going into that OR as soon as it's cleared."

Then she reached into a small pan sitting on a table. The pan was filled with gauze pads soaking in water. Putting a small wad across my lips, the nurse said, "But what you get out of that, I don't know about."

I didn't say anything, I was too busy sucking the moisture out of that gauze pad. Then I noticed somebody smoking a cigarette nearby. I didn't bother wondering what he was doing smoking inside the hospital tent. And I didn't care either. That person came over when I asked and gave me a couple of drags from that cigarette. Let me know if you're out there, guy—I owe you a cigarette.

Now they gave me a shot in my good arm and the world was going away for a while. While I was drifting away, I remember thinking that I was only hurt in my arm. Actually, my arm was so bad that it was masking the other wounds.

I woke up in the recovery room. Gradually, I became aware of my surroundings. I could hear people talking but couldn't make out the words very well. Then there was the feeling of somebody taking my blood pressure. But I couldn't move, or open my eyes. Everything had an unreal quality to it. Had I died?

The voices were getting louder as I struggled inside to wake up. Then I finally managed to open my eyes. There was a nurse bending over me taking my blood pressure. This had to be the most beautiful woman I had ever seen in my life. Perhaps the Army puts its best-looking nurses in the recovery room on purpose. If so, I've got to find the guy responsible for that policy and buy him a drink. This woman was lovely, soft hair framing a beautiful face with eyes that could melt your heart. The face of an angel, and a body wrapped in a crisp white uniform that made you think anything but angelic thoughts.

"I'm dead and I'm in heaven," I croaked. Hell of an original line, isn't it?

"What are you talking about?" the vision asked with a puzzled look.

"No, I mean it—somebody as pretty as you must be an angel."

"He's all right," my angel said. "Orderly, put him on a ward."

So much for impressing the nurse. Now I was being moved into a ward with a number of other wounded. My sense of time was all screwed up—it could have been morning or late afternoon for all I knew. It had been just a little before ten the night before when the mine had gone off. When the orderlies took me off the gurney and placed me on a bed, I just went to sleep.

Waking up the next day was a little more normal, but the surprise waiting for me was nowhere near as pleasant as that nurse had been. I felt like a screen door somebody had run through. My arm was the major wound, but my legs, feet, back, and head were all bandaged. The blast and flying fragments had torn me up pretty badly. I thought I must look like a mummy. I lay there in my bed trying to get into a comfortable position.

Now I started getting visitors. My PRU agent, George, my interpreter, the town chief of Nha Be, and the district chief all came in to see me. The orderly had helped me get into a sitting position, with my arm braced on the bed. My visitors had a pillow with them with the Vietnamese flag on it.

When I saw the agent, I asked him about the other guys who had been by the mine. "I know they didn't make it," I said. "But . . ."

"No, they're gone," said the agent.

There was nothing found of two of the EOD men. They had just ceased to exist at the instant of the blast. The third man's torso had been found. The next thing the agent said set me back a bit.

"The VNs here want to give you the Vietnamese Cross of Gallantry with a Silver Star," the agent said. "None of their people got hurt. You pulled them all out. They know that if you hadn't gone in there, they would never have gotten the support they needed. You did your job." The agent shook my hand. "They're going to be

moving you out of here this afternoon. You're on your way to Japan."

"What?" I said. The shock of the situation was still settling in.

"Your arm's a mess. I know you haven't seen it yet, but I talked to them about it. They're sending you to Japan to a larger hospital. You'll be all right, but it's going to take a bigger place than this to give you the proper treatment."

The VNs awarded me their medal with all the respect and ceremony they could, given the surroundings. They pinned the medal on my bandages, and the group of officials stood around me for pictures. It was quite an honor, one I certainly hadn't expected. But a bigger surprise was right there.

A man came up from the back of the group. He was from NOS-GRUP–V (Naval operations support group–Vietnam) in Saigon. "Hey, Chief, here's your pay record." He handed me a large envelope. "Hang on to this," he said. "At least when you get home, you'll have money."

They had brought me my pay record! It was known throughout the Navy that if you got hit, your pay records stayed in Vietnam, and God only knew how long it would take them to catch up to you. Until they did, you could only draw a limited amount of money against your pay. This man had done me one hell of a favor, and I didn't even know who he was.

What had probably happened was that my PRUs had hit the VC before they could get to Hanging Tree and place their mine. The mine could be floated in place until it was located where they wanted it. By puncturing the two flotation chambers at either end, they could sink the mine to the bottom. With the mine in place, it could be detonated either from the shore or by a timer. We would never know exactly how the operation would have been carried out. The mine was gone, and everybody connected with it, except for me, was dead.

When my PRUs ambushed the mine crew, one of the crew must have pulled the pin or started the pencils, just as the SEALs would have done. The last thing you can do is arm the bomb. Maybe you can take some enemy with you. Those VC would never know how successful they had been.

Only a few hours later I left the hospital in Ben Wha. They put me on a big C-141 headed for Japan. Being wounded was awful. You lose all your dignity being handled like a product. Even when they are doing their best for you, your own frailty keeps reminding you of what happened. Just going to the bathroom can be a humbling experience. I had to urinate very badly, but I couldn't get out of bed. The nurse brought me a bedpan, hose, and body attachment that looked as if it had been designed for some weird sexual activity. The damn thing didn't work and in general made a miserable mess.

What a way to fly the friendly skies. As a litter patient who can't even get up. Good-bye, Vietnam.

CHAPTER 10

Recovery and Return

It was maybe eight or nine in the evening when I arrived in Japan. I was sent to the 106th General Hospital in Yokohama and assigned to a bed in ward 6-A. My bed was the second from the end on the north side of the northeast wing. An advantage of the location was that I could see Mount Fuji in the distance.

It was going to be some time before I appreciated that view. I thought that my Navy career was over. Depressed doesn't come close to describing how I felt just then. And it showed.

The three men who had been killed didn't occupy my thoughts at the time. I was too busy feeling sorry for myself, one of the worst things you can do in that situation.

There was a young nurse on the ward who must have noticed how I was feeling. That evening she approached my bed with a medic and a gurney. "Come on, fella, we're going for a ride," she said.

It had to be after ten o'clock—Taps had already sounded. Maybe they're going to operate on me some more, I thought. They had only stitched up the few frag wounds on my head. All the injuries on my legs, arms, back, and chest were open. I still hadn't figured out how I got the frag wounds on my chest.

Traveling through the hospital, we entered a ward where most of the lights were out. The first bed on the left held a patient who was still awake. This kid couldn't have been much more than eighteen years old. His bed was cranked up, and he looked at us as we came in. When he saw me, the kid shook his arm and said, "The bastards didn't get this one! Semper Fi!"

He shook his right arm because he didn't have a left one, and it was obvious that there were no legs underneath the sheets. He was a triple amputee. Here I was, this big, tough-ass SEAL chief with a serious case of the sorries. And there was a young Marine who couldn't be far into his second year in the service, if that. That young man was a credit to the Corps.

The nurse never said a word, she just wheeled me back to my ward. The medic put me back into my bed and left the room. Reaching over to me, the nurse put her soft, cool hand on my head. I could hear the clean white cloth of her uniform rustle. She said, "You needed that."

"Yeah, I sure did," I answered quietly.

"You're going to be all right," she said. And then she left the room.

That wasn't the only incident that night to give me something to think about. After I was back in the ward, I got the word that there was a phone call for me from the states. Now who would know where I am this quickly? I thought as I was wheeled over to a phone at the end of the hall. At the other end of the line was a waitress I knew at the chiefs' club in Little Creek!

"You big sonofabitch!" she cried. "Are you all right?"

That woman had called five different hospitals in Japan looking for me. If I hadn't been lying down already, I probably would have fallen over from shock. "Just how did you find out what happened to me?" I asked. At the time, the SEALs were still very classified, and our casualty reports were big-time secrets.

She explained that Bob Gallagher had walked into the chiefs' club just a short time earlier. Bob and I were close, so it didn't take long for this lady to suspect that something had happened. After one look at Bob, she said, "What happened to Jim?"

"What are you talking about?" asked Bob.

"I don't give a shit about your secrets, Bob. All I want to know is if he's all right."

Taking her away from the bar, Bob led her into the back area and told her what had happened. "He got tore up pretty bad," Bob said. "But he'll be all right. That isn't the problem. They don't know if they can save his arm or not."

Not exactly the subject I wanted to talk about at the time. But I told her that I was going to be all right and that everything would be fine. Now if I could just convince myself of that! After a little more conversation, we said goodbye and I was taken back to my bed. Marlene and I had been having problems. She didn't call me at the hospital and I didn't feel like calling her. Finally, I went to sleep.

The next morning, I woke up to the bustle of activity that marks every hospital. It was about 8:00, after breakfast, when a nurse came in for me. She was a short little redhead, just buzzing with activity. Later I would learn that she was a major. Greeting me, the nurse called out, "How are you today, Sergeant?"

She must have thought I was a sergeant because of my age. It didn't take me long to set her right.

"I'm not a goddam sergeant, I'm a chief in the United States Navy."

That nurse came over to my bed and put her arms around my neck. Kissing me solidly, she said, "You've got to be a SEAL. I love you guys. I've been with you in the chief's club."

Well, sonofabitch, looks like I've got a friend. And with what I was facing, it looked like I could use a friend. In a military hospital, there's no time for sympathy. They don't pamper you and they don't pat you on the ass either. But they can give you respect on occasion.

During my stay I got a close look at the kinds of people who run a military hospital. There was the Red Cross worker who passed out shaving kits and toilet articles to the men in the ward. When she learned that I had no money to buy cigarettes and not much chance of getting to a pay office, she went and bought me a carton of Pall Malls out of her own pocket.

There was the first sergeant of the ward, who had me wheeled into his office the day after I arrived. First thing he did was let me know that there was no rank for the patients in a military hospital. Then he made certain his people called me "Chief" and that I knew where his coffeepot was.

That was the last bit of dignity I was given for a while. Later that day, I was told they would operate on me in the morning. The operation itself took place in another building. It wasn't serious surgery, mostly closing up the wounds in my legs and doing what they could for my arm. I still hadn't seen my arm. It had been wrapped all this time. This was not something I was looking forward to. But the anesthetic took hold, and I was in their hands.

I woke up back in my bed on the ward. If there had been any time in post-op, I couldn't remember it. My arm was in some kind of sling, with a lamp glowing down on it. I was later told that the wound had to be exposed to the air and the lamp was ultraviolet to keep the germs down. Now I could see what had happened to my arm. It was anything but a reassuring sight.

There was no graft or anything to block my view. The blast had peeled away the tissue from underneath most of my left forearm. The bone was exposed almost from the elbow to the wrist. A few stitches held the remainder of my arm together. The doctors had removed all the tissue I had held so tightly those few days ago.

No wonder they hadn't let me look at it before. Hell, I didn't want to look at it now. Checking out the rest of me wasn't much better.

The doctors had used "continuous wire stitches." I looked as if I had been caught in an explosion in a spring factory. There were stitches everywhere! Large wounds in my legs and side had been closed, along with a number of smaller wounds scattered all over my body. Boy, is it going to be fun when they pull these bitches out, I thought.

A doctor came in to check on me and see how I was healing. As the doctor worked on my wounds, he kept telling me how everything was doing fine. "But what about my ears?" I asked.

"What about your ears?" the doctor asked, puzzled.

Summoning my vast store of medical knowledge, I told him. "They're screwed up. I believe the one eardrum is blown completely out."

"How's that?" the doctor questioned, skepticism plain on his face.

Not bothering to answer, I took a drag on my cigarette. Then I proceeded to blow smoke out of my ear. That managed to get his attention.

"Oh! They'll take care of that when you get back to Portsmouth. We haven't got time to play with things like that here."

"Oh, okay!" And that was the end of it. There just wasn't much argument in me. I was damned glad just be be alive. Smoking my cigarette, I watched the doctor work or looked at Mount Fuji outside the window.

A couple of days later, my doctor was back. It was about four days after the operation and my doctor figured it was time for the stitches to come out. Talking to another medic, the doctor said, "They look good. Go ahead and take the stitches out."

Dr. Nicholson, the medical officer in charge of my case, wrote up the extent of my wounds from the mine. The doctor diagnosed MFW (multiple fragment wounds) to my left shoulder, left forearm, and left leg with left ulnar nerve palsy. The wounds were considered received by indirect hostile action—a polite way of saying I screwed up and Charlie got me.

After all of the stitches had been removed, I stayed on the ward for a couple of days. EOD sent over a man to interview me on the mine incident while I was recovering. I dictated the whole story to a yeoman, who typed it up for my later signature. The EOD man told me they had decided that the mine's design was Russian and it had been built by the VC from local materials.

The nurse in charge of rehabilitation, a major, sent over a Special Forces sergeant to work with me while we were both laid up. The sergeant had taken a round through his hand while operating up in II Corps as a member of an A-team, the twelve-man operational detachment of the Army Special Forces.

As soon as I had healed enough to use a wheelchair, just a couple of days, the sergeant and I were able to travel around the hospital. Wheeling me down to another office, the sergeant helped me take advantage of a regulation I had been told about. In the basement of another building was the office of a Marine gunny sergeant.

"How are you doing, Chief?" the gunny said. "I heard about you. You're a SEAL, right?"

"That's right," I answered.

"You know," the gunny remarked, "if you're a corpsman I have to outfit you."

Reaching over with my good hand, I shook hands with the gunny. "Just call me Doc," I said.

"You got it, Chief." That's how I was issued three full sets of fatigues from the skivvies out, including a new pair of boots. Not that I was going anywhere real soon. But the uniforms gave me something other than hospital-issue pajamas to wear all the time.

Somebody went out and even had name tags made for me that said WATSON and SEAL 2. There was some trouble getting me a proper set of jump wings, but they gave me a set of silver ones for my uniform. The object was to help my morale, and being able to dress like a SEAL did make me feel better. After I was squared away, I at least felt that I looked a little better. Even though I hadn't been able to put the boots on, wearing a uniform was a big improvement over those loose linen pajamas.

I was walking by the time I left the hospital. The only injury that was still real bad was my arm, and they had worked on that quite a bit. Taking some of the skin they had removed from my leg during my first surgery, the doctors had done a skin graft to cover the underside of my left arm. The rest of my repairs would be done back in the States at the hospital in Portsmouth.

The medevac flight to the States ended at Andrews Air Force Base in Maryland, where I spent some time in the base hospital. It was cold and nasty at Andrews, a big change from Vietnam, but at least it was home. The ward they put us in was very plain, not much more than a row of beds for us "in-transit medevacs."

One nice thing that happened almost right away was that the Red Cross showed up with portable phones. Each patient was allowed a three- or five-minute call anywhere in the continental United States. I was having trouble with my wife at home, and the only people I would have wanted to call were my parents. It wasn't that big a thing for me to call New Jersey. There was a young Marine from the Midwest who wanted to call both his parents and his girlfriend. I asked the Red Cross representative and she agreed to give my call to the Marine.

At the airfield in Norfolk, there were ambulances for the litter patients coming in on my flight. For those of us who could walk, there was a bus ready to take us to the hospital. I had an additional surprise waiting for me to arrive.

When I walked off the plane, there were two of the waitresses from the chiefs' club at Little Creek. Both of the ladies had large purses with them, and inside the purses was another surprise for me. Each purse held two rum-and-Sevens, in the glass, without lids. The drinks had been bought at the chiefs' club, and the ladies had carried them all the way to the airport without spilling a drop.

Now it was time for me to go to Portsmouth. The Army hadn't paid me using my Navy records—it had been willing to advance me up to a thousand dollars against my ID card, but would not mess with my records at all. So as soon as I was finished with the doctors, I was heading to the disbursing office to try to get some money. But first the doctors.

They admitted me to neurosurgery. The skin graft on my arm wasn't taking properly and was getting infected. The wound was draining constantly and starting to smell. This was not a good sign. Dr. Larson, a lieutenant commander, was in charge of my case, and we started to get along pretty well. It was obvious that they were doing as much as they could for me, but I was starting to get a little clausty and wanted out for a while.

During the course of one of our conversations, Dr. Larson asked me where I lived.

"Right across the river in Virginia Beach," I answered. "Is there any chance of me getting out of here?"

"Those bandages have to be changed every four hours, Chief," Larson said. "The wound has to be cleaned with saline solution and closely watched. We're starting to lose the skin graft. A decision is going to have to be made real soon about further treatment."

"Look," I said, "if I can't do it myself, I'll get somebody else to do it. Can I get out of here?"

"If you can get into a uniform," he said, "come and see me. My office is just at the end of the ward."

This was a situation that sounded familiar. I called home and talked to my wife. My sister Joy was living with us at the time, so she was at the house too. I told them to bring my uniform and stop on the way over and pick up a set of ribbons. Since Marlene had an ID card, she would be able to pick up the ribbons I needed at the exchange. I gave them the list of decorations and they said they would be over as soon as they could. It was about noon and I might be able to get out that day.

Marlene and Joy came up to my room and started helping me get my uniform on. While Marlene and I were working on getting me dressed, Joy was putting my ribbons together, grinning from ear to ear. "What are you grinning about?" I asked.

"When I was buying these ribbons," she answered, "the woman at the counter said, 'These can't be all for one man.' 'They sure are,' I told her. 'He's my brother.' "

"Oh, he must be a SEAL," the clerk said as she packed up the ribbons.

The uniform worked, and Dr. Larson allowed me to go home.

At the house, my youngest daughter, Pat, jumped up and ran over to me. She wanted to be her daddy's nurse. Pat-Pat was only six years old at the time, but she changed my bandages right on schedule, every four hours. I was on sick leave from Portsmouth from March 5 until March 31.

I was about to receive a decoration that I never particularly wanted. Getting hit was a learning experience that I could have done without. And now I'd have this medal that would tell everyone that I hadn't ducked at the right time.

Not one man who ever followed me in my platoons was hit and earned the Purple Heart, a point of some pride for me. Now the Navy awarded me a Purple Heart. Fellers ended up meeting me at the Portsmouth hospital after I had been sent home. It seemed that Chuck just couldn't stay out of trouble after I'd been hit and went home.

The Team had set up procedures to follow back in 1967 after the first platoons went to Vietnam. The procedures were about notifying a man's family and were unique to the Teams as far as I knew.

A man's closest friend, in my case Bob Gallagher, would be listed as the one who would speak to an injured man's family. I was listed as the man to talk to Bob's family when something happened to him. And Bob got hit three times.

That wasn't the only way the Team saw to a man's family. Whenever someone was away from Little Creek, whether it was a regular deployment or a tour in Vietnam, there were people to help his family. All that the family would have to do was call the Quarterdeck, the front office at the Team, and the crew would go over to take care of the problem. That was how tight Team Two was.

During the tours Bob put in over in Vietnam, his wife, Tina, got to know me better than she wanted to. Marlene saw Bob only that one time, but I had to go over to see Tina twice.

Tina never did get excited. She would just ask me, "How bad is it?" and "Is he alive?" When Bob went over to my house, it was a little different for him.

Bob had been stopping at the house quite often to make sure that everything was all right with my family. But that one time that Bob pulled up to give Marlene the bad news about me, she only had to look at him once before she asked, "How bad did he get it?"

"What are you talking about?" Bob answered.

"Jim's been hit," Marlene said.

"Why don't you give me a cup of coffee and we'll talk about it," Bob said. That big Irishman just couldn't come right out and say I had been hit. He told Marlene that I was tore up pretty bad but there was no danger to my life.

Casualties were classified Secret in the Teams. Whenever a man was hurt or killed, only his immediate family was allowed to know that anything had happened. Charlie thought the SEALs were some kind of supermen, and we didn't want him to know that we could be hurt or killed. Reputation can mean a lot in a fight, and we wouldn't let ours get tarnished.

Reputation or not, I was wounded and the situation sucked. One good thing came out of it—I finally had a decent excuse to get out of Rudy's PT. But I still had to make the runs. The treatment of my arm had stopped the infection, but a lot more work had to be done. By April, it was time to go back into the hospital.

There was a whole team of doctors working on my case now. A doctor from PHIBLANT, Dr. Larson, and a number of others consulted on what had to be done to repair my arm. The whole underside of the arm was just covered with a thin layer of skin and not much more. The chances of infection setting in and my possibly losing the arm were serious enough that the doctors wanted to try a new surgical procedure on me. Calling me into his office, Dr. Larson told me about the "pedicle flap" they were going to try.

This was really going to be fun. The doctors were going to attach the underside of my left arm to my left chest, effectively doing a tissue graft. As the graft started to take, they would gradually cut the tissue away from my chest as it grew into my arm. The first thing they had to do was cut the three sides of the tissue square free of my chest. Once they had the section of tissue separated on three sides, but still alive, they would graft it onto my arm. Dr. Larson figured this would give me the best chance of not losing my left arm at the elbow and maybe even get full use of the arm back. This was a chance to stay in the Teams. I would have done the procedure myself with a pocketknife for the chance to remain an active SEAL.

The operation was done under local anesthetic, and this was one of the few times I had nerve enough to watch. I normally don't even like to watch myself get a shot, but this was important enough for me to overcome that. Now I had an excuse to get out of Rudy's runs too.

One of the few pluses was that I had my own room at the hospital this time. Also, if you were a combat WIA and had a weight loss, according to your records, you were authorized a special ration, as long as you weren't on medication, for two cans of beer a day!

"Hey Doc!"

"Yes, Chief."

"I seem to be losing a lot of weight. Don't you think I should be put on a beer ration?"

"Well, you do seem to be losing a bit of weight. I'll go ahead and write it into your orders."

After some problems with the graft—they ended up packing it in ice for a while—things started healing okay. I was sure glad that the graft was starting to work because if it didn't take, they would have to cut the tissue off and try again. The only other place they could have tried another flap would have been my left leg and that would have really been uncomfortable. Would have looked a little silly too.

A slight infection set in, but they were able to get it under control. Now came the pleasure of physical therapy and trying to work the arm. But hey, if it would keep me in the Teams, bring it on.

It seemed that the Teams needed me too. All my time leading my platoon and squads, I never had a man hit who was following me. I leave the platoon in Nam and what happens—a man gets hit. Chuck Fellers got wounded in the left hand.

Chuck ended up losing his left index finger. When the doctors decided to amputate Chuck's finger, they removed the stump and stitched his hand together so that sometimes it was hard to notice that Chuck was even missing the finger. But old nine-fingers decided that he didn't want the doctors to keep his finger. He wanted to steal his finger back from the lab.

In proper SEAL fashion, Chuck laid out his operation to steal back his finger. He even had a taxidermist in mind to mount his finger so that he could wear it around his neck. But Chuck got caught in the lab before he completed his op. It did make for a great story, though.

And good stories were what was needed to lighten the atmosphere around the hospital. Now the Team had four of us in there. Me with my arm, Chuck and his hand, and Bob Gallagher had gotten his legs chewed up by fragments and Jim Cook had lost an eye in combat. At the time I had this real tiny little second car, an NSU Prinz with a two-cylinder engine. The four of us were going to commute back and forth from the hospital to the Team whenever we could.

This commuting quickly became the joke of the Team. I would drive the car, working the pedals and turning the wheel with my good arm. Since Bob's legs were screwed up, he would operate the shift with his good arms. Chuck and/or Cook would be in the back seat acting as navigator. Teamwork got the bunch of us around in that little car. Some SEALs were convulsed with laughter when they saw our road show.

After one of our drives, Bob and I took some time off at the chiefs' club. Bob was hurting pretty badly right then. This was the third time he had been wounded. Three Purple Hearts were enough for any man.

"Jim," Bob said, "this shit just isn't worth it. Look at us. I'm full of holes and you're full of holes. We've paid our dues. This war isn't worth it. Nothing is. Nobody gives a shit about what we're doing over there anyway. Let's you and me sit back and just run the Training Platoon. Too many of the guys have bailed out and didn't do anything anyway. We've earned our place in the Teams. That war isn't worth our lives."

This coming from a man who had just been awarded the Navy Cross, after he had been put in for the Medal of Honor! This was not like anything Bob had ever said to me before. But there really wasn't any argument against what he was saying. Being in the same condition he was, wounded and in pain, I agreed with him. We decided against ever going back to Vietnam.

That decision didn't last out the year. Neither Bob nor I had to prove anything to anyone else. But we needed to prove we could go back to ourselves. When I left Vietnam at the end of my third tour, who went over there to relieve me? Bob Gallagher, the other SEAL who swore he would never go to war again.

But before I could go back, or even stay in the Teams, there was a lot of work for me to do. As it was, I had been in the hospital for over ninety days, and now I had to report to personnel for possible reassignment. I had reached an agreement with the doctors at Portsmouth. They had agreed to let me return to the Team, but I would still be listed as an outpatient at Portsmouth. Other restrictions included my not being able to jump, dive, or operate. Lyons, our skipper at the time, didn't care about my restrictions. He wanted me back to help teach the new guys before they went on a combat tour. My experience was valuable to the Team.

I was running the Training Platoon, getting other men ready to deploy to Nam. The training had changed for the better. The pop-up courses were more sophisticated, and the ambush techniques had been improved. The Team had learned a lot since those early days back in 1966. Bob Gallagher had been constantly improving things as combat experience grew.

While charging around as chief of the Training Platoon, I was wearing a set of tigerstripes from Vietnam. I hadn't worn them over in Nam—they just weren't available when I was there. But one of the platoons had brought a whole mess of tigerstripes back from one of its tours, and a number of us picked up some sets.

The only place that tigerstripe uniforms were being made at the time was in the Philippines. You could buy them in Vietnam, but they weren't available in the States. This made the uniforms something of a status symbol. Wearing a set of tigerstripes meant that you were a combat vet, you had been to the mountain and seen the elephant. Personally I liked the way the jagged black, brown, and green stripes blended in with foliage, especially in the wavering shadows cast by the plants in Nam.

The SEALs became the most highly decorated single unit of the

Vietnam War. You would be told when an award came in for you, but you wouldn't be given the medal right away. There were so many awards coming in that the Team would save them up until there were enough for a good-sized award ceremony.

At the ceremony all the men receiving awards would be standing in a group. Men not receiving awards, usually the new guys who hadn't deployed to Nam yet, would stand as the Team. Most of the time this resulted in the Team appearing to be only about ten men or so. All the rest of the Team would be standing in the awards group. Ninety percent of the Team would receive awards while the other 10 percent passed out programs.

The running joke became that the SEALs would spend six months in Vietnam, come back to get decorated, and then go back for more decorations. There were some odd situations. If, like me, a man had already received a number of Bronze Stars, he would put small stars on the ribbon to indicate the additional awards. I received four Bronze Stars during my time in Vietnam. Consequently, some guys, myself included, would ask for other ribbons when someone put us in for an award. "Don't put me in for the Bronze Star, sir, I already have some of those. Put me in for the Navy Commendation Medal or even the Navy Achievement Medal."

At least those were different ribbons. In 1965 and 1966, having a single row of ribbons, three awards, was considered really something in the Teams. By 1969, if you didn't have at least four rows of awards, you had to be screwing up somewhere. You were either real new or not an operator. I pulled a good stunt on one of my new men later on in Vietnam. This kid was a real operator and a brave sonofabitch. He earned several Bronze Stars during his tour. I had the kid convinced that all he had to do was win a few more Bronze Stars. When you had five Bronze Stars, you could trade them in for the Silver Star. Or so that kid believed—after all, his chief had told him that.

During the winter months, I spent time working my arm and getting back in shape to carry my share. Now I wanted to go back to Vietnam. It was something like the old falling-off-the-horse story. If you fall off a horse, the best thing to do is get right back up on one again.

Team One had an accident with a Stoner in Vietnam that had

bad results for the SEALs. Apparently, during an op, the weapon fell over from where it had been leaning against the side of a boat. When the Stoner hit the deck, it started firing uncontrollably. When a SEAL jumped on the gun to stop it, he was shot through the finger. The injury wasn't severe but, as a result, the Navy would no longer purchase more Stoners or even spare parts for the ones we had. The word was put out to all the SEALs to be real careful with our remaining Stoners due to what had happened to the West Coast people.

Up in I Corps area, a Stoner was recovered from a VC weapons cache in early 1970! That was probably the only Stoner the VC ever had and was one that had been lost in a river down in IV Corps area. When the weapon was received by Team Two at Little Creek, it was all screwed up. The parts were rusted and it was obvious that it had not been maintained at all. After spraying the weapon with WD-40, we took it to the range and it fired fine, no problems. The only reason the VC hadn't used it was that they couldn't get any linked 5.56mm ammunition. Our Stoner men were still picking up their links whenever they had the chance.

Cadillac Gage, the manufacturers of the Stoner, heard about our recovered weapon in their headquarters near Detroit. The fact that this weapon was still operating was a good selling point for the system and they wanted the piece back. The company offered two brand new weapons for our one. Now we were in a good position and we bargained for three weapons, the short-barreled version, and some spare barrels. I think the bargaining finally finished at two guns and several spare barrels for our recovered weapon. For myself, I hand carried the recovered weapon to Cadillac Gage in Michigan. A fine state to visit, but not in February. All that snow gets a little too deep for this SEAL.

Team Two was soon going to receive a new commander. Lieutenant Commander John Ferruggiaro was going to relieve Lieutentant Commander Lyon. Having a new commander who wasn't familiar with the Team gave me an opportunity to try a stunt. All of my agreements with the hospital—not jumping, operating, or leaving the Creek on deployments—were verbal. There wasn't anything on paper other than my records listing me as an outpatient from Portsmouth. This was my chance to get in with a deploying platoon.

It wasn't that I was trying to prove anything to anybody, except maybe myself. But how could I train new men to go to Vietnam when I couldn't go myself? My style of leadership had never been "do as I say." I had seen other so-called leaders use that safe style of leadership. My method has always been "do as I do," and that method had done very well for me and my men.

I still didn't have full use of my arm, but I knew I could carry my share of the boat. If I went over with a platoon, I would be giving them an edge with experience—my injury wouldn't make me a sea anchor.

Just before the Sixth Platoon started to beef up for deployment to Nam, I asked to be made the platoon chief. The Team didn't have all of its platoons up to complement. There were always holes in a platoon when it was back at the Creek. But when it came time for a platoon to be deployed, especially to Vietnam, they were brought up to complement quickly. It was a heart-stopping couple of moments with Ferruggiaro in his office, but when I left the meeting, I had a platoon!

Predeployment training gave me some trouble. My arm still wasn't what it had been and might never be as good as it was. But if I had thought I would be a drag on the platoon, I would have quit in a heartbeat. All my arm really meant was that I had to work a little harder. Lou Boink and Bud Thrift, the Sixth Platoon's officers, were glad to have my experience, and I was glad to give it.

The platoon had a good number of veterans in the unit, so we had more than just my experience to draw on. Chuck Fellers was with us—he had healed well from his last tour. Eddie Leasure was in Sixth, and his last tour had been as a PRU adviser. Out of thirteen enlisted men in Sixth Platoon, seven were veterans of at least one tour in Vietnam. Dean Nelson was my senior first class in the platoon and was the platoon PO (petty officer).

The platoon was a good one. We had Chuck, Doc Hammer, Dean Nelson, John Porter—we called him Little John—and "Fast Eddie" Leasure, a real good hustler with a pool cue. And Duke Leonard—another hunter—Leigh Barry, Dennis Sprenkle, and Dave Hyde, a country boy who just loved the M60. Hyde had built himself a backpack with a flexible feed chute on it that would attach to his M60. In the backpack, Hyde would put anywhere from six to eight hundred rounds of 7.62mm ammo for his M60.

As officers we had Bud Thrift and Lou Boink. Bud was a known factor and a real good leader to have with us. Lou Boink was quickly proving to be a very competent operator and would soon shine as the leader of the most successful Team Two platoon ever to deploy to Nam. We had two officers and thirteen enlisted men, up a bit from the new platoon size of two officers and twelve enlisted. As before, the odd man was so we could assign a man as a PRU or LDNN adviser without shorting either of the squads.

There was some more schooling the higher-ups wanted us to take. The whole platoon packed up for Vietnamese Language School, several weeks of intense instruction in speaking and reading Vietnamese. When the yeoman came over to me for guidance in filling out the orders, I told him what I wanted: authorization of transport by personally owned vehicle to Bragg, where the school was, individual orders, and advance per diem, travel pay, if he could get it.

"But how do you want your orders filled out, Chief?" he asked.

"I'm not going," I answered. "I'm already fluent in three dialects. I've been to Nam twice, and I am not wasting my time at any language school."

That finally drove the yeoman off, but he wasn't very happy. The XO was very hot on language school and he wanted the entire platoon to go. When Jake Rhinebolt, the XO, came into the chiefs' club the next Monday, he was all hot for my ass.

"Jim," Rhinebolt said, "I've been with you in Vietnam. What's this shit about you speaking Vietnamese? Outside of being able to order a beer and talk to the bar girls, you don't speak any more Vietnamese than my dog does. What's this three dialects bull?"

"I speak three dialects, Jake—5.56, 9-millimeter, and 7.62. It's the only language the VC understand."

Well, that worked. Jake had been ready to have me flown down to Bragg to join my platoon at school. But he liked my answer and let me skate this time. I wasn't going to be able to put anything over on Jake again, though.

Things were running smoothly. I had two good leading petty officers, Nelson and Fellers. Whenever I asked if something had been done, packing weapons or preparing certain equipment, before I could finish the question they would answer, "It's done—here's the paperwork, sign it."

One day it was about nine-thirty in the morning and we were ready to go. All of the CONEX* boxes had been loaded, the manifests made out, everything was squared away. There was nothing more to do. "All right, guys," I said, "Tell the men to hit the beach. Don't make any waves about it. I'll see you in the morning for PT."

We had gotten to know Lou Boink real well. He was cool—nothing could rattle him. Fast Eddie started calling him the Marlboro Man, and the tag really fit. Just a few days before we left, Lou decided to throw a party for the platoon. He had a nice little bachelor pad down on Virginia Beach, and we were all to gather there. When we offered to kick in, he said no, the party was on him.

When we arrived at the house, Lou had another surprise for us. I don't know how many cases of Ripple and Cold Duck Lou had bought, but it was more than enough for all of us. After we had all gotten in the house, Lou locked the doors. "It's party time and nobody can leave until all the booze is gone," he said.

Not wanting to disobey orders, the platoon set to obeying Mr. Boink. I don't think we actually finished all that booze, but we sure tried. After that, it was off to Nam.

---

*The CONEX container is a large, heavy steel box used to secure materials for transport. Boxes, weapons, equipment, even ammunition, could be shipped in CONEX boxes. Once on site, the CONEX, with its thick steel walls and securely locked door, could be used as a small shed.

Third Tour

On April 8, 1970, I left for my third tour of duty in Vietnam. Sixth Platoon was a reinforced platoon with an extra man to act as a possible PRU or LDNN adviser. As usual, we traveled to California for a few days of paperwork with Team One. Then it was on to the rivers, jungles, and mud of Vietnam.

The platoon was made up as follows:

Alfa Squad

LT Louis H. Boink
EO1 Orlin D. Nelson
SM2 George E. Leasure
GMG2 Leigh D. Barry
BM2 Dennis G. Sprenkle
EN2 David E. Hyde
BM2 Robert W. Lewis

Bravo Squad

WO1 Henry S. Thrift
QMC James D. Watson

HMC David D. Hammer
AE1 Charles W. Fellers
EN2 John G. Porter
MN2 Wellington T. Leonard
QM3 Slaytor C. Blackiston
QM3 Elliot G. Tesci

Landing at Tan Son Nhut air base on April 15, we all went down to Nha Be to say hello. Ca Mau was going to be the platoon's primary area of operations, relieving Lieutenant Woolard's platoon. Leaving the rest of the men at Nha Be, five of us, the officers, chiefs, and Chuck Fellers, went into Saigon to check in with the NAVSPECWARGRU-VN. There was now a commodore in charge of SEALs operations in all of Southeast Asia as well as a third Special Warfare Group to support our operations.

The commodore was Captain Kane, and his chief of staff was Commander "Stormin' Norman" Olsen. We were checking in and making sure everything was set up for the platoon to begin operations. After checking in, we went back to our platoon and set up shop in Ca Mau, right in the middle of the Ca Mau Peninsula, the rice bowl of Vietnam.

Platoon headquarters was quickly set up at Ca Mau, and almost immediately we were sent to Song Ong Doc. There was an ATSB (Advanced Tactical Support Base) for the PBR sailors at Song Ong Doc. The base was a barge with shore facilities and huts right at the mouth of the Song Ong Doc River where it emptied into the Gulf of Thailand. The base had been having trouble with VC sneaking into the base and near the barge at night. Not having any real intelligence on the area, we were going to set out some ambushes and listening posts, static posts for the most part, just to see if we could get lucky.

Lieutenant Woolard went with us to Song Ong Doc. After his platoon had returned to the States, he stayed back to acquaint Boink, Thrift, and me with the political end of operations, introduce us to district chiefs, things like that. He also familiarized us with the operational clearance procedures for our AOs. That familiarization was a big advantage to the relieving platoon. When the platoon being relieved left, it would normally leave either an officer or a chief behind to help settle in the new platoon.

Introductions helped a lot, especially with some of the native officers and politicals we had to deal with. Far better than walking into some district commander's office cold was to have the man who had been working closely with the commander introduce you: "This is my relief, sir. He has been sent over to further assist you in operations in this area." That sort of thing, as thick as it had to be laid on sometimes, was a lot better than trying to break the ice on your own.

And Rick Woolard always went the extra mile when working with the new platoon. Going with us to Song Ong Doc was a good example of Rick's attitude. Way over on the west coast of the Ca Mau peninsula, Song Ong Doc was about twenty-five miles west of Ca Mau and 175 miles southwest of Saigon.

Our first operation was a simple one. Four of us went on a prisoner snatch deep into the Delta. Inserting from a PBR, we traveled during the day to reach our target site. The plan was to travel during the day, find the target, lay up with the target under observation, and pull off the snatch at night.

A fairly simple op for us. There was only one problem. There are almost no landmarks in the flat Delta land of the Ca Mau Peninsula. By that afternoon, we were a little confused. Swamp and brush surrounded us. I thought I knew approximately where we were, but when you're wandering around in Charlie's backyard, approximately isn't good enough. It was about three o'clock and time to find out our exact location. One of those tricks they taught us in the Gunfire Support course came to mind.

A Coast Guard cutter was offshore, acting as our primary fire support with her 5-inch gun. I called her on the radio and put in my order for fire: "This is Whiskey Sour. I want one round, Willy Peter, on my command, center of sector."

While the cutter was loading up I spoke to the rest of the squad. "Everybody watch for smoke and listen for the noise. Pay attention to your compass when you see or hear anything."

Slaytor looked at me and asked, "Are you really doing that?"

"Yeah," I answered.

Just then the cutter called back "Ready!"

"Shoot," I called back.

"Shot," was their answer, and the round was on its way.

"Okay, everybody pay attention. It's on its way."

"Hey, Chief?"

"Yeah, Slaytor."

"What happens if we're standing in the center of the sector?"

"Slaytor, bend over and kiss your ass good-bye. It's a 5-inch Willy Peter round."

We weren't in the center of the sector. In fact, we were roughly where I had figured we were on the map. None of us saw the smoke from the WP round, but we heard the explosion and had a good idea where it had landed. Paying attention to the time of flight of the round and what we heard gave us a good indicator of our general position. It turned out to be a dry op, the target never showed. But I don't think Slaytor ever wanted to use "center of sector" again.

The platoon had inherited an interpreter from Woolard's platoon. Fast Eddie and I both thought the man was double-crossing us. We had caught him lying to some of our VN intelligence sources. What he was doing was misinterpreting what we said to agents and other people who wanted to sell us information. The man had been with the platoons for about a year and had been giving trouble for some time now.

Since almost all of our interpreters were supplied by the Agency, we had a hard time letting them go. Finally, I had just had enough of this one man. His fabrications, telling people what we would do to them and what they might get paid, were undermining our intelligence-gathering for the platoon. I convinced him that perhaps there were other places he might prefer to go.

The barge we were working off was anchored in the river. To defend against enemy swimmers, there were open boxes of fragmentation and concussion grenades on the bulkheads spaced every five or ten yards along the deck. If a swimmer was spotted in the water, any crew member could shout out a warning. Within seconds of a warning, anyone who was near a box would start tossing grenades into the water.

One evening, I took the interpreter over to the edge of the barge. The man just acted cocky when I tried to explain the situation to him. As far as he was concerned, he was an Agency employee and there was nothing I could do. Suddenly I grabbed him by the shirt and leaned him way out over the water. The Vietnamese are just little shits and I had no trouble holding this man exactly where I wanted him. The Agency had issued him a Browning automatic, and I took it from him.

"Let me tell you something, fella," I said, holding him out over the water. "I can fuck you up real easy. I'll just drop you into the river and shout 'Swimmer in the water.' " He suddenly stopped struggling, the meaning of what I had just said sinking in. His eyes were huge as they pleaded with me not to let him go. His squalling grated on my nerves, and I told him to keep quiet. The sound of that brown water gurgling by was all you could hear for a moment.

Sticking his weapon into my belt, I told him to find his way back to Agency headquarters in Saigon, one long walk away. Basically, I fired him on the spot. Not much argument from him, and I heard little about it from our Agency people.

Now we were assigned a new interpreter by the name of Füks. Füks proved his value to us almost right away. He had the valuable skill of translating not only what you were saying, but also the inflection and what you meant to say. Some interpreters will just translate what you say into another language without giving any special attention to the meaning. Hence the old saying "It loses something in the translation." But Füks would make sure what we said didn't lose anything in translation.

One day, a young couple came over to the barge where our headquarters were. They had some information to sell and knew that the Americans were buying. The guard at the end of the gang-way came back to our part of the barge—on the southwest corner, right next to the head—to ask if we wanted to see this couple. He told us they seemed legitimate to him, so we said to bring them on in.

That couple just thought they were selling information to the Americans—they had no idea that they would be talking to SEALs. We wore standard fatigues with our names and U.S. NAVY above the pockets and that was it. We kept a low profile and appeared to be regular PBR sailors.

We were sitting around a small table in a ten-by-ten-foot metal-walled room. Lou Boink, the Marlboro Man, was sitting at the table quietly, smoking a cigarette. Lou's more than six feet of height and broad shoulders were disguised somewhat by his sitting down. But there was no mistaking the quiet menace that he could bring into his voice when he wanted to. Fast Eddie sat to the boss's left and I sat to his right on opposite ends of the table.

Füks brought the young couple over to the table and sat them down across from Lou. These two kids couldn't have been far out of their teens if they were that old. Moving over to my right, Füks sat between Lou and me, ready to translate for us. It was obvious that these kids were a bit nervous, but they thought they were in control. The reality of their situation was soon going to hit them like a truck out of the darkness.

Intel was important to us for our operations, but there was no way we would take any chance with these two. While just staring down at his hands on the table, Lou cross-examined them like a deadly, green-dressed Perry Mason. What did they know that they wanted to sell us?

The answer was that they knew where some weapons were and possibly some people, and what would we pay for the information? Did we know anyone that would possibly want to go after the materials? Did any of our boat sailors want some war trophies? Generally they were giving us a bit of a runaround without saying anything specific enough to get our attention.

Lou just sat and smoked his cigarette. Never looking up, the Marlboro Man just asked his questions in a quiet voice. Now Lou figured it was time to end the games and get some answers.

"Füks," Lou said, "Ask them if they have ever heard of the 'men with green faces.' "

That was a name the Viet Cong had put on us a few years earlier. That name was absolutely dreaded by the VC. They had no idea of who we were when the SEALs started operations in Vietnam. They knew we couldn't be Army personnel, because the Army always moved en masse. To the VC's knowledge, there were no Marines in the Delta, and besides, the Marines didn't operate the way we did. Sailors were on boats on the rivers. So who the hell were we?

All the enemy knew was that whenever someone saw us, and lived to tell about it, we were heavily camouflaged. When we put on the green-and-black makeup to help hide our faces, we barely looked human. Popping up from concealment in the bushes or the water, we could send the Creature from the Black Lagoon running, screaming with fright.

When Füks asked those two if they knew of the men with green faces, all the blood just drained from their faces in a heartbeat. Shock, and more than a little fear, was all they showed. Eddie and I had been looking at them as Füks asked them the question, and Lou had glanced up too.

Then Lou really dropped a bomb on them. Slowly taking a drag from his cigarette and then exhaling, Lou said, "Füks, tell them that's who they're talking to."

Those two people changed their tune in a hurry. Now they didn't want to be paid anything for the information. Everything they knew they would tell us. Now it was time for us to get down to the nitty-gritty. Lou told them that they would get paid, depending on what we found, but they were going to have to lead us in.

The young man balked quite a bit at that. It was obvious that we had scared him, but not enough to make him ignore his own good sense. He would lead us in, but there were two conditions. The first was that he be given a weapon for the operation. The second was that his girl would stay behind.

"No problem," we answered. "We'll give you a weapon, and the girl can stay here." Giving him a weapon didn't bother us at all. We even had an M16 specifically for agents whose loyalty we questioned. He could check the weapon, even see that the ammunition was live. But he probably wouldn't notice that the tip of the firing pin had been ground off.

The op went well. The weapon was there, and we picked it up. The person that the agent pointed out to us as VC was snatched cleanly. A nice clean op, no shooting and no casualties. It went like a Union Camp training operation. The op and the prisoner led to another op and those led to more. We ended up pulling about eight to ten operations out of Song Ong Doc before we pulled out and went back to Ca Mau.

And it turned out that we hadn't left Song Ong Doc too soon. Within a week of our leaving, the barge was shelled with mortar fire. We got the word that our compartment and the head were gone. The part of the barge that was hit was just the southwest corner, where we had met that young couple.

That incident taught us one good lesson—be very careful about who we brought home. Our living quarters and working areas would stay off-limits to anyone that there was even a slight question about.

The barracks, actually a small villa, we stayed in at Ca Mau was also where the PBR sailors on the base stayed. The villa, an H-building, with two long wings connected by a short cross hall, was a good-sized place, and we had the part closest to the gate. The other end of the building had also been available for us but we had turned it down. Bad mistake—in the section of the villa next to the spot we had turned down was stored all of the beer for the base!

The reason the men had turned down that section of the building was its lack of ventilation. The ventilation was closed off because of all the stacked cases of beer. And the only thing separating the two sections was a half-inch plywood wall. Eventually a "door" did appear in that storeroom wall for our use. But we could have arranged it so that the walk was considerably shorter.

In our own compartment, we built a little bar and had a refrigerator. No warm beer for the SEALs, even if the price was pretty good. We always had a bar tab book, and our liquor was paid for on the honor system. Every payday, each man would give what he thought he owed in the book—usually we didn't even bother to look it up. Most of the time, we ended up with more money than was needed. Whenever we could, we stocked the bar with booze, and beer was always available.

Not everything went as well with our living quarters as we would have liked. Every week the air conditioners had to be cleaned. And I mean cleaned—taken out of the walls and hosed down. That tropical climate in Southeast Asia could grow some of the nastiest crud in a very short time.

The platoon operated out of Ca Mau for only a short time. Bud Thrift went down to Hy Yen to see about operations in that area. The district adviser connected Bud with a Chinese Catholic priest named Father Wa who lived in Hy Yen. Father Wa had his own group of indigenous people who would operate with Americans. The unit Father Wa had assembled wasn't a PRU; they weren't Vietnamese or LDNNs. What they were was the meanest bunch of bastards I had ever even heard about. Arms and equipment would come to Father Wa through "unofficial" channels, and his men never seemed short of arms or ammunition. For all I knew, they could have been stripping out VC arms caches.

Most of Father Wa's people were either ex-VC, ex-NVA, or whatever. And these weren't Hoi Chanhs either. (The United States had instituted the Chieu Hoi [Open Arms] program by which Viet Cong could surrender and eventually work with the U.S. forces as scouts. VC who had taken advantage of the Chieu Hoi program were called Hoi Chanhs.)

What Father Wa had done was develop his own surrender program. Charlie knew that he could come into Hy Yen, with his weapon slung, and not be accosted. That first time, a VC could come in and get a meal, some extra rations, some light medical attention, and even a little bit of money in some cases. Father Wa would take the man's picture and enter him in a big book. Then Father Wa would tell the man:

"I have done this for you and will do it again. But if you come back again, it is obvious that the people you work for cannot pay or take care of you. If you return, then you work for me. The job is here if you want to stay now, or come back later. I have fed you, and this is what you can take with you. If you come back again, there is no choice—you will work for me."

That is how Father Wa built up his force. As a Chinese priest who walked around carrying a Remington 12-gauge, Father Wa had a greater knowledge of unconventional warfare in Southeast Asia than the whole of SEAL Team Two. The history of Father Wa's assumption of control of a VN village was quite interesting.

After World War II, the Communists in China were chasing out or killing all of the Chinese who wouldn't accept the new government. Coming down to Vietnam, then French Indochina, Father Wa was given jurisdiction over the small village of Hy Yen. Over the years, Father Wa's influence grew. His brother ended up being the village chief and became a high-ranking VN. By the time we came around to Hy Yen, even the bad guys respected Father Wa.

And Father Wa supposedly knew about the men with green faces and what we did. The SEALs were still a very secret organization, and few outsiders knew much more than the rumors we helped circulate. Father Wa had a great deal of respect for us, and that worked out in our favor. Father Wa had the best intelligence-gathering network in South Vietnam, probably the most effective network of the whole Southeast Asian war. And he was willing to give us his information! That was an absolute gold mine for the SEALs and for Sixth Platoon in particular. The platoon mined that gold with enthusiasm.

We hadn't done much operating out of Ca Mau before Bud Thrift came back with his report of the situation in Hy Yen. Soon Bravo Squad was on its way to Hy Yen for fun and games with Father Wa's people.

Point men and agents were supplied to us by Father Wa. One of the men he gave to lead us in on an op was a thin man, tall for an Asian, who had obviously been around war most of his life. His glittering black eyes had seen an eternity's suffering, and his careful, deliberate movements showed that he had lived in a hostile environment for some time. Father Wa spoke to Bud Thrift and me the first time we went on an operation with this new man.

"This is a new guy who knows the area very well. He's taking you to a target. If he moves wrong or even blinks and you don't like it, if you have any hesitation about his loyalty at all, don't bring him back. Don't worry about it. If you come back without him, you won't have to answer to me." Father Wa could play hardball with the best of us.

The man ended up being one hell of a point man. He scouted for us a number of times and led us through some bad areas. He knew all the signs of booby traps, caches, and safe trails. He should have—he'd been an NVA company commander before joining Father Wa's group!

We pulled six or more operations in a row without ever firing a shot. We kept hitting pay dirt and doing the job clean. Just like it was supposed to be according to our training—go in, hit, and pull out without anyone but the target ever knowing we had been there. Perfect SEAL operations, and we were snatching our people and finding the weapons caches. The Song Ong Doc operations had been much the same way, only we hadn't hit the target as often. Normally, this kind of luck is nothing to complain about. The only trouble was that some of the new guys, those who hadn't been in combat before, were getting a little too cocky.

One operation we went on took us deep into enemy-held territory. We were eight to ten klicks inland following one of Father Wa's agents. Duke and Chuck both had Stoners. I was running rear security for the squad. Bud Thrift was up front. Fast Eddie was running point moving with the agent. When we were less than five hundred yards from the objective, standing in the middle of an open rice field, things started happening.

The jungle is normally pretty quiet at night. The occasional greenish-yellow light from a firefly. Grunts and noises of night wildlife moving about. And the air is chill against your skin, moist with the humidity of the tropics. The SEAL squad moves silently. No one speaks a word. Any necessary communications are made by hand signals or very close in whispering. My skin started crawling with awareness of something more than the breeze blowing.

All around us, lights started going on. Village dogs were barking. The pucker factor was getting big. Going up to Bud, I told him, "Boss, get the fuck out of here!"

"We've only got a couple of hundred yards to go," Bud said. "The guide says the hooch is right over there."

"Boss," I insisted, "something's wrong!"

"What are you talking about, Chief? Anything happens, we can handle it. We've got two Stoners with us."

The man had never been shot at. The operations had been going as if we were training back in the States.

"Bud," I said, "the Stoners make you Jesus Christ, they don't make you God. Something's wrong. Here it is, two, three o'clock in the morning, and all those lights are coming on. Those are kerosene lamps being lit by somebody. Why? Everything I know is saying, 'Get the hell out of here!' Whatever is going on, we don't want any part of it."

Apparently my little speech did some good. Bud turned the squad around and aborted the op. The only person upset about turning back was the agent. He seemed a little disappointed. Intelligence came out later that the operation was a setup. The agent had been sent in to sell us information that would lead us into a trap. If the ambush had been successful, it would have been a real plus for Charlie. Not only would the VC have gotten rid of a local unit, they would have taken out a bunch of green faces. This was not something that we ever wanted to deal with again. I believe Father Wa's people dealt with that particular agent.

But I had to deal with my officer. Bud Thrift was a good leader, and he was showing the makings of a good operator, if not a hunter.

But Bud needed a talking-to, and I hoped he was ready to listen.

"Hey, Boss," I said in private, "don't get me wrong, you're doing a great job. But this isn't Union Camp or Camp Pickett. This is Vietnam, and this shit is for real. If you screw up, Charlie will put your head on a stick. You have to realize that those guys out there are trying to kill you before you kill them. This is fucking Vietnam! This is war!"

Bud never did get excited. He just looked and listened to me. After I was done, he said, "You're just excited, Chief."

Damn, that was frustrating. All the more so because I was leaving. It had been decided that I would be going over to relieve a lieutenant in charge of a group of LDNNs. My next operations were scheduled to take place in Cambodia. We were going to cross the border and mess with Charlie in what he thought was a safe area.

If I had been over there with a green platoon, I would have never thought of asking for the LDNN adviser slot. But the platoon had a large percentage of combat vets and a deep pool of experience to draw on. I had gone to Bud Thrift and Lou Boink and asked for the assignment, and received it. But before I went, I had to be sure that Bud knew what I felt was wrong with the situation.

You can only talk to a man so much, then you have to let him go on his own. Bud learned. I hadn't been gone a week before Bud had a message sent to me. He had walked into a trap with the squad right alongside of him. He was just too confident because he hadn't been shot at yet. The ambush took care of that. The squad didn't get hurt—they fought their way out. But Bud learned his lesson. Now he had been shot at and wouldn't feel quite as immortal and overconfident as he had before. The message he sent to me ended with: "You were right, Chief."

But before I left for my adventures with the LDNNs, there had been another little problem I had to clean up. My medical records still had me listed as an outpatient from Portsmouth Naval Hospital. This hadn't seemed much of a problem when Sixth Platoon had left the States. But while in Vietnam, I realized that my enlistment was up in May. I had to take a reenlistment physical. My injuries hadn't kept me from doing my share in the operations with the platoon. But there was no way they would get by a medical officer.

Through a bit of luck, we were able to do a favor for a Coast

Guard ship that was operating nearby in the South China Sea. The favor wasn't much, just a bit of diving to check on some possible hull damage. Nothing was wrong, but the skipper of the ship felt he owed me a favor. Now was my chance.

I leveled with the skipper, told him my situation. It turned out that there was a doctor aboard the Coast Guard ship who would be glad to help me out.

The physical was approved, and I was certified for reenlistment. Going up to Can Tho, I took the oath of enlistment and filled out the necessary paperwork. Chuck Fellers was with me, and we ran into Harry Humphries in Can Tho. We all tied one on pretty well, and Chuck the most of all. When Truxell, the CO of Det Alfa at the time, gave me the oath of enlistment, a picture was taken of the little ceremony. It's a good thing they weren't running a tape of my reenlistment, because I think my Jersey accent was a little thick that night. It's also fortunate that the photographer didn't have a wide-angle lens on his camera. You can't see in the picture where Chuck is passed out on the floor between Truxell and me.

On my way to my LDNN assignment and Cambodia, I stopped off in Nha Bey to meet Ronnie Rodger. Ronnie was learning his assignment and had gotten word to me that if I wanted a Stoner for my ops in Cambodia, he would lend me his. With my going over to be an adviser to the LDNNs, I wanted all the firepower I could get. Roy Boehm had told me a long time ago that the LDNNs weren't the most reliable troops in the world, and all I had heard since then reinforced that.

Ronnie had one of the short Stoners, the Mark 23 Mod 0 model with a 150-round belt drum. After removing the stock and tying a sling onto the weapon, I had 150 rounds of firepower available in a two-foot-long package. The LDNN knew very well the destructive power of the Stoner and treated anyone holding one with respect. Along with the Stoner, I had Sweetheart, my eight-shot pistol-grip 12-gauge. Now I had enough firepower to operate safely with the LDNNs, and without shorting my own platoon a Stoner.

Ronnie and I spent a couple of days taking some liberty in Nha Bey. We went to a party being given by the Agency people, and Ronnie had a particularly good time there. The people at the party had thought that Ronnie was a chaplain! One commander even gave Ronnie his confession.

This was a scream. Ronnie and the commander were in the men's room, the commander on his knees confessing his sins. And Ronnie played it to the hilt, placing his hand on the commander's head and solemnly saying, "I forgive you, my son."

Later on I told Ronnie that if he ever met that commander again and he was wearing the uniform of a second class bosun's mate, "Sell the shithouse, because that commander will have them weld the cell door shut."

Perhaps Ronnie shouldn't have pushed the joke so far. He did end that tour wounded. Maybe God got a little mad at him. There are some people bigger than the SEALs.

But now it was time for me to move on to my new assignment. I had my Stoner and was now feeling a lot more comfortable about the assignment.

The platoon had come over to Vietnam well armed. Each squad had two Stoners, and later in the tour, when I returned from Cambodia, I showed up with a fifth Stoner. That was a tremendous amount of firepower for the platoon.

We had heard that new weapons had been shipped over, specifically the M203 grenade launcher. The M203 was an improved version of the earlier XM-148. We didn't receive any of the new launchers while I was there; the platoon used the XM-148s we had brought with us from the Creek.

Team Two had received a number of Hush Puppies and each of our officers had brought one with them. I personally never used the Hush Puppy in the field, but thought a lot of it. During my first tour, the M3A1 greasegun with the World War II OSS silencer was the only suppressed weapon we had been able to get our hands on. And the operation we had the suppressed greaseguns for was scrubbed. The Hush Puppy was a great addition to the platoon. Those quiet pistols would fire a single shot that could hardly be recognized as a firearm shot twenty yards away.

When we originally asked for a suppressed pistol—the powers that be did not want the term "silencer" used—we were asked what we wanted it for. Since killing men with a suppressed handgun was considered somehow "unsportsmanlike," we told them the weapon was wanted to shoot dogs. Every VN village had dogs hanging around that would sometimes bark as we approached. Since the weapon was intended to silence dogs, and any other vermin who happened to get in front of it, the pistol was named the Hush Puppy. Because of that name, after a while, all silencers came to be called Hush Puppies.

Only Bud Thrift and Lou Boink normally had the Hush Puppies in Sixth Platoon. The image of the Marlboro Man, the archetypal SEAL, face all covered with green and black camo, coming out from concealment holding a suppressed pistol, his eyes as cold and deep as glittering death, was enough to give anyone a moment's thought. To a VC, he would be a demon out of some nightmare. The last nightmare that Cong would ever have.

On May 27 I arrived on the USS *Benewah* (APB-35). The *Benewah* was a self-propelled barracks ship anchored way up in the Mekong River near Cambodia. The *Benewah* had berthing, feeding, repair, and resupply facilities for the Brown Water Navy and Seawolf detachments assigned to her. On board the *Benewah* I was going to join Detachment Sierra, the SEAL LDNN advisory group.

When Sixth Platoon had hit country, we had done a few ops as a platoon. For Team Two in Vietnam, full platoon ops were not the normal way of doing things. Team One did a lot of operations as a full platoon while it was in the Rung Sat. What we did was spread out as squads and have a few Americans assigned to PRUs as advisers. This style of operation allowed Team Two to make the maximum use of its people incountry. Now I was breaking off from the platoon to operate with the LDNNs, the South Vietnamese version of the SEALs.

President Nixon had authorized U.S. troops to enter Cambodia earlier in the month. In two weeks of fighting, the combined U.S. and ARVN forces captured thousands of tons of supplies, weapons, and ammunition. The U.S. troops were allowed to go only up to twenty-one miles into Cambodia proper. But the ARVN forces were not held back by this constraint, and the LDNNs were also South Vietnamese forces.

On board the *Benewah* was a lieutenant who had been working as the adviser to the LDNN group I was picking up. The lieutenant was a real hot operator, as good a hunter as anyone I had known. When I arrived at the *Benewah*, he already had my fourteen-man LDNN unit ready for me to take over. From what I heard later, when Admiral Matthews saw that a "Chief Watson" was relieving a lieutenant, his comment was, "A chief relieving a lieutenant?"

One of the officers with the admiral knew me and explained the situation. "Admiral," he said, "there is not going to be any problem with this chief relieving an officer. Your problem is going to be just keeping track of this man. He likes to move and move fast. He likes to operate."

That apparently was enough for the admiral. I didn't hear anything further about my assignment. My team was LDNN Group Alfa operating under the direction of the commander of Task Group 194.0 (Rear Admiral Matthews), and I was the senior U.S. naval adviser to the LDNNs. The naval aspect of the Cambodian operation was named Tran Hung Dao XI.

All of this had little practical effect on me as I prepared to operate with my new unit. The LDNNs had their own compartment deep inside the *Benewah*. As the adviser, I had my own little stateroom that I shared with the lieutenant I was replacing for a few days while he settled me in.

Those first days were a break-in period while I learned about my troops, what areas we would operate in, how to handle the intel we would receive, and all the other things I needed to know to operate properly. Chief Ba was the senior LDNN and ran the men.

The routine was that I would gather the intelligence on a possible target and give it to Chief Ba. Ba would write up the patrol order for his men and give it to me first for suggestions and corrections, so that I wouldn't have to change Ba's orders in front of his men. Then Ba would brief his men, giving them all the intelligence and orders for the mission with me just standing there.

The first LDNN op I went out on was a VCI body snatch. The target was a VC finance chief who was supposed to be coming out of Vietnam with the money he had collected. The finance chief would be coming to a central meeting point in Cambodia.

The agent who had brought us the information drew out the trail the finance chief would follow and traced the route on an aerial photo. Going up in a chopper, we conducted an air recon, and the agent pointed out where we could find the finance chief.

With all this intelligence, Chief Ba put together the plan for the patrol. The operation would be an ambush with the intent being to kill the target. The LDNNs were just like the PRUs in that respect. The easiest way to deal with the enemy is just to kill him. That was also how you got loot and weapons with the least exposure to yourself and your men. But you also lost any intelligence that the target could have given you.

We would insert for the operation by STAB. These were not the earlier STABs that Team Two had brought over in 1967. The Mark II STAB was also known as the LSSC (Light SEAL Support Craft), but was most commonly called the STAB, this time for Strike Assault Boat. These new STABs were everywhere; they didn't stand out as the early Mark I STABs did. Everyone and his brother seemed to use the damn things.

Since they were so common on the rivers, I had no qualms about riding the new STABs, especially since the average STAB carried three M60 machine guns, two Mk 20 40mm machine guns, an M79, and the personal weapons of the four-man crew.

We inserted without any trouble. I had my Stoner with me and was prepared for any trouble that might come up. And I wasn't just looking in the jungle for trouble to appear. The squad of LDNNs I was with hadn't earned my trust either.

The first LDNNs had been trained by Roy Boehm back in the mid-1960s. Right before graduation, over half of the class went over the hill to North Vietnam. A week after those first LDNNs deserted, a ship was sunk in the harbor at Da Nang. Roy's only printable comment was that they had done the job just as he taught them. It was Roy's warnings and my own innate combat paranoia that kept me from trusting the LDNNs much at all.

After we inserted, we walked in to the target site. Coming across a cornfield, we walked between the furrows, the tall stalks helping to conceal us. Besides my Stoner, I had a radio on my back, so I was pretty weighed down on this patrol. Here I was, deep into Indian country, patrolling with a squad I didn't really trust, and all that kept going through my head was part of the title song from *Oklahoma!*: "The corn is as high as an elephant's eye . . ." Singing has never been my strong point. Hell, I was looking around for an elephant to see if the song was right.

We finally cleared that cornfield, and I managed to get that song out of my head. Traveling along, we went through woods, clearings, and rice paddies. After the amount of time I had spent in Vietnam I barely noticed the wet, earthy smell of the woods, the rustle and swish of the high grass in the clearings, or even the stink of the rice paddies. The thought of running into an Asian two-step—any of a number of very poisonous snakes, usually a banded krait—in the grasslands wouldn't even enter my mind now. In all my time in Vietnam, I had never had any real encounters with the native wildlife. Even walking through the mud of the rice paddies, stepping into the footprints of the man in front, was now second nature to me.

Besides, I had enough to worry about just keeping an eye on my LDNNs. This was our first op and I was being doubly cautious.

Coming up on a trail, Ba stopped the patrol and spread out the squad. He was setting up the ambush! Going up to Ba, I said, "You're not there yet. What are you doing? We have at least another two klicks to go."

Looking at me suspiciously, Ba said, "What do you mean?"

Now I was really wondering what the hell was going on. "This is just a trail," I said. "You've seen the maps and aerial photos, you even went on the aerial recon. There's a Y in the trail where the target spot is. It's on that compass bearing"—I pointed out the direction—"about another two klicks, according to my pace count. Now saddle the guys up and let's go."

Ba stared at me and said, "Remember one thing. You are my adviser, not my boss."

Oh, really! I thought. Not saying another word, I went over to the other side of the trail, where all the men were, and charged my Stoner.

The scrape-click-snap of a Stoner being cocked is a very noticeable sound, especially when the weapon is right next to you. All those men knew exactly what a Stoner could do, especially at the eyeball-to-eyeball distance we were facing each other at. Nobody was moving, and I had their absolute attention. "Ba," I said, "come over here and sit with your men. If I hear one sound, I will list you all as KIA"—killed in action—"and make a hero out of myself for getting all the bodies out."

That was the way we spent the night, the LDNNs staring at me like one huge eyeball, and me with about eight pounds of pressure on my Stoner's ten-pound-pull trigger. If there had been one sound out of that group, I believe I would have pulled the trigger. All I carried was the 150 rounds in the drum of the weapon. But that would have been enough. I just didn't like the bastards. It seemed that many of the Vietnamese were like their flag—what wasn't Red was yellow.

By the next day, it was time to move back to the extraction point. This time I pulled rear security, moving along at the back of the patrol. Only thing was, I wasn't covering the squad's rear, I was covering my own.

When we got back to the *Benewah*, I had it out with Chief Ba. Seriously pissed only comes close to describing my state of mind. After I'd gone round and round with Ba, we finally came to an understanding. I would leave and the VNs could do whatever they liked with their country if he wasn't going to listen to me. I didn't need this shit and would go back to the Delta with the rest of my platoon and we would do our own thing. Only trouble was that when I left, the support we supplied would leave with me.

While the other members of the platoon were operating in their respective areas, I began getting somewhere with my LDNNs. There was an agent, a real skinny young kid, who wanted to work for us full-time. The kid was a little hyper, but claimed that he had enough information to keep us busy for a while. Neither fully Vietnamese nor Cambodian, the kid lived right on the border near the area we wanted to operate in.

Since he wanted to work with us so much, anything that we could pay him would be fine. Whenever he went along with us, he would always wear a mask if there was a chance someone would see him. He was always concerned that someone would recognize him and that his parents would suffer for it.

Now information started to come to me that there were a couple of Red Chinese advisers living in a particular village near a pagoda, up in Cambodia.

After the Agency had given me all it had on the situation, I turned my masked marauder loose on the problem. I figured that the kid could infiltrate into the area and give me more recent, detailed information on the Chinese. He came back a couple of days later with the information I wanted.

As things went in Cambodia, anytime I wanted specific information, I could just let this kid go and filter into the target. Since he was half Cambodian and half Vietnamese, the kid could blend in anywhere on either side of the border.

After the kid came back, he laid out the information for us. Making a drawing of the village and comparing it to aerial photographs, we had a good idea of the target area. Now we knew where the two Chinese were all the time. They lived in a small brick-and-stone building that looked like a pagoda but was really a dwelling.

Now it was time to go on the op, and this looked like a big one. To my knowledge, no one had captured a Chinese adviser to the North Vietnamese or the VC. We knew that they were around, helping to guide the war effort, but we hadn't caught one yet.

This was going to be a good op, and I was looking forward to it. Going out on an aerial reconnaissance, I checked the target area. The village was a medium-small one with some permanent-style buildings, about twenty-five miles southeast of Phnom Penh.

The target was only a few miles inside Cambodia, and I had no trouble getting support for the operation. The higher-ups had code-named my op Operation Safari, a subordinate operation to Tran Hung Dao XI. Whatever I needed was made available to me, and the op was a go for May 31.

Operation Safari had six guns (helicopter gunships) laid on for air support and two slicks for transport. More slicks were on call if we needed them. All of the LDNNs and the agent were going in on the op. When we dropped into this little village, the group would break up into two-man teams. Teams would bust into each hooch, search it, and then move on to the next one. The operation could quickly dissolve into a first-class cluster-fuck given the troops I had to work with. And these were supposed to be among the elite fighting men of South Vietnam.

But one rule was established with the LDNNs. Anytime that shooting erupted during the operation, the men were to "rally 'round the flag." It did happen that I, the chief, was the flag. But I had no problem enforcing that suggestion. I had the radio and could call for the bus home.

The helos had the most fun on the operation. After we went in, they circled the area for targets of opportunity, much as on a parakeet op. One Loach pilot in particular had a great time. The Army Loach that the pilot was flying, a Hughes OH-6 Cayuse, was armed with a minigun on the left side of the aircraft.

The pilot actually captured a prisoner with his helicopter. Seeing a man running from the village, the pilot swung his Loach over and gave chase. Catching the man on a small bridge, the pilot knocked him down with the bird's landing strut. Leaning out of the cabin with a pistol, the Loach pilot forced the prisoner to grab hold of the strut and hang on. That's how the pilot brought the prisoner to us, hanging on for dear life from the bottom of the helicopter.

Going through the village, I came on what looked like a schoolhouse. There were desks, a blackboard, and a larger desk at the front of the classroom. Shouting out to Ba, I asked, "Has the schoolhouse been searched?"

Ba bellowed back that it had been searched, and he continued on his way. I was pretty loaded down with my Stoner and the radio, and I just couldn't force the drawers of the big desk open. The drawers were locked, so I knew that the LDNNs hadn't searched the schoolhouse. They were absolutely paranoid about booby traps and would bypass anything that even looked like a risk.

Thinking that Ba had just lied to me pissed me off a bit. Flipping the desk over, I started kicking the bottoms of the drawers out. Those LDNNs hadn't searched this desk all right. Pouring out of the kicked-in drawers was money! Lots of Cambodian money. Jamming the bills into my pockets, I stripped out the desk and continued with the operation.

As the rest of the village was being searched, I kept the information about the money to myself. Finally, we called in the extraction choppers. We now had thirty-some prisoners, including two Chinese. Not a shot had been fired at us, and now we were heading back home. This was the kind of op I loved. The air support had a ball. To the men in the choppers, the whole operation was like a three-ring circus. All during my time on the ground I had been in constant contact with the gunships, and they had been talking to me.

"I've got a guy over here," a pilot radioed. "What do I do with him?"

"If you can't bring him to us, shoot him," I answered back.

Anyone who was running was fair game. The whole village had been full of materials, VC, and NVA troops. They were bad guys, so screw them. If they wanted to surrender, all they had to do was put their hands up. A lot of the enemy did put their hands up, and now we had to move them.

Into each chopper full of prisoners, I put two LDNNs to guard them. It had been prearranged before the mission that we would extract to a Special Forces A-camp, a forward area base for an A-team, just inside of the Vietnamese border.

Arriving at the camp, we ran into a new problem. The Special Forces men at the A-camp balked at the number of prisoners we had. "You have got to be shitting us," they complained. "We're not here as a goddam prisoner-of-war camp!"

I said to the OIC of the A-team, "Captain, you don't understand. I haven't got anywhere else to take them. I can't take them on board my ship. There just isn't any room. Besides, we have to wring them out, especially those two Chinese."

There was a mustang Marine lieutenant at the camp who was real interested in who I had. That officer was ex-recon, and he wanted a shot at the Chinese. "We'll wring 'em out," he said. A regular hard-core Marine recon grunt. They could do anything the SEALs could, only not as well.

Neither that Marine nor I was a trained interrogator. An unnamed government Agency was supposed to have had an interrogation team waiting for me to arrive at the camp. Separating the prisoners, I put the LDNNs to work guarding the POWs. This pissed off Ba—his people weren't sentries and they were not supposed to guard people. As time went on, Ba and I had more and more clashes.

But I had other things to concern myself with besides Ba's injured feelings. We tied the prisoners' hands behind their backs, then, taking a line, tied all of the prisoners together. One person could now watch all of them without any trouble.

Now it was time to deal with my real prizes, the two Chinese officers. The younger member of the pair was maybe in his midthirties and more than a little scared. The older Chinese, maybe in his late fifties or early sixties, was one tough sonofabitch. That older Chinese was obviously a bigwig with the NVA and North Vietnamese government. In the older man's pockets we found Polaroid pictures of Ho Chi Minh's funeral in Hanoi! Shots of Uncle Ho, who had died in 1969, lying in state in his glass coffin. Polaroid pictures don't have negatives—this man had taken the shots himself!

All kinds of materials were in these guys' pockets—postcards from North Vietnam, things like that. Even a real nice picture of Mao Tse-tung. Later on, I passed the picture on to my Naval Intelligence representative in Can Tho, and he saw to it that the picture was given to Major General Hal McCown. I received a letter thanking me for the picture.

The military thought that our capturing the two Chinese advisers was dynamite. We ended up taking most of the prisoners back to their village two days later. The two Chinese stayed with us.

The younger of the two Chinese broke during interrogation, telling us everything he knew, even volunteering things we hadn't asked for. The old man was a different story. He was *not* going to break. That old man was ready to die for what he believed in, no matter what we did. A hard-core professional, that Chinese was not going to tell us anything.

Giving that Chinese the chance to be a martyr to his cause was not something I was rushing to do. My experiences in that Marine E&E course told me that somewhere down the line, somebody could break this man. But I had the world of respect for that old man's professionalism and courage.

One of the advantages we had was having Füks as an interpreter. The first thing the Chinese tried was to tell us they didn't speak Vietnamese. Fine—Füks started speaking Cambodian to them. No, no, that wasn't right, they didn't speak Cambodian either. Oh, okay, what language do you speak? Chinese. And Füks started talking to them in Chinese.

Using the money I had taken from the schoolhouse, I paid Füks extra for what he was doing during the interrogations. Füks was paid by the South Vietnamese navy, and his base pay wasn't much. But a better interpreter I couldn't have asked for.

The money caused some problems with Ba and the LDNNs. Ba swore that I had taken the money for myself and put it into my pocket. After we went round and round on the subject for a while, Ba had the rest of the LDNNs convinced I had taken the money from them for myself. Some of the problems I had brought on myself. When we arrived at the camp and were settling in, I had waved all those bills in front of Ba and his men, saying, "You searched that schoolhouse, right? Then how could I have found all this?" Perhaps not the most diplomatic thing I could have done, but the performance of my LDNNs was less than I would have expected from a bunch of Hell Week trainees. I had a lot more respect for that Chinese officer, my enemy, than for these "men" of mine.

The Marine officer and I interrogated that Chinese officer for seventy-two hours straight. There would be a treasure trove of intelligence for operations from the old man if we could get him to talk to us. But he never did. The younger man had told us the older man was a general, high up in the Chinese army, and an adviser to the NVA. Finally, we turned our two prisoners over to the South Vietnamese military. From what I heard later, that Chinese general barely broke stride going through ARVN headquarters. In the front door and out the back. The South Vietnamese system in the rear was so corrupt that you had to go into the combat zones for a breath of fresh air.

On one op later, Füks and I were resting, deep inside of Cambodia. With his overview of the war and deep involvement in it, Füks had come up with his own answer to dealing with Vietnamese corruption and deceit. "All we have to do," Füks said, "is put all the good Vietnamese on board a ship. Then we go down to the Delta and move north to Hanoi, killing every sonofabitch we find. Then we go back and sink the ship."

Füks's bitterness was easy to understand. We had risked a lot to capture that Chinese adviser, and then the people in the rear just let him buy his way out.

Many of the South Vietnamese people were good folks. The unending years of war had taken their toll on the country. What the people faced from the NVA and the VC was much worse than the corruption of their own government, so we fought on. But it was for some of the country people we fought, not for the VNs back in Saigon.

But the Cambodian operations were putting a real dent in Charlie's operations in Vietnam. We ended up pulling about eleven operations in Cambodia. While I was still at the A-camp, we operated with some of the intel we had gotten out of the younger Chinese. The information was about another Cambodian village where there was supposed to be a weapons cache. This was a good target, and my LDNNs and I prepared to go.

Earlier, a few days after I arrived at the camp, I had been sitting down in one of the bunkers having a couple of beers during the hot part of the afternoon. The CO of the A-team, a Captain MacMillan, joined me. "Chief," the captain said, "Don't you remember me?"

"Excuse me, sir?" I said, looking at him closely.

"You don't remember me, do you?" he said, grinning.

"No, sir, I'm afraid I can't say that I do. Should I?"

"Well," he said, "forget the bars on my shoulders. Put some stripes on my arm and stick me in the water. Still nothing? Underwater committee, Fort Bragg."

"Well, I'll be damned," I said. He had gotten himself a field commission. We spent the rest of the afternoon catching up on what had been going on in our respective units.

When I was putting together the weapons cache op, Captain MacMillan looked me up again. The op was going to be heliborne—I like to operate out of a helo; they get you in and out fast. The captain said, "Hey, Jim, can I go with you?"

"Wait a minute now, sir. You're an officer in the United States Army. I'm a chief petty officer, an E-7, in the Navy. If you go on an operation with me and things start happening, you're going to turn around and be an officer. With Army gunships overhead, you're going to insist on being in command. No. When I go on an operation up here, especially with these people, I'm in charge. If I get killed, I want it to be by my own fuckup, not someone else's."

This was only going to be the third op I had pulled in Cambodia, so things were still running tight. But Mac still insisted on going. Finally I relented and gave him the rules. "All right," I said, mostly in jest, "if you're serious, you can be my backup radioman. Carry a PRC-25 and have no markings on your uniform just like us." At the time I was wearing Levi's and a black pajama top.

"Okay, okay," Mac agreed. Now I had another American going on the op with me. It was June 30, and off we went on a daylight op.

Going in by helo, we had two slicks full of men and were covered by the gunships. It was similar to a parakeet op, but we were coming in hot, balls to the wall and as fast as we could move. Only trouble was, when we came up on the village, there wasn't anyplace for us to land. I was up in the cockpit with the pilot. "Shit!" he said. "Where the hell am I going to put you down?"

I could see a little pontoon dock extending out into the river next to the village. "On there!" I said. The only trouble was that the end of the dock had a little outhouse on it. "Oh hell!" I said, spotting the outhouse. "That little hut. There isn't enough room."

"No problem," said the pilot. And he proceeded to knock the outhouse into the river with his struts. Now there was room on the dock, only it was the pilot's turn to see a problem.

"Those wicker pontoons will never take the weight of this bird," the pilot said. "I can't set her down."

"No problem," I answered. "Hover it."

He held that chopper just off the dock, and we bailed out the sides. As soon as we were free from the first bird, the second chopper swung in and did the same thing. Now all my men were on the ground, and we moved into the village.

Mac was right alongside of me and having a ball. It had been a long time since he had gone on an op without having the responsibility of leadership. Without the pressures of watching out for everybody, he could just operate and carry my spare radio.

I had my shotgun, Sweetheart, with me, so Mac and I took a hooch out, just blew the shit out of it. Meanwhile, Ba and his men were policing up the area. The informer was telling us who was in charge of what. As we grabbed the people, Ba and his men secured them. We ended up taking three enemy troops prisoner, but we couldn't find the weapons cache. Suddenly, we started taking sporadic weapons fire from the west side of the village.

Hitting the deck, I called in the gunships over my own radio. I looked over at Mac and said, "Look, I'm going to go over to Ba and make sure we have the prisoners ready for extraction. You call in the guns and direct them." Mac was Special Forces—he wouldn't have any trouble calling in targets to the gunships.

But when I saw Mac reach for his handset, I could see his hand trembling. "Okay, Jim," he said. "You've got it."

Now it started going through my head that I had never operated with the man. I knew his background, but what was he like in combat? I just couldn't understand how, with the little bit of fire we were taking, this man could be so shook. It was plain that his hands were shaking. This didn't add up.

Shit happens. We extracted without problems and went back to the camp. Mac had controlled the gunships and suppressed the incoming fire properly. The prisoners were put away for interrogation, and we took some time off. Mac and I were having a few beers, just sitting quietly. Thinking about what had happened that afternoon, I decided to ask Mac about it. Just as I was starting to speak, Mac reached across the table for another beer. I could plainly see his hand trembling again!

"Well, I sure feel good now," I said with relief.

Looking at me, Mac's face suddenly lit up with understanding. "My hand," he said. "That's why you've been acting funny today."

Putting an arm around a fellow warrior, I said, "Yeah, Mac. I just could not understand. A man with your background. This is what, your third or fourth tour? I just couldn't see how, with that little bit that was happening there, you could get excited."

"Okay," he said, and we embraced each other. In my eyes, the man was a hunter, as I was. Mac understood what I meant and said that he would have felt the same way. "But why didn't you say anything out there?" he asked.

"Because, Mac," I answered, "that was neither the time nor the place to get into a pissing contest over a guy showing he was scared."

But the operation was successful in a way. Though we didn't find the weapons cache, we had one enemy KIA and three prisoners. The information from the prisoners led to another operation.

Documents we were capturing on almost every op would lead to another target. One after another, we pulled operations in Cambodia, capturing enemy personnel and collecting intelligence. We were at the A-camp for about ten days total. Toward the end of our stay, I had some visitors show up.

A white-and-blue Air America chopper arrived with a load of plumbers. A runner came charging into my quarters telling me I was wanted on the pad. I headed out to speak to those representatives of an "unnamed government agency." Füks went along with me. Though Füks was my interpreter, these "visiting dignitaries" didn't know that. To them he was just another gook with an AK.

I was pissed. They had left my ass hanging out with that Chinese general, and I was not happy with their job performance. When they whipped out their funny little ID cards, I just gave them a cursory glance. "I know, your names are Smith and you're plumbers."

Ignoring my sarcasm, they said, "We're looking for a Chief Watson. Are you him?"

"Really," I said. "Who?"

"Chief Watson." Now they were starting to get annoyed. But they had a long way to go to get to my level of pissed off. These idiots and their damned games had gotten people killed!

"Let me give you boys a piece of advice," I said in a reasonably friendly way. "That's a civilian aircraft, and I advise you to get back on board and fly out of here. My bodyguard here," and I indicated Füks, "doesn't speak any English. If he hears me start to raise my voice, he gets excited." And with that, I started to raise my voice.

Of course, Füks understood every word I said, and he showed it too. As soon as I raised my voice, Füks snapped off the safety on his AK—*clack.*

Before the sound of Füks's safety snapping off had faded away, those plumbers were back on their aircraft and lifting off. I knew what those men had wanted—they wanted my ass. Admiral Matthews had let me know what was going on. The U.S. State Department had been taking some heat for my capture—my "international kidnapping"—of those two Chinese officers. They wanted my head on a platter.

But for the time being, I couldn't worry about what might happen later. I wanted to continue pulling ops, kicking ass, and taking names in Cambodia.

Sixth Platoon hadn't been standing still either. The reports of operations going back to the Creek started to get a little out of hand. Some people back at Team headquarters started to question the level of success the platoon was having. Father Wa's intel was so good that if the target wasn't a high-ranking VCI man, the platoon just didn't bother with him.

Boink and Bud were sharp, and I was up in Cambodia just raising hell. Finally leaving the A-camp, I returned to the *Benewah* and continued operation with my LDNNs. The admiral and a captain on the *Benewah* had heard about the Stoner and wondered if I had one. When I told them I did, they asked if they could shoot it. A chief turning down an admiral's request just doesn't happen in the Navy, so off to the fantail we went.

My customized eight-shot Ithaca shotgun with the pistol grip and duckbill muzzle attachment really impressed the admiral. But he didn't want to shoot my Sweetheart. Both the captain and the admiral did fire the Stoner. They were impressed with the obvious volume of fire that the weapon could put out. I didn't mind the little demonstration—brownie points for me if nothing else.

Admiral Matthews was a good man, and that bit with the Stoner wasn't the only favor I did him on that tour. There were some midshipmen on board the *Benewah*, fresh from the Naval Academy. One of the middie's fathers was an admiral stationed in D.C. and also a friend of Admiral Matthews. The middies wanted to go into Cambodia in the worst way—telling their fellow cadets about that back at Annapolis would mean a great deal to them. Matthews asked me, as a personal favor, to take these two young men into Cambodia.

"Chief," the admiral asked, "do you think you could run these two men up to that town in Cambodia? Just set them on the beach for a while and have a few beers?"

The two middies were wearing middie-type uniforms that didn't look anything like the regular uniform of the Brown Water Navy. "Not in those uniforms I can't," I said emphatically. "If they get into some regular fatigues and look like PBR sailors, maybe." Turning to the middies, I addressed them directly. "Do you know how to handle a .45?"

Those two middies wanted to go armed to the teeth. I was just going to take my shotgun. "And the big thing you have to remember is this. You two may be middies, but on this op and up there, if I say 'Shit,' you just ask how much and what color. Correct?"

They agreed, and I took the responsibility of taking those two officers into Cambodia. We didn't do much, just boated around a bit and checked things out. After we returned, I continued with my duties. I don't remember those two middies' names, but I'll bet they remember mine. I usually remember someone I just met for a little while only if he was a screw-up or the excelling type.

As I say, I still had operations to run with my LDNNs. The intel said that a VC courier would be traveling along a trail at a certain time on his bicycle. This could be an ambush my LDNNs could handle. Getting into position along the trail in Cambodia, we set up our ambush. Using commo wire we had brought with us, we stretched a tripwire across the trail. Since we wanted to capture the guy and not decapitate him, we strung the wire about three feet off the ground.

Now it was time to wait, and we didn't have to wait long. Ba and I had discussed the different ways we could stop the bike—throwing things into the spokes, stuff like that. The tripwire seemed to be the easiest and most workable plan we could come up with. Not very original, though.

Low and behold, here comes this bicycle, just boogying down the trail. Zap . . . bam . . . boom, and we had him.

I can imagine how that poor guy must have felt. Here he was, just chugging along on his bike, and zap. He gets knocked backward by something he never even saw. Before the shock of landing wears off, here come these six apparitions from the woods around him. Green-and-black-camoed faces must have looked unearthly to this poor bastard. Without a word being spoken, he gets knocked down and tied up, all under the threatening muzzles of six silent weapons.

We didn't find any documents on the man, but that didn't mean he wasn't who we were looking for. Füks wrung him out a little bit with a little impromptu interrogation. The guy convinced Füks that he was exactly what he appeared to be, just a guy out for a bike ride. We let him go.

Afterward, the joke was made that we should stick closer to water for our operations. When we went inland, things just didn't work out for us. But the operations in Cambodia were big news for everybody back in Vietnam. The Cambodian side of the border had been off-limits for so long that now that it was open, everyone wanted to have a part of the action.

One man showed up at the *Benewah* wanting to go into Cambodia. This SEAL was one of the first men qualified as a male nurse in the Navy who also qualified as a SEAL corpsman. There had been a program in which corpsmen could take the training they had and apply it to becoming a male nurse. Not quite an RN, but much more trained than a regular corpsman.

This man knew Ronnie Rodger and Bob Gallagher, and when he had the chance to go to the *Benewah*, he looked me up. He wanted to go on a Cambodian op in the worst way. "Bud," I told him, "you're not a corpsman anymore. You're a qualified medical officer. You and I would both be in a world of shit if I took you on any operation, let alone crossed that border with you."

But the man just wouldn't let the idea go. Finally, I relented and said he could go with me.

Taking Ba and four other LDNNs, we went across the border on a simple operation. The op was something like the clothesline bicycle ambush—sit along a trail and wait for the target to show up. A static ambush, not my favorite method of operation.

We sat there all night, and the target never showed up. A dry hole. When daylight finally broke across the horizon, the SEAL nurse was really upset. All he had wanted to do was get his M16 a little warm. Be a combat soldier again for a while.

I asked, "You really want to get into it, don't you?"

"Yeah," he answered. "The reason I came up here was to get into Cambodia. I heard of your reputation, that you're the kind of man who makes things happen. Being raised under Gallagher puts you in a different category from the other SEALs."

Who says flattery won't get you anything? I said, "Come on, let's go. Since they won't come to us, we'll go find them and have some fun."

This was not the brightest thing I ever did. We had been staked out along a half-assed road waiting for our target. Calling this path a road might be giving it delusions of grandeur. If a jeep traveled down this road, it would scrape against both sides of the trail.

But off we went, traveling down the road. I had Sweetheart with me and my radio on my back. That other SEAL just kept on trucking right along side of me. Then we came to a small village. Pulling me over to the side, the nurse whispered to me, "I heard you were crazy. But this is nuts. Are we going to have some fun now?"

"If there are bad guys here, we are," I answered. "Let's go shake some bushes and see what falls out."

The village turned out to be a dry hole too, but that SEAL nurse had a great time, even if he didn't get to warm up his M16.

My LDNNs and I had gone back to the Special Forces A-camp after a short time at the *Benewah*. Some intel had come in and we were running some ops into Cambodia. Nothing much was turning up and we were continuing to operate when a message came in for me from the *Benewah*. The message read, "Return to *Benewah* for return of LDNNs to Saigon."

Well, enough's enough, I thought, They're shutting down the operation. Guess they'll send me back to my platoon.

This was going to be my last time with these LDNNs in the field. I told the men to just pack their stuff when we got back to the *Benewah*—they were going back to Saigon. This was a happy bunch of troopers. The mission was over, they had been reasonably successful, and now they were going home.

We couldn't fit all the unit on one STAB, so I was riding in another boat. While we were cruising down the Mekong to the *Benewah* another message came in for me over the radio. The admiral wanted to see me as soon as I arrived at the ship. One does not keep an admiral waiting. I was wearing Levi's, a black pajama top, and coral shoes and had my 12-gauge Sweetheart hung around my neck.

Arriving at the *Benewah*, I climbed up the accommodation ladder to where the admiral was waiting. At the top of the ladder was a civilian type, snapping pictures with his 35mm camera. The last thing I wanted was my picture taken in Vietnam, especially coming in off an op. Rick Marcinko had his picture published, against his wishes, in a magazine back in the States. The article was a lurid account of the SEALs. The result was that a wanted poster appeared in Vietnam with his name on it. The VC offered fifty thousand piasters to anyone who could kill Rick!

Rick and I had competed in a lot of things, but I had no wish to see if I could get a bigger bounty placed on my head. As I hit the top of the ladder, I reached out for the cameraman. He offered little resistance. I took his camera, hit the open button, and stripped the film out. I suppose I was a fairly intimidating sight to a civilian right then. Face expressionless and hard as a rock, pale green eyes glittering like two chips of jade, and a very nasty-looking exotic shotgun hanging within a few inches of my hands.

After I let him go, the photographer stood there for a moment with his mouth hanging open. Turning to Admiral Matthews, who had been standing nearby and had seen the whole episode, the photographer said, "Admiral, did you see what this man just did?"

The admiral just looked at him. "Yes. It's obvious that the gentleman didn't want his picture taken." The admiral turned to me, and what he said next just floored me. "Sir," he said, "would you please accompany me to my quarters?"

Sir! Me? From an admiral? The admiral knew I was a chief, but he would not let on in front of the civilian. It turned out that the civilian was an Associated Press photographer. I hated newsmen from my experiences with them in Vietnam, and I still hold some reservations about most of them.

Opening the door to his large stateroom, the admiral said, "Come on in, Chief."

"Sir," I answered, "I can't go in like this. I'm filthy and I'll dirty up everything." I still had mud on me from my last operation. The only parts of me that were clean were the inside of my shotgun and my eyeballs.

"Don't ever apologize to me for being in working clothes, Chief," he said. "Now what kind of beer do you want?"

Opening up his refrigerator, the admiral handed me a beer and waved me to a seat. He told me how pleased he was with our operations in Cambodia. In fact, he said that he had submitted the papers to have me promoted on the spot to E-8. His reason was that everything I had done made him look better. Admiral Matthews had been the commander of Task Force 194.0, Sea Lords, in charge of the American portion of Tran Hung Dao XI.

Matthews thought that the sun rose and set on the Navy SEALs and had a high respect for one particular SEAL chief's operations. Not too bad for Marcinko's Misfits' old point man. It had been the admiral who had originally questioned a chief's relieving a commissioned officer. The admiral told me now that he had no regrets on that decision.

In fact, Matthews told me that he had put me in for a high decoration for my Chinese operation. But word had come back to him that my capture of those two officers had made me some enemies in high places.

The Plumbers' Union was seriously pissed at me. I had made the local station chief look bad or something. At any rate, the Agency had turned the whole thing over to the State Department. Since I had taken a foreign national, with whose country we were not at war, from one country, which we weren't at war with, into another country, against his will, the State Department wanted me charged with international kidnapping.

The admiral wanted to know what I wished to do about the situation. I didn't have to give it a lot of thought. "Get me the hell out of here, sir," I said. "I'll go back to Saigon with the LDNNs. I don't want to have anything more to do with them anyway. After that, I'll go back to my platoon—they're way down in the Delta on the South China Sea. As long as you don't tell anyone where I went, nobody will ever know."

Matthews agreed with my idea. Now we discussed what I wanted to do about getting my people back to Saigon. He offered to help me in any way he could.

"Well, sir," I said, "I'd like to get them back by air. It's a long way back to Saigon in a PBR or Mike boat."

The admiral was true to his word and had three slicks put on to take my people back to Saigon. Before I left, the admiral told me that COMNAVFOR-V (Commander Navy Forces—Vietnam) and NAVSPECWARGRUP-V (Navy Special Warfare Group—Vietnam) both wanted me in Saigon for a debriefing on the Cambodian operations. Admiral Matthews assigned his own personal helicopter to take me into Saigon for my meetings.

The chopper landed at Tan Son Nhut on June 21, and my Cambodian adventures were over. There was a jeep and driver waiting to take me to Saigon and Navy headquarters. When I climbed out of the helicopter I was still in my Levi's and black pajama top. I had my shotgun slung around my neck and was wearing an LDNN beret with lieutenant's bars on it. This was the way to go into Saigon.

As I went over to the jeep, I saw that Rudy was driving it. He was over in Nam on a tour and just happened to be available to pick me up. As I walked over to the jeep, an Air Force colonel stopped to talk to me.

"Excuse me, mister," the colonel said, "but what's that hanging around your neck?"

"That's my Sweetheart," I said. "My 12-gauge."

"I've never seen a weapon like that before."

"No, sir," I said. "It was custom-made for me at Frankfort Arsenal. This is the only one there is." I had made the pistol grip myself, cutting down a regular wood stock. But the rest of the weapon had been one of the first duckbill Ithacas with a special magazine extension to come out of Frankfort Arsenal back in 1968.

"Sir," he said, "do you realize that shotguns are against the Geneva Convention?"

In fact, shotguns themselves were not against the Geneva Convention, only soft lead bullets, such as buckshot, were. But I just looked at this twerp wondering where the hell he thought he was. "Colonel," I said, "if they ever send me to Geneva, I'll leave her home. But between now and then, she and I just don't part company."

"What did you say your rank was again?" he questioned. By now the colonel was getting a bit hot under the collar. I just don't have time for these self-important assholes, and I guess it showed.

Still moving toward the jeep, I called back over my shoulder, "You had it right the first time, Colonel—mister."

I jumped into the jeep and off Rudy and I went. I don't know what that colonel was thinking, don't really care. But I must have confused him. Here was a man in civilian dress, armed with an exotic weapon, being picked up in a jeep with a Navy master chief as the driver. Sometimes, this job can be fun. Rudy just had a big grin on his face during the whole thing.

At NAVFOR-V, I spent a long two days being fully debriefed on the Cambodian operations. Commander "Stormin' Norman" Olsen and, I believe, Red Cannon were both there during the debriefing. It was a lot of questions and discussions in a second-floor office in the NAVFOR building.

My LDNNs had gotten back to Saigon and had checked in with their own headquarters in the city. The men wanted to get together with me before I went back to my platoon. Not thinking anything of it, I agreed to meet that night. Then a West Coast SEAL looked me up to let me know what the real story was. "Watch your ass, Chief," he said. "Ba and a bunch of his LDNNs are planning to take you to downtown Saigon and get you killed. He feels you screwed him over on the money."

This was a bit of a shock. "What?" I said.

"Didn't you pick up a whole bunch of money in Cambodia on some op?" he asked.

"Yeah," I said, just shaking my head.

"Well, Ba is telling every LDNN who'll listen that you put the money in your pocket. Did you?"

That was a bit much. "Hell no!" I said, getting a little hot. "I used the money to pay Füks with. He had earned it, and it was the best use I could think of for it."

That night, I took the SEAL's warning to heart. I did go with the LDNNs for a beer-drinking dinner party. They were hosting their American adviser who had helped them on a successful series of operations in Cambodia. And at no time during the evening did they make any kind of move to take me out. Of course, the fact that I had brought my own Sweetheart to the party may have affected things a little bit.

That was the only time I pulled liberty armed to the teeth. I had my shotgun and a Smith & Wesson strapped to my hip. Eight rounds of #4 hardened buckshot with a horizontal four-to-one spread would put a dent in anyone's plans.

Rudy was working out of Nha Be, if I remember correctly, and he and I had some time in Saigon as well. Walking into NAVFOR-V headquarters for the debriefings, Rudy and I ran into Captain Watkins as he was coming out. Watkins had been the commander of the Amphibious Base back at Little Creek when the SEALs had been put together back in 1962. Watkins made no secret of his low opinion of the UDT, let alone this new bunch of animals called SEALs. But when we passed him on the streets of Saigon, Watkins stopped us for a moment.

"Excuse me, Chiefs," Watkins said. "You're from Little Creek, aren't you?"

"Yes sir," we answered.

"Do you remember me?"

"Yes sir, we do."

"Do me a favor when you get back, will you?"

"What's that, sir?"

"Back at Little Creek, please give the men in the Teams who remember me my apologies. But I still have a question. How can a bunch of hooligans like the SEALs be so goddam professional?"

Rudy's answer to Watkins is one I'll remember for a long time. "Sir," Rudy said, looking straight at Watkins, "there's one thing about being in the Teams. I don't care if you send us to Pennsylvania to dig coal. Give us five days and we'll be digging coal better than any sonofabitch who ever lived."

That was the success of the Teams. Watkins had no answer to Rudy's statement. But he agreed with us in the end.

The debriefing finally ended, and the people in Saigon were satisfied. NOS (Naval Operations Support) group had given me permission to head back to my unit. Bob Gallagher had nicknamed that outfit the NOSE group a long time before. Our other name for them was the Headquarters Guerrillas. A bunch of paper-pushers who made the plans and policies that we had to operate with in the field.

Admiral Matthews saw to it that a letter of commendation about the Cambodian ops made it into my service record. The letter listed the official results of our missions. In the eleven SEAL operations we conducted, we listed three VC KIA, one VC WIA, forty-one VC detained including two VCI, and eight kilos of documents and one grenade captured. All of this with no friendly casualties. Not a bad way to end a series of cross-border ops.

One the way back to my platoon, I was first going to make a stopover in Hy Yen. The operations in Cambodia had been an adventure, but my opinion of the LDNNs hadn't changed much. Now it was time for me to go back to rampaging around with my platoon. I had been reading some of the after-action reports from the two squads, and the guys had been doing dynamite. Both squads were just kicking ass and taking names. Charlie definitely knew we were there.

In Saigon, they told me there was no scheduled flight to Hy Yen, but I could go out to Tan Son Nhut and hitch a ride on one of the supply flights. There was a squadron of HC-46s at the air base that made daily mail and supply runs to all of the outposts. I went out to the air base, put my name on a list, and was able to jump a flight that day.

Landing at Ca Mau, I headed over to the little PBR base where my men were staying. The base wasn't far from the river and convenient for our operations. Dean Nelson had been left in charge of Alfa Squad, the Sixth Platoon squad at Ca Mau.

Walking into the little PBR base, I had a bit of a shock. A couple of the guys called out to me, "Hey, Chief, how are you?" They looked like Joe Shit the ragman. They needed shaves and haircuts, and their uniforms were terrible. This was not right. Not saying anything to the men, I went looking for Dean Nelson. It was not correct for me to say anything to the men, not looking the way I did. But I had just come off an operation where I was working with indigenous personnel. In a situation like that, you don't want to look like a sailor. Blending in is very important in a combat zone.

The men told me that Mr. Boink was off at the TOC checking on some intel. Ops had been happening so fast and well that Mr. Boink had practically moved into the TOC. Since Lou was busy, I wanted to take the chance to speak to Nelson.

Going over to the hooch, I first changed into a fresh pair of fatigues. When Nelson came in, I asked him what the problem was. Why were the men walking around without haircuts and un-shaven? I wasn't exactly Rudy Boesch, but I knew the importance of a man's appearance. My men were not going to look like this much longer.

"Come on, Chief," Nelson said. "This is a combat zone. You can't expect the men to stay spit-and-polish out here."

"Hey," I answered, "you're on a military base, you look military. Not everybody knows that you're SEALs, but you should be proud anyway. And pride shows in a man's dress."

"Well, Chief, I think—"

I cut him off. "Nelson," I said, "when you make chief and get your own platoon, then you can let them dress anyway you want them to. But until then, I am the chief of this platoon. Before I leave here tomorrow, I want each man standing tall with a haircut, clean-shaven, and squared away."

He didn't like it, but he carried out my instructions. Later on, after I had left the Teams, Dean made chief. As I was told later, Dean ran a sharp platoon.

A new program was developing in Vietnam for all of the U.S. forces—Vietnamization. The people back home wanted us to push it. Bravo Squad came up from Hy Yen for a week to help in the setting up of our initial program.

The South Vietnamese Army was going to be taking over some of our operations. To help them get a head start, we set up a series of lectures and demonstrations of small-unit operations, counter-insurgency tactics and techniques, and weapons. We explained to the ARVNs how we operated.

One of the biggest problems we had with the program, besides the general attitude of the ARVNs, was the size of the groups they wanted to field. Where the SEALs would use a patrol of four or six men, the ARVNs would send a hundred or more men at a time.

Besides the lectures, we also took the men on field problems. One of the things we tried to instill in the men was the importance of air support. Without air support, you're just another idiot wandering around with a rifle in your hands. The big upper hand that we had, especially as a small unit, was air support. If Charlie had had air support, the whole war would have been a different ball game. Charlie was good—never underestimate your enemies.

We spent about a week on the program. We had a small airport available where slicks would come in to take us all out on operations. The senior VN officer would have a SEAL with him and each platoon would have a SEAL instructor along. In the field, we explained how the SEAL squad was broken down, did recons, and so forth. One thing we didn't tell them was where we got most of our intelligence. The Agency and Father Wa's group were supplying us with some of the best intel of the war. But if those men wanted to supply the ARVNs with intel, it was their own business.

The sweep operations we would go on with the ARVNs were a laugh. ARVN intel would report that bad guys were in a certain area. Our unit was to sweep the suspected area. Using slicks, the unit would go in and land on the dike line at the end of a bunch of rice paddies. On either side of the paddies there would be a row of trees, lining the dikes.

The ARVNs would go into the rice fields and spend all day walking through the paddies and on the dikes. At the end of the day they would pull out and report that the area was cleared—it had been swept and no enemy forces had been found.

Never once did the ARVNs go into the tree lines! What the hell did they expect, Charlie to be out in the open fields? When we suggested that they send men into the tree lines to check them, they wouldn't do it. They said that we were there as advisers only. We were not their boss. Our job was to teach them and they would conduct the operation as they saw fit.

The ARVNs went their own way, and Bravo Squad went back to Hy Yen. And I went along with my squad.

By this time, Bud Thrift was just hauling ass with the squad. When I first arrived back at Hy Yen, Bud came over to me and put his arm around my shoulders. "You got my message about what happened right after you left, didn't you? We got ambushed!"

"Yeah, I heard about it," I answered.

"You were right, this is for real. But Chief, we're kicking ass and taking names."

Bud had gotten real close to Father Wa by now. I hadn't had much in the way of dealings with Father Wa directly; all my work with him had been through Lou Boink or Bud Thrift. Bud made sure I was properly introduced to Wa and his brother, the village chief. The security of the camp was explained to me. There were little OPs—observation posts—and small bunkers all around the village. Claymores had been set up, and I was shown the command post where the claymore firing devices were.

Our quarters had been set up on the northeast corner of the village. Looking out of our hut, you could see along a dike to an OP off in the perimeter. We were the inner perimeter of the village for that corner. The hut was made of native thatch, probably to give the bugs somewhere to sleep. The back wall was made of rough-cut boards of local wood. We slept on regular Army cots, each of us with weapons and equipment laid out around him.

Everybody slept with his weapons right by his cot. I damn near slept with my shotgun in my arms, and there was a loaded Stoner alongside my cot. If the VC got through the wire and into the perimeter or inside our hooch itself, I would need the shotgun for close-in work. If we had to get up and go poke out the windows, the Stoner would be the thing. Especially with the case of ammunition I had right next to the Stoner. We kept plenty of bullets available inside the hooch. There really wasn't any evacuation or contingency plan made up. The only course would be to make for the TOC bunker in the center of the village.

There was an unwritten rule that you didn't touch another man's gear, especially his weapon. Messing with a man's weapon was like messing with his 'lung back at the Creek. It just wasn't something you would even think of doing.

Rarely did I have to step in and tell a man not to take something he wanted. Setting up a patrol order, you would assign weapons according to where the man was in the patrol and what the mission was. But for general operations, you didn't involve yourself in a man's choices very much.

Hyde was a big North Carolina lad who really loved his M60 and was very good with it. He had built an aluminum ammunition can inside a rucksack and harness so he could carry and feed lots of ammo to his weapon. Trouble was, Hyde also thought the world of hand grenades, and a sidearm, and any other weapon he could strap on. Finally, I had to put my foot down.

"Hyde," I said, "all you are going to carry is that M60. The grenades we'll pass out among the other members of the patrol who are walking lighter than you. I don't care if you can handle it. That's the way it's going to be."

That was the most I did this tour with getting involved with a man and his weapon.

During breaks we just hung around the hooch. You could lie back in your bunk and watch the geckos hunting bugs along the roof. Those little buggers could climb anything to get at a bug, and when you startled one, he barked at you. Just like Vietnam. Even the lizards have to put their two cents' worth in.

Now it was time to go on an op. The squad was doing a lot of heavy operations in sampans. This was not something I particularly cared for. The men assured me that this was the way to go and was one of the reasons the platoon was having such success. Instead of calling in a PBR for an op, the men would use sampans and get up all the thousands of little bitty canals all over the place.

Coming up to VC outposts at night in the sampans wasn't a problem either. All of the men we were working with were either ex-VC or ex-NVA, and they knew the passwords. Coming onto some VC in the dark, the SEAL would be hidden, lying down in the middle of the sampan, covered up with mats or nets. Father Wa's men would give the proper passwords and we would be allowed to go on our way. The system worked, but the pucker factor sure was high for a minute or two.

The regular sampan was enough for most operations. We borrowed them sometimes from the village's fishermen. When Bud or I would go on a sampan op, Father Wa's men would say "boo coo mot"—that meant we were big sonsabitches and they would have to get a larger sampan. Bud and I would sink a regular sampan all by ourselves. The usual sampans were around ten to fourteen feet long and about a foot and a half wide. Two natives and a smaller-statured SEAL could use one. Small sampans were either made from a hollowed-out log—dugouts—or built up from planks. The larger sampans, for Bud and me, were about eighteen feet long, two to three feet wide, and a couple of feet deep. All of the larger sampans were plank construction.

The sampans had no motors. The two agents would paddle them along. Coming back from an op, if we were in a safe area, the SEAL would help with the paddling. The sampans were very maneuverable and could get into places none of the riverine boats could go. They were also the most common watercraft in Vietnam. But operating in those tiny boats was some of the hairiest time I spent in Nam.

It was the parakeet ops that I preferred. With the quality intelligence from Father Wa and his people, the parakeet op was a fast way to go. The sampan ops were stealthy and could slip us in anywhere in the Delta region. But they were slow and took all night. It was the parakeet op and quality intelligence that led to my POW camp raid and the first Bright Light mission of the war.

We had grabbed a VC security chief on a parakeet op. A security chief knows a great deal about his area, and we knew there was an active POW camp somewhere around. With Füks's help, I persuaded our prisoner to tell me where the VC would be holding their POWs. I think pushing the man out the door of the helicopter and letting him look down at the jungle fifteen hundred feet below had something to do with his deciding to talk to us. There wasn't a chance of the man actually falling from the bird, but he didn't know that.

POW camp rescue operations were so important to the U.S. military that they had already established a procedure to follow in case we developed intelligence on one. The operations were to be code-named Bright Light. As far as I knew, no one had gone out on a Bright Light operation yet.

It was about two o'clock in the afternoon. This security chief VC had told us which camp would have the prisoners in it and how many of them there were. According to him we could expect about twenty-five or thirty VNs in it, and possibly three Americans!

This was it, a Bright Light operation, my first one and possibly the first one of the war! The word had gone out that you needed clearance from God to put on a Bright Light. But if you said you had the information for a Bright Light, God wanted to talk to you! So I flew up to Ca Mau, and when I couldn't find Lieutenant Boink, our platoon leader, I jumped a shotgun flight and went straight to Saigon.

After a fast meeting with the powers-that-be in Saigon, I had permission to put on the Bright Light op. I would have ten slicks to carry my men and every piece of air and fire support available at my command. Flying back to the platoon, I checked in with Lou Boink. After going over my plan, all Lou said was, "You've got it, Chief. Take the other squad with you."

Getting the platoon together, I outlined my plan. Eight VNs and a SEAL would be in each slick. In the lead birds would be two SEALs and a VN squad. To give us the needed manpower, we had almost every man Father Wa had available. Almost a hundred men would be going in on this op. Four empty choppers would be following several miles behind the assault group to bring the "Harvest," liberated prisoners, home.

A last-minute argument by John Porter resulted in his going with me in the lead bird. Chuck Fellers and Duke Leonard were riding in on the number two bird. Everything was looking good, up until our chopper got shot down on the insertion.

The chopper crash and subsequent messing around did more than just abort my Bright Light operation. I was more than a little nervous about getting in a helicopter for a mission again. Both Porter and I were shook. After all, we had just learned that a dead helicopter has the glide path of a rock. A heavy rock.

Back in Ca Mau, Boink had gotten the word that we had gone in. The platoon was saddled up and ready to go back into the area and get us out. When they heard we had gotten out okay, things went back to somewhere near normal. John Porter and I had talked about our little adventure without the rest of the men around. We decided that the only thing to do was get back up on the horse. We had to go out on another helicopter op, the sooner the better.

So we both went to Ca Mau that night, and went out on an op the next day. It was Dean's operation, and I did for Dean what Boink did for me. I just went as a tag-along. The op had been developed, planned, and put on by Dean, and he led it. It was a successful operation. We found the cache and confiscated twenty-one carbines and five Mausers. A good op, and I was over any helicopter problems I might have had.

Everything was cool. John and I had both gone out and come

back okay. Within yourself, you had to find out if your nerve was gone. No one can say how he will react until it happens to him. But when you're faced with a life-or-death situation that you have no control over, it will affect you. I had to go back up to see if the crash had affected me too much. If I'd lost my nerve, it was time to go home. I wouldn't be of any use to anybody.

But there was still a point I had to make with Dean. This was one of the few times that I stepped on Dean hard. The operation had been more of the Vietnamization training program that we had put together before I went back to Hy Yen. What Dean was going to do was give all of the captured weapons to the Vietnamese. It was Dean's way of showing faith to the VNs.

"No, no," I said. "That isn't the name of the game. How many of the men in your squad have a Mauser or a Chicom carbine? How many even have a war trophy to take home? All of these weapons are bolt-action. They're all legal to take back to the States."

"Well," Dean said, "it would be good politically. You know, just buttering up the Vietnamese a little bit."

"Fuck the Vietnamese," I said heatedly. "We've done enough for them. You watch out for your own men first. You first make sure that every man in your squad has what he wants, but no more than one apiece. Anything left over after they're done, you can use to play politics with the VNs. But your own men come first! I know it's your squad, but it's my platoon. If you want me to act in the position of platoon chief, I can direct you to do that. But I don't think it will be necessary."

"You're right, Chief," Dean said. "I have to think of my own men first."

"Keep that in your head, fella. There will come a time when you're the platoon chief. Your men always come first."

Dean Nelson became one hell of a chief and retired from the service as a master chief. He always looked out for his men.

But getting over my helicopter crash wasn't the end of my problems with the Bright Light op. That colonel in the C&C bird had me formally charged with direct disobedience of an order in the face of the enemy. Holy shit, I was going to be court-martialed!

During the preliminary hearing, I was assigned a Marine major as my defender. During the entire proceedings, while all the Army people were making their statements and accusations, my defender just sat there not saying a word! To hell with this, I thought. Get rid of this guy and get me Perry Mason!

After all the Army people were finished, my defender stood up with a military manual in front of him. His question to the court was simple: "In any operation, who is the ultimate commander in charge?"

Reading from the manual, he stated the answer: " 'It is always the ground commander, regardless of rank.' And who was the ground commander on the operation in question? Chief Watson. That is all I have to say, gentlemen." And he sat down.

For a second, I just stared at him with my mouth open. That op wasn't the only time my mouth overloading my brain had gotten me in trouble. But it had sure looked like it would be the last time in the military. The charges were dismissed, and there was no record of the charges ever made. That colonel had been made to look like a fool, and everyone involved wanted to forget the incident.

Other operations went much better than my Bright Light op. We had intel on a probable VCI member in a small hamlet. The place wasn't even large enough to be a village, just a couple of hooches close together. Intel also said that there might be a munitions cache in the hamlet. This looked like a good thing, so we went in on a daylight helicopter insertion.

We piled out of the helicopter right next to the hamlet. Running along the main path, we ran into no resistance. There was a small bunker in the middle of the village, and I pumped a tear-gas round into it as I went by. Special tear-gas ammunition had been made for us that we could fire from our 12-gauges. I had left Sweetheart back at Hy Yen, because you couldn't fire the tear-gas rounds through the duckbill attachment. The rounds proved great for clearing out bunkers, holes, and hooches without using lethal force.

One man came up to a hooch door, and we snatched him up. Two of the VNs with us ran into the hooch and almost immediately came out with the man's weapon. That was it—he was a bad guy, no question.

Duke took charge of the prisoner and started discussing philosophy with him. Would the man like to tell us where the cache was, or would he like to set the new record for holding his breath underwater? Duke was aggressive but cool under pressure. Minh, another of our interpreters, was right with Duke, making sure the prisoner understood the questions. During the discussions, Duke did manage to scare me once.

While Leonard was giving this guy a stress test, I reached down and grabbed hold of Duke's arm. "Hey," I said, "if this prick drowns, he can't tell us anything."

"Don't worry, Chief," Duke said. "I have the situation under control." Just then Chuck came up, and he wanted to get in on the discussion. Instead of that, Chuck and I started searching the rest of the hamlet. The VNs were checking some of the other hooches as well, but I told them I wanted that first hooch, where they had found the weapon, gone over closely. The VNs assured me they had done so, and we continued with the op.

Coming back to me, the VNs said that they had gone over the entire village real well. "The hell with it," I said. "We've got a bad guy and a weapon. Burn the hooches."

It was Mark 13 time. As the VNs were setting fire to the huts, Duke and Chuck were still talking to our prisoner. They were trying to convince that VC that it would behoove him to tell us where the munitions cache was. A second later, it was no longer important that the prisoner talk to us.

Ka-boom! The first hut, which had been burning merrily, had a high-order detonation. Getting up from the ground, I figured that we had found the cache. But now I was seriously pissed at the VNs. They'd said they had searched that hooch! I think they'd missed something.

Later there was going to be some review of searching procedures. But now it was time to get out of Dodge again. Anybody nearby would have heard that detonation, and we could have uninvited guests any moment. He who runs away, comes back to kick ass another day.

We called in the extraction birds and got ready to pull out. Setting up a fast skirmish line, we waited for the bird to show up. While we hung around the hamlet, a medium-sized pig was charging around squealing. The pig ran past the bunker and drew my attention to it again.

Going over to the bunker, I had the interpreter holler in for anyone inside to come out. I didn't have any more tear-gas rounds with me, and something just didn't feel right about that bunker.

Most of the hooches had small mud bunkers built into the rear walls. We had searched them and pumped in tear gas without any reaction.

"Well," I said, "if there's anybody in there, a frag grenade won't hurt anyone. There's no one to be hurt." That comment was translated but there was still no reaction from the bunker.

Going as close to inside the bunker as I could, I threw an M26 frag grenade around the blast wall inside the doorway. With the explosion came a blood-curdling scream from inside the bunker. But now the choppers were here and we had to pull out. The area was a free-fire zone and no one was supposed to be living there. The detonation of the hut proved who had been working in the village. It was time to go, only the VNs didn't quite want to leave.

Father Wa took care of his people, but they didn't always eat as well as they would have liked to. All the VNs were eyeballing that pig still running around the area. It was obvious what was in their minds—that little oinker on a spit over some hot coals. Turning to Minh, I said, "I know what they're thinking, and it's okay. But don't let that pig interfere with us getting the hell out of here."

My VNs might not have been good at searching hooches, but they trussed the pig up for travel in an eyeblink. All four legs tied together, that barbecue on hooves was the first thing tossed on the chopper.

It was a good-sized little pig, maybe about eighty pounds. Now we were going to have a barbecue. Arriving at Hy Yen, I told the VNs to have the pig killed, and the Americans would throw a party. As the VNs went off with the pig, we took care of the prisoner, weapon, and after-action paperwork.

Bud Thrift was filling out the after-action report on the op and didn't know quite what to say about the pig. In a flash of inspiration, it came to him. Looking to me, Bud said, "Let's have some fun."

Under "Captured" in the report, Bud listed ONE VC MOBILE FOOD CACHE (PIG). Then he sent the message on to Saigon.

Olsen was the chief of staff up in Saigon. After they read the report in NOSGRUP, they wrote us back. Bravo Zulu, good job, well done, all of the usual stuff. Then they added something more: "Our sense of humor is what helps keep Support Group going."

Bud sent them another note. "Thank you, it's not your support that keeps us going."

Busting balls in Saigon was always fun. Besides, supply could be a pretty dicey thing with us. One day you would be eating fishheads and rice, the next day steak and lobster. We had no refrigeration in Hy Yen, so we made do with what we could.

For the party, we thought we would be barbecuing a pig. As it turned out, our share of the pig for the cookout was the head, feet, and innards. The rest of the meat had been sold. All of Father Wa's people were ex-VC or ex-NVA, and they weren't treated very well by the other Vietnamese. Father Wa did the best he could by them, and they were good fighters. There wasn't much we could say.

Still we were going to have our barbecue. Our grill was a fifty-five-gallon drum, split in half, at the back of our hooch. When we had the coals going good, the rest of the people showed up. Here was Father Wa and his brother and all of our buddies who were on the operation.

It was Bud's idea—that sonofabitch is a lot crazier than I am, no matter what people say. "We have to show these people how big, bad, and mean we are," Bud said to me. "They need to know that nothing bothers a SEAL. We're going to eat the head, Chief."

"We're going to what?"

"I'll take a big bite off his nose if you do."

"Yeah, right. You do it first."

I shouldn't have said that. Bud picked up the head from where it had been roasting over the coals and *chomp*—he took a big bite out of the nose. He handed it over to me and I did the same thing. The VNs went absolutely bughouse, clapping their hands and jumping around, shouting at each other. Later on what they had been saying was translated for us. It came out something like "Look at the crazy Americans."

Some days a Seawolf would call down that it was going out to an LST just offshore, and did we need anything? Food, ammo, supplies, things like that. "Hey, just bring us what you can," we'd usually answer.

Instead of landing, the birds would normally just pass by low and slow and toss the stuff out of the bird. Sometimes it would be a case of J5 rations (steak), sometimes a case of lobster tails. Occasionally a case of C rations, but not very often. The Seawolves didn't like our shooting at them when they dropped off C rats.

One day I asked a passing bird to take me if it could. There wasn't any problem. The bird landed at our little pad and took me out to an LST supply ship. The Seawolves would leave the major portion of their ammunition back at the base on these ops. Less weight so we could carry more stuff back.

On board the T, I talked to the cook about what we could get. Some potatoes sounded good. The cook told me to leave him my shopping list and come back in about fifteen or twenty minutes. Sounded good to me, so I just went wandering around the ship.

It was down on the tank deck that I made my big discovery. Just walking around, seeing if there was anything useful I could scrounge, I walked up to pallets of ammunition. All kinds of food for bullet launchers was there—.50 caliber, .45 ACP, some 9mm, 5.56mm linked, 7.62 . . . *5.56mm linked!*

There it was, linked Stoner ammunition. Cases of the stuff. Hell, there were pallets of it. Linked Stoner ammo was hard to come by. Many a night the squad sat up cleaning links and linking up 5.56mm. The Stoner was a big chunk of a squad's firepower, and here was enough ammo to burn out all our barrels.

As I started tearing open a pallet, another chief came up to me. I wasn't paying any attention to anything else. All I wanted to do was get as many cases of this stuff on board the chopper as I could. Screw the food—this was stuff that could kill gooks. "Hey, hey," the ship's chief yelled, "get away from that. We're saving that stuff for the SEALs."

"Thanks a lot, Chief," I said. "You just found us. Where have you been?"

"What do you mean?"

"Look," I said, "I don't want to be a hero or anything. But we haven't been able to get this stuff. We're over there relinking salvaged links to feed our guns. Here you are with a whole damned tank deck full of it."

"When we loaded up, all they did was put this stuff on board and tell us to save it for the SEALs. Nobody told us where to find you."

"Well, we're found. Take me to your radio room."

I called up to Ca Mau and reported what I had found. Boink sent birds down to pick up what he could. I loaded up our bird with as much as I could and planned to make more trips. There was more Stoner ammo on that one ship than six platoons could have used in a year. They had just been sailing up and down the coast, carrying supplies and looking for the SEALs. God only knew how long that ammo had been floating around looking for us.

Getting back to Hy Yen, I had remembered to bring some food back with me. No potatoes, but I did have a case of frozen lobster tails. When Chuck and Duke saw the ammo, they flipped. "Holy shit," they said. "No more sore fingers."

But we really didn't expend that much ammunition. We were mostly capture-oriented. Most of the guys in the SEALs were that way, both Team One and Team Two. We all knew that you could get more from a guy by talking to him than by killing him. It didn't matter how low on the totem pole that VC was. He would at least know who his boss was. And that was who we wanted, the bosses, what we called the VCI.

The Americans and South Vietnamese may have lost the Vietnam War. But the SEALs won their part of the war. We had Charlie so shook he didn't know where he could operate safely. And nowhere was safe from the SEALs. Charlie never knew when he could lay his head down safely. Sometime during the night, the men with green faces just might kick the door in.

The intel from Father Wa we would put to use almost immediately. Now we had a number of ways to operate. Bud Thrift and I would go on sampan ops whenever they looked like the best way to go. The maneuverable little boats had proved their worth often enough. Most of our sampans came from the fishermen of Father Wa's village. There wasn't much trouble with our borrowing the few we needed for operations. The boats had a nice used look to them too. They didn't stand out at all on the waterways.

Bud Thrift took us deep into enemy territory on an op that ran almost all night. The mission was a body snatch of a high-level VCI. It was almost dawn when we reached our target and snatched him and his bodyguard up. Moving back to the sampans, we got ready to pull out. Then the shit hit the fan.

Fire started coming in from all sides. Taking cover, we called in Seawolf. When Seawolf came in, he had some bad news for us. "There's no way you're getting out on those boats," the pilot called down. "I've got some slicks on their way."

There was nothing for it but to hunker down and wait for the extraction birds. When the slicks showed up, we got ready to leave. Looking at the boats, Bud said, "if we have to leave them behind, we don't want to leave anything Charlie can use."

With grenades and gunfire, we made sure those sampans couldn't ever be used against us. On the way back, though, all we could think of was that we'd borrowed those sampans from the local fishermen.

Bud looked at me and said, "How are we going to go back to Hy Yen without those sampans?"

There had been about six boats that we reduced to kindling. Shit happens. When we landed at Hy Yen, we started walking into town. A bunch of the local fishermen came running up to us. We had flown back—where the hell were their sampans? All the jabbering and arm-waving didn't help the situation at all.

Going to Father Wa, we asked him what to do. Father Wa said that he didn't have the money to buy half a dozen sampans. Bud Thrift flew up to Saigon to see if he couldn't get the money from someone up there.

Bud came through with the money, and we ordered a bunch of sampans from the local sampan builder. It was a couple of weeks before the boats showed up. For those two weeks, it was very hard for us to borrow a sampan from the locals. Father Wa put a stop to that real fast. He asked the locals which they would have preferred—our dumping the sampans and coming home as we did, or our trying to bring the sampans home and getting killed. If we had been killed, there wouldn't have been anyone for them to have a grievance against.

Our philosophy was "If in doubt, wipe them out." If we destroyed something or killed someone by mistake, at least we would be around to try to correct things. If we guessed wrong and they were the enemy, we wouldn't be around to do anything but fill a body bag. It's a harsh rule to follow, but it's also a rule that brought us home.

Now the sampans were ready and delivered to us. Since we had ordered them, the boat builder saw to it we received them. The little canal next to our hooch looked like a regular marina with all those brand-new boats in it.

We decided to have a regular change-of-command ceremony for

the boats. On a certain day, the fishermen were told that they could come down and take command of their new boats. These were nice, white, new boats, not a mark on them. Bud Thrift stood tall and issued each man his paddle with proper ceremony. After saluting, Bud would snap out the man's paddle and announce, "Congratulations, you now have command of sampan number X."

The fishermen didn't know what the big deal was. They didn't care either. All they wanted was their sampans back. Everyone was smiling, and we had a little party. Within a few days the fishermen tried to hustle us out of caulking and more work by the boat builder. But that didn't last long. They had new boats, bigger than the ones we had destroyed.

The sampan ops were working well for us. We operated, on the average, twice a week. On August 20, I went out on an op that I will long remember.

The op would be going deep into enemy territory. All the land was rice paddies and canals with very few tree lines, and the whole area was a free-fire zone. If it hadn't been for Father Wa's people, we could never have operated this way. For the op there were only three SEALs, five of Father Wa's men, and the agent who was leading us in. The target was a VCI and his bodyguards. Army intel had said there was nothing in the area, no VC, and definitely no NVA. So here we were, going after a target the Army said didn't exist.

The last friendly area we passed was a small outpost at the mouth of the canal we entered to continue on our way. Di-di-mauing (moving fast) along the canal, we had entered bad-guy country. The small canal opened into a larger canal, almost a small river, that you still couldn't get a PBR into. Once we entered the large canal, we still had another six or eight clicks to go along that. We were one hell of a long way from home back at Hy Yen.

All the way while in bad-guy country, each SEAL lay back in the middle of his sampan. We had been covered with woven thatch matting. Lying there on your back, all you can do is listen to what is going on around you. My shotgun was across my chest and I had about ten pounds of pressure on Sweetheart's twelve-pound trigger.

None of us ever talked to each other about what we thought while lying under that matting. Every man lived within himself.

For myself, I was scared spitless just lying there in the dark. It wasn't really tough to breathe, but sometimes the weight of the matting seemed suffocating. And the air wasn't very pleasant. These sampans were working fishing boats, especially the big ones I rode in.

The boat would rock under your head and you could feel the movement of the water. There was always a trickle of water in the bottom of the boat to soak into your uniform. I would usually wear fatigues or dungarees on these ops. We'd save the few tigerstripes we had for when we went home. They helped us look like heroes. But I felt like anything but a hero, lying under that stinking matting in the suffocating darkness, listening to my heartbeat thundering in my ears.

Every now and then, at least three or four times on this op, you would have something else to hear besides the slow soft splash of the paddles and the beating of your heart. From the banks of the canal would be called out a password in Vietnamese. It was the VC manning an outpost!

Father Wa's men knew the correct answers to the challenges called out from the shore, but it would be a heart-stopping moment before the sampan continued on its course. We couldn't see what was happening. But once you trust your men, you go with them all the way. Father Wa's men never once let me down. That's more than I can say about some SEALs!

Charlie just couldn't change his passwords quickly enough to prevent our men from knowing them. The VC communications system wasn't fast enough or complete enough. Once the password system was set in place, it stayed in place.

But while we trusted the men we had with us, we didn't trust the VC. If there had been a shot fired, or if the sampan had rocked as if a man was getting in or out of it, we would have all come out firing. But that never happened. We just kept going, every now and then pissing our pants when a challenge was called out.

Landing near the village, we grounded the sampans and moved in on foot. When we came up on the village, the agent pointed out the two target huts. We wanted to hit both of the huts at once. One hut held the bodyguards, the other our target. To do the operation meant I had to split my forces, something I hated to do. But there was no other way to hit these two huts at the same time. They were too far apart.

There was a dike line we could follow to go into the village. If we hit at the same time, we could be sure of getting our target no matter which hut he was in. I took the interpreter and some of Father Wa's men with me. Duke, Chuck, and the rest of the force went after the other hut. The hut Chuck and Duke were hitting was supposed to hold the bodyguards. Since the bodyguards would be armed with AKs, that strike team needed the heaviest firepower. Duke and Chuck had Stoners with them.

Moving along the dike line, we followed the path on top of the dike. Dead ahead was the hut Duke, Chuck, and their men were to hit. The path made a ninety-degree turn to the left and went toward my target hut. At the turn we split the group up.

Approaching my hut, I held my shotgun, Sweetheart, at the ready. On my back was the radio if we needed to call out. As we approached our target, we started to hear a commotion at the other hut. This wasn't good. Then a man came to the door of our hut with a weapon in his hands.

What kind of weapon it was never even registered. All I could see was that he was armed and right in front of me. I snapped my shotgun up and cut loose a blast. *Blam*, and the flash lit up the night.

Sweetheart was loaded with XM-257 rounds. Twenty-seven pellets of hardened #4 (.24 caliber) buckshot roared out of her muzzle. The duckbill attachment on the muzzle spread out the pattern to ninety-six inches wide and twenty-four inches high at thirty yards. Only this man wasn't thirty yards away, more like five.

The buckshot load hit him like a runaway buzzsaw blade, almost cutting him in half. I wasn't the best shot in the Teams, but Sweetheart more than made up for it. The remaining seven rounds in the magazine I cut loose at the house. The shit had hit the fan. The target was up and armed, and I had no idea what else would be waiting for me on the other side of that thatched wall. For all I knew, I had the bodyguards' hut.

Blam . . . clack-chunk . . . *Blam* . . . clack-chunk . . . *Blam* . . . clack-chunk . . . On and on my weapon roared, almost making the hooch a split-level. Finally the weapon clicked on an empty chamber. I rapidly stuffed more rounds into the magazine and chambered a round. I carried a couple of spare rounds between the fingers of my left hand to help give me a fast reload. Now it was time to clear the hut.

Absolutely none of my training had, or could, prepare me for what I found in the hut.

I found the bodies of a mother and her small baby. The child had been suckling at his mother's breast. It didn't matter that the child could never have even felt the storm of shot that took his life. That father had brought the war home, where his family was. Goddam him!

Inside the hut we found several more weapons. The man had an AK-47 on him and two more SKS semiautomatic carbines in the hut. There wasn't much question that this was the man we had come for. Most of his bodyguards didn't last any longer than he did. One of my men came running up from the other group.

There was a lot of noise coming from behind the other hooch. They had a prisoner—where was mine? I told him that all we had was some weapons and that my VNs had picked them up. The ball game was sprung. Now it was time to get the hell out.

We all ran up the paddy dikes, automatic weapons fire coming in from all around us. It was obvious there were more of them than we could handle; 7.62mm bullets from AK-47s and SKSs were snapping all around us. Charlie didn't know exactly where we were—they were reconning by fire. By shooting up the area, they were hoping to get us to shoot back. When we did, they would have us pinpointed.

Running along the path on the dike, I was probably the most scared I had ever been in my life. Even that torpedo tube on the French submarine was better than this. But just when I thought I couldn't get more scared, I fell into a punji pit.

As the earth broke open beneath me, I knew that this was it. When I hit those spikes at the bottom of the pit, it would all be over. My men would probably be killed trying to pull their thick-skulled, bucket-footed chief out of this hole. Some point man I was. All of this took less than a second and I hit the bottom of the pit.

Wap! No spikes. The pit had just been covered over. The punji stakes, usually sharpened bamboo stakes dipped in rotted excrement, hadn't been put in place. The pit was only chest-deep, about four feet. I scrambled out of the hole and continued running along the dike.

While we hauled ass along the dike, I was calling in on the radio. "Seawolf, Seawolf. This is Whiskey Sour. This is Whiskey Sour. Do you read me? Over."

Somebody from the TOC broke in. "Whiskey Sour, what's your problem? Over."

Before the operation, we had set up support with the Seawolves of Detachment Six in Song Ong Doc. Instead of just putting in the paperwork for air support, the SEALs liked to talk to the pilots personally whenever possible. We felt that when a pilot could put a face to a code name, he tried just a little bit harder.

The Seawolf pilot jumped in on the conversation. "TOC, clear the air. Whiskey Sour, where are you? This is Seawolf Six Two. Over." When we were operating, the pilots slept in their birds, ready for situations just like this.

"We are at Home Plate en route, Home Plate en route. Over."

"What's happening? Over."

"Bring it, Bud. We're in a world of shit. We walked into a hornets' nest. Over."

"Hang in there, Whiskey Sour. We'll be there in one zero. Over."

"Roger that, Six Two. We'll be here."

There was nothing for us to do but wait. We had been running along a dike between two rice paddies. On the far side of either paddy was a tree line. Behind us was the village we had hit. Passing a dike going diagonally to the one we were running along, we ducked into the corner of the two dikes. Now at least there was cover between us and the village and one of the tree lines.

We used different codes on operations. For me, Home Plate was usually the target. First Base could be the insertion point. Second Base could be a checkpoint that was a permanent landmark—a canal junction, a village, or something else fixed. You could use baseball, colors, whatever you wanted. But you tried to switch the code words around. You never knew when Charlie might have a radio and be listening in.

We were all excited. The head VN was handling the prisoners, so Duke and Chuck wanted to go up on the dike and lay down a field of fire with their Stoners. "Don't fire those fucking Stoners," I said. If we opened up with the Stoners, Charlie would know exactly who we were and where we were. Nothing else in that war sounded like a Stoner.

But Duke and Chuck were insisting. "Come on, Chief," they said. "Let's take some of them out."

"Just get down in the fucking mud," I answered.

Now Seawolf was overhead. We carried strobe lights that had directional heads. We could use the lights to signal a chopper without the light being seen from the side.

"All right, Six Two," I said, "I'm going to put it on you. Identify."

We had lenses of different colors for the strobe lights. When you were identifying yourself, you never told the color you were using over the air. You always had the overhead people identify the color.

"Whiskey Sour, I have a green strobe. Over."

"You got me, Hoss, that's us."

"How tight are you?" He was asking how small the landing area was.

"We're tight."

"Where are you taking it?" From what direction were we taking fire?

"All around."

"Recommendation?"

"The tree line north of us. Hit it."

He came in on a gun run for the tree line. We could see the green tracers lifting up toward the Seawolf from where the enemy was.

"Hey, Bud," I said over the radio, "don't come in so low. You have it coming back at you."

But we were laying in the fire from the helicopters onto the enemy positions. Duke and Chuck still wanted to open up on the enemy with their Stoners. "Let me shoot, Chief!"

"Hey," I said, "when they come over the dike, we take them with us. Until then, hold your fire."

We were as flat into that mud as you could be. The dike was only about four feet high, and we used every inch of it. Fire was still coming in all around us. But now there was the heavier sound of the Seawolves' guns and rockets. The gunfire drowned out what little noise we might make talking, and the enemy still didn't know exactly where we were. Now Seawolf was back on the line.

Seawolf Six Two had scrambled two more detachments to back

us up. Each detachment was two helicopter gunships. Over the radio, the pilot told me that we had fire in the woods all around us. He was running low on fuel and ammunition and would have to go back to rearm. The two detachments Six Two had called up would be on station before he left.

We still wouldn't shoot back—the biggest gun we had was my radio as long as a Seawolf was in the air. And Six Two was not going to leave us alone. Six Two had called in to the VNs for a slick to get us out at first light. At the time, the only slicks in the area were controlled by the ARVNs. And they wouldn't release a bird to come and get us!

Seawolf Six Two had to leave us to rearm. But before he went, he called in a detachment of Black Ponies. The Black Ponies were OV-10 Bronco fixed-wing aircraft intended to back up the Seawolves and Navy forces. Armed with 5-inch Zuni rockets, 7.62mm machine guns, and lots of bullets, the Black Ponies were a nice sight to see in the Vietnamese skies.

Now it was about four-thirty in the morning. The VNs now said that they didn't have a slick they could cut loose. They had an operation going out at first light and they needed all their birds. It was really because we had Father Wa's people with us that the ARVNs wouldn't help us. The South Vietnamese had no use for the PRUs or Father Wa's people. Which was stupid, because they were the best fighters the South had! None of Father Wa's people lost their heads. Minh, the interpreter, kept everyone cool. And the funny thing was that Father Wa's men could have just laid down their weapons and slipped away. They had all been the enemy once, they could join him again.

But instead, we rode out the night. Seawolf Six Two just would not leave us. I could hear him calling over the radio that he would join us down on the deck rather than leave us. By first light, the Black Ponies showed up. The VC around us were starting to keep their heads down. But there was still plenty of fire coming our way. Now Seawolf Six Two left us to rearm, or so we thought.

What Six Two did was go back to Song Ong Doc, refuel his bird, and strip all the heavy weapons and ammunition off her! Six Two turned his bird into a slick! Heading back into that hornets' nest with just one door gunner, Seawolf came to get us.

Over the radio, Six Two told me what had to be done. I had to make sure that only one man at a time got aboard the bird. The area was real tight, and Six Two wouldn't chance setting down in the paddy. He would hover the bird as low as he could, using every bit of cover that the dikes provided. If he lost control of the bird, it would crash, taking him, and probably us, out with it.

That was August 20, 1970, and he got us out of there. For my part in that operation, I was awarded my fourth Bronze Star. But I knew who deserved more medals than I could give them for what they did. All we had was the weapons we had captured on the op, AKs and SKSs. Since the Seawolf people didn't have the chance to pick up any war trophies, we gave the weapons to them.

Father Wa's intelligence later came back on who had faced us on that op. The airstrike had seriously messed over one full NVA battalion that had been in the tree lines around that village. We had put a dent in Charlie's day that time. The NVA troops had infiltrated from Cambodia and no one had known they were there.

Seawolf Six Two was part of Detachment Six out of Song Ong Doc. The bird's ID was Seawolf 312. Three weeks later, Seawolf 312 was shot down while escorting an Army medevac bird. Killed in the crash was the pilot, Lieutenant (jg) William A. Pederson, and crewman José P. Ramos. I will never forget the courage of Seawolf Six Two.

While I had been busy with other things, Lou Boink and Alfa Squad hadn't been standing still either. After gathering the intel needed, Lou put on a Bright Light op, and it was a successful one. On August 22, Sixth Platoon, along with a number of South Vietnamese, raided a POW camp. After a short, fierce firefight, the carefully planned air support and naval gunfire drove the VC guards away. Though no American POWs were rescued, twenty-eight South Vietnamese were released. Some of the prisoners had been held for over four years.

Sixth Platoon just kicked ass while in Vietnam. We were so successful that the Navy awarded Sixth Platoon, SEAL Team Two, with the Navy Unit Commendation, the only SEAL platoon to be so honored. And it wasn't just the quality of the intelligence we had developed. It was the skill and professionalism of the officers and men of Sixth Platoon in using that intelligence. They took the war to the enemy.

Operations were going on all of the time with both squads. We went out on one sampan op in the very early morning. The target was well west of Hy Yen, the first time I knew of our operating in the area. We set up on shore at the end of a canal. We could see up the one canal that we knew the target was supposed to be traveling on. What we didn't know was whether he would turn right or left directly in front of us.

The point we chose gave us a good view up the target canal. The target was supposed to have weapons in the sampan. Just as the intel said, at about ten-thirty in the morning, here came our target. Popping up from the reeds, we drew down on the man in the boat. Up went his hands—no problem.

Inside the sampan, we found the weapons the man had been transporting for the VC. Tying the captured sampan to our own, we paddled home. It was a broad-daylight sampan operation. We weren't covered up, but I didn't like our asses hanging out in those little bitty boats in the open light.

That was our only daylight op in sampans. Getting back to Hy Yen, I was told there was a phone call for me. A phone call? Who would be calling me in the middle of the Delta? I went over to the communications hut and took the call.

It was my kid sister in Neptune, New Jersey. My maternal grandmother had passed away. Sis was a little broken up, and she said our mother was taking it bad. The platoon was short—we had only about four weeks to go in our tour. I explained to my sister that it would be ridiculous for me to even try to get home. By the time the paperwork was done and I could get back, the funeral would be over. But she told me that Mom was taking it very, very hard. Anything that I could do would help. Besides her own mother's death, this was my third tour, and with what had happened last time, Mom was very worried about me.

As I was telling my sister that I would be home in a few weeks, but no sooner, somebody cut in on the line. It was a Support Group officer up in Saigon. He had been listening on the line. I'm not sure who it was, but I think it was Commander Olsen. "That decision is not yours to make, Chief," the voice said. "There is a shotgun en route to your position to pick you up now. He will take you to Ca Mau. There is a Huey in Ca Mau to take you to Ben Wha air base. Your orders will be brought to you at the airport. You have a seat on the first C-141 going to McGuire."

Well shit, I didn't pack any of my stuff or anything. I changed into a clean pair of camouflage fatigues and threw a few things into a small handbag. There was a VC flag we had just captured recently that I was going to give to my nephew, and I threw that into the bag as well.

A shotgun flight is a spotter craft for air strike, artillery, and naval gunfire. The plane is just a little two-seater Piper Cub. I had never flown in one of those before and I don't think I ever will again. The plane is armed with a few spotter rockets and that's all. There isn't much room for anything else anyway.

As I climbed into the plane, the pilot asked me, "Have you ever flown in one of these before? No? Well, don't get excited when we take off. The first thing I have to do is push the stick forward to get the tail off the ground. Once we do that, the stick goes back and up we go."

We charged down the runway, just a dirt road really. When we got up some speed, forward went the stick and up came the tail. We moved along like that for a while, then back came the stick and up we went. Landings and takeoffs in the Republic of Vietnam were something else. Secure areas to land in were few and far between. A pilot would drop from the sky as fast as he could when he came close to the ground. On takeoffs, the plane would almost stand on its tail to gain altitude. Charlie liked shooting at planes. And I had left Sweetheart back at the base. All I had with me was a .45 automatic, and I had to turn that in.

The Ca Mau portion of my trip lasted only a few minutes. Into the Huey and off to Ben Wha. At the airport, there was a man from Saigon with my orders home and my pay record. I was on my way. Customs at Ben Wha took my .45 and gave me a receipt for it. It was August 29 and I was on my way home. First stop, Japan.

In Japan I was able to pick up a shaving kit, one of the many things I hadn't packed with me. Cleaning up a bit during the couple of hours we were in Japan made me feel more human. Back on board the plane and on to McGuire. Inside my AWOL bag was the VC flag and a few pieces of gear.

We landed at McGuire and I was back in the States, home from my third tour in Southeast Asia. And this time I walked off the plane just fine.

But my troubles weren't over yet. Back in the world there are all sorts of things to deal with. Now I had to go through Air Force Customs. It was midafternoon on a sunny warm day. At least the weather knew how to greet a returning warrior. But the Air Force sure didn't.

At Customs, this Air Force sergeant was going to take me through all the Mickey Mouse shit. Pulling out my VC flag, this self-important asshole stated it was contraband Communist material and could not be brought into the country. As far as I knew, he would take the damned thing for himself. I had just left a combat zone, and I didn't have the patience for this shit. Picking up the flag, I loudly blew my nose in it. "This isn't a flag," I said, "it's my handkerchief." And I jammed it into my pocket. He didn't give me any more flak and I cleared Customs.

Now I had to meet my dad. He was going to be at the base when the plane set down. We were going to drive into town in Dad's big LeBaron. There was a small opening, wide enough for two people abreast, you went through to get on the base proper. Two air police were on either side of the gate. Wearing my camouflage jungle fatigues and LDNN beret, I headed for the gate.

"Where are you going?" one of the guards asked.

"I'm going home," I said. "Here are my emergency leave papers."

Beyond the door, I could see my dad and brother waiting for me by the car.

"Excuse me, Chief," the guard said, "but you can't leave the base in that uniform. The regulations state Class A's or civilian clothes."

"Let me explain something to you," I said. "See these papers? Can you read where they say 'Emergency Leave'? One day ago, I was on a combat patrol in the Mekong Delta of Vietnam. If you want to stop me from leaving this base, you had better be prepared to use that weapon on your side. That is the only way you're going to stop me."

I walked right past him and into my father's car. Driving off, I left Vietnam behind me.

EPILOGUE

What first motivated me to become a UDT man was the desire to always be with the best. That desire stayed with me when I was a young boy playing ball or in the drum and bugle corps. I wanted to be a winner and would work to be with the winners.

In 1952 I saw the movie *The Frogmen*, with Richard Widmark. What impressed me most about the film was the men's teamwork and their devotion to get the job done regardless of the odds. The UDT was a challenge to me, and I have always enjoyed a challenge; I still do. This story is the proof of that. To me, this book is the biggest thing that I have done in my life.

As a young man, in 1953, I won the Tri-State Baritone Bugle Individual contest in Reading, Pennsylvania. That was the big day in my life at the time. When I enlisted in the Navy and graduated boot camp at Bainbridge, Maryland, in 1955, that was a big day and the highlight of my life to that time. After three years, and many requests, in 1959 I was finally accepted for Underwater Demolition Team Replacement training at Little Creek, Virginia.

I reported for training along with 125 other volunteers. We all thought we could pass training and join the UDT. I decided that the only way I was going to wash out was if they killed me, and I thought that was against regulations.

There was no way that I would quit—they couldn't make me quit—but a couple of times I did think they might kill me. As the days and weeks went by, our numbers shrank. The instructor told us that he was going to graduate our class in a telephone booth.

On graduation day from UDTR there were eighteen very proud young men left of the original 125 volunteers. Among those eighteen were two foreign sailors. One of these men, Finn Volke, I have heard has since become an admiral in the Danish navy.

The day we reported to UDT 21 was again to me the biggest day of my life. Two years later, I was one of the enlisted men chosen to form the ranks of the first SEAL team, Team Two. And as I hear the protests from the SEALs of Team One, yes, we were the first because there is a three-hour time difference between Coronado and Little Creek.

I went on to many military schools, most of which seemed to either beat you, starve you, or both. Later I became a member of one of the first SEAL Mobile Training Teams and deployed to Turkey. I was one of the first SEALs to attend certain military schools to help evaluate them for the Team—the Army Ranger, Marine escape & evasion, and jumpmaster schools among others.

Later I was to be a member of one of the first Team Two platoons to see combat in Vietnam . . . to capture the first Team Two AK-47 from an NVA Medal of Honor winner . . . to capture the only, to my knowledge, Chinese military advisers to the NVA and VC ever taken prisoner.

I was also honored to serve with such legends among the Teams as Lieutenant Commander Roy Boehm, Chief Warrant Officer Bob Gallagher, Master Chief Boatswain's Mate Rudy Boesch, and Commander Richard Marcinko.

Such were the major events of my life up to my retirement from the Navy in 1974. Since retirement I've become a Mason and have worked my way to the shrine as my Uncle Buck did earlier. I have also taken on the awesome responsibility of being the curator for the UDT/SEAL Museum in Fort Pierce, Florida, and of keeping the history of all the Teams alive for future generations.

So that's my life, until now. With this book, telling the story of my years with the SEALs, I have completed the biggest challenge of my life. It is with no little wonder that I sit now and ask myself, "Now what?"

J.D.W. III

Index